Court,
church
and
conflict

David Loades

HENRY VIII

Court,
church
and
conflict

The National Archives

First published in 2007 by
The National Archives,
Kew, Richmond,
Surrey, TW9 4DU, UK
www.nationalarchives.gov.uk

This paperback edition published in 2009.

The National Archives brings together
the Public Record Office,
Historical Manuscripts Commission,
Office of Public Sector Information
and Her Majesty's Stationery Office.

A catalogue card for this book is available
from the British Library.

ISBN 978 1 905615 42 1

Jacket, page design and typesetting by
Ken Wilson | point 918

Printed in Singapore by
KHL Printing Co Pte Ltd

Jacket image
Henry VIII,
attributed to Joos van Cleve (c.1485–1540/1)
The Royal Collection
© Her Majesty Queen Elizabeth II

Contents

Preface 7

Chapter 1 THE RENAISSANCE PRINCE 10

Chapter 2 THE KING'S COURT 35

Chapter 3 THE KING AT WAR 61

Chapter 4 THE KING'S GREAT MATTER 88

Chapter 5 THE KING'S LAWS 112

Chapter 6 THE KING'S GOVERNMENT 133

Chapter 7 THE KING'S ENEMIES 156

Chapter 8 THE KING'S OTHER ISLAND 180

Chapter 9 THE KING'S RELIGION 202

Chapter 10 THE KING'S LAST YEARS 229

Notes on the Text 250

Further Reading 264

Index 265

Picture Credits 272

Author's Acknowledgements 272

Preface

HENRY VIII has always been a little larger than life. Physically he was a very big man, and in later life gross, but that is not really the point. The image that Holbein created for him is still the first that springs to mind when the word 'king' is mentioned. He is notorious, even among those with the most minimal knowledge of English history, for having had six wives, two of which he executed. Those with slightly more retentive memories may recall that he removed the Church of England from the papal jurisdiction, and brought to an end almost a thousand years of English monasticism. To his contemporaries he was awe-inspiring, even terrifying, and to later historians either a bloodthirsty tyrant or a great national leader, according to taste or prejudice. His admirers have credited him with the foundation of parliamentary government and the Royal Navy; his detractors have accused him of cultural vandalism upon a gigantic scale. The one thing that no one has done with Henry VIII—not even Jane Austen—is to ignore him.

Studies of different aspects of his life and reign are legion. Peter Gwyn has examined Henry's relationship with Thomas Wolsey, Richard Marius with Thomas More, and Diarmaid MacCulloch with Thomas Cranmer. John Guy has examined Wolsey's influence on Henry and the country, and Geoffrey Elton that of Thomas Cromwell. Each of these works, and particularly the last, has stirred up controversy among historians that has rumbled on for years. Henry's various marriages have been picked over even more industriously. Garrett Mattingly's classic work on Catherine of Aragon is now over sixty years old, but has not been replaced.

Eric Ives has written two excellent and exhaustive studies of Anne Boleyn; Anne has been approached from a different angle by Wretha Warnicke, who has also written on Anne of Cleves. The brief and tragic career of Catherine Howard was examined many years ago by Lacey Baldwin Smith, while much more recently Susan James produced a biography of Catherine Parr. Henry's marriages in general, and the succession problem that they reflected, have been written about in a more popular vein by David Starkey, Antonia Fraser and myself. Novels, plays, films and TV dramas based upon the lives of Henry's various wives and mistresses are numerous, while Beverly Murphy has written an excellent study of his illegitimate son, Henry FitzRoy.

Almost every Tudor historian of repute has written about Henry, or some aspect of his career. The best biography was written in 1968 by Jack Scarisbrick. More recent research has to some extent dated it, and the appearance of a new edition in 2000 created opportunities for revision that were unfortunately not taken. Nevertheless it remains the standard work. In 2005 George Bernard, a scholar with a notable track record in early 16th-century studies, approached Henry from a slightly different angle. The king, he argued, has been too often overshadowed by his ministers and servants. The English Reformation was not created by Cranmer, or Cromwell, much less by imperfectly visible ecclesiastics and preachers, but by the king himself. This thumping assertion of the royal supremacy will not, of course, be the last word on the subject. Some writers have already expressed reservations, and the debate about Henry's religion, no less than the debates about his marriages and his foreign policy, will persist as long as the Tudors continue to fascinate us.

This book is not intended to emulate professors Bernard or Scarisbrick, much less Elton or MacCulloch. It is, I hope, based on sound research and a great deal of thought, but the intention is to offer some useful perspectives on Henry for the benefit of those who find him interesting but who have no specialist knowledge of the period. In one respect it also differs from its predecessors.

Henry's reign saw an enormous increase in the quantity of surviving documentation. There are chronicles, narratives and State Papers of various kinds in unprecedented profusion. The papers of those arrested for treason, such as Thomas Cromwell, were seized when they were imprisoned, and remain to be read. The continuous registers of the Privy Council begin during this reign, and there are records of the new courts, Star Chamber, Requests and Augmentations. The narrative here is supported by a selection of these documents, which I hope will not only illustrate some of the points being made, but also convey a flavour of this unique period in English history.

This paperback edition coincides with the 500th anniversary of Henry VIII's accession. In the spring and summer of 1509, England rejoiced in a new, young and handsome king. It was also the year of his marriage to the beautiful Catherine of Aragon and they were crowned together on midsumer's day. This was a time of hope that those who witnessed it did not forget, in spite of the thunder that later rolled around the throne.

DAVID LOADES

§1 The Renaissance Prince

GREAT KINGS ARE RARE. Some were great because dynastic circumstances, or the wealth and power of their realms, made them so; some because of their own heroic dimensions. Henry VIII started with few advantages. His father had been a parvenu who had struggled to establish his claim, and the England into which Henry was born on 28 June 1491 constituted, even by contemporary standards, a very small and not particularly stable world.

The population of England had declined catastrophically from the end of the 13th century, when it may have stood at nearly 6 million, to the middle of the 15th century, when it barely exceeded 2 million. The main reason for this had been bubonic plague—the so-called Black Death—of 1348 to 1350. However that was not the only cause; population had been falling gradually for half a century before that, probably because the resources of arable land were overstretched, and simply could not feed the numbers that had then been reached. Plague was to remain endemic in England until the later 17th century, but it was never again as virulent or as widespread as it had been in the middle of the 14th. The population showed no signs of recovery for nearly a century after the worst outbreak had subsided. Around 1450 there were probably fewer people in England than at any time since before the Battle of Hastings. Thereafter, for reasons that are not at all clear, a slight recovery began, which had probably lifted the level to about 2.5 million by the time Henry was born.[1]

There had been a number of knock-on effects from this demographic crisis. Labour was in short supply, and that had freed the market, leading to the abandonment of many feudal customs and the virtual end of unfree tenantry, 'villeinage'. Instead of being personally unfree, and tied to services in the manor of his birth, the typical 'husbandman' (as the social rank below yeoman was termed) became a free man, selling his labour in an open market. This did not happen all at once, and was bitterly resented by conservative landowners, but it was an irreversible tendency from the late 14th to the late 15th century. With tenants in short supply and the wool trade flourishing, many lords converted part or all of their estates to sheep ranching. At the time this was relatively uncontroversial, but as population levels recovered it became a grievance, and 'sheep devouring men' was a popular theme by the 1520s.

All this was important, because England was overwhelmingly rural. No more than 10 per cent of the population could be classed as urban, and there were no more than half a dozen towns with 10,000 inhabitants or more. Only London, with 50,000–60,000, was a true city by European standards, and most towns that considered themselves to be such had fewer than 5,000, including the 150 or so parliamentary boroughs. At the same time, London, with which the court was in close and regular contact, was a wealthy cosmopolitan centre, and growing fast. It held substantial resident communities of Italians, Flemings and Germans, and smaller numbers of French and Spaniards. Its aldermen were as wealthy as peers, and it sucked in apprentices and workpeople from all over England. Its literacy rate was far higher than that of the surrounding counties, and every sort of idea, new, eccentric or downright mad, was canvassed on its streets and in its markets. London had its own social structure, which was basically an oligarchy of wealth, and its own semi-autonomous government,[2] which was imitated on a small scale by those other towns that had pretensions, such as Norwich and Bristol.

In the countryside a freer labour market had to some extent disrupted the hierarchies of village life. There were now opportunities for free husbandmen to acquire wealth and to rise in the social scale, so the yeomanry was a growing class, and it was from their ranks, along with craftsmen such as blacksmiths, that offices like those of constable and churchwarden were filled. So the village constable was less likely to be the lord's man, and the greater access of free men to the king's courts reduced the lord's courts to mainly economic functions.

Higher up the social scale, a rather similar development was taking place. In theory there was a very strict division between the noble and the non-noble, but in practice the boundary was highly permeable. Many yeomen prospered from running sheep on their small estates, bought more land and acquired social aspirations. They sent their sons to school and to the universities, not necessarily to become priests but rather lawyers and what would later be called civil servants. In the process they became gentlemen, and many a 16th-century knight, or even peer, had a yeoman for a grandfather.

However, at the very highest social level there had been less change, thanks partly to the political turmoil known as the Wars of the Roses, and partly to the conservative ethos of the royal court. Only deeply entrenched families such as the Percies, the Fitzalans and the Courtenays could command the traditional loyalty that created the retinues with which those wars were fought, and ancient lineage continued to be respected, especially by those who did not possess it. Edward IV had fostered this respect by governing largely through a small number of noblemen.[3] The chivalric tradition, enhanced by organizations like the Order of the Garter, placed great emphasis upon the right to bear a coat of arms, and although arms were granted by the king, they were generally regarded as signs of lineage, and of course of military prowess. From 1483 onwards the College of Heralds guarded these practices with a jealous eye. It was not until Henry VIII had been several years on the throne that this aristocratic preoccupation with ancestry began to wane, and to be replaced with what is generally called a 'service nobility'.

How a subject was governed at the beginning of the 16th century depended to a large extent on where he, or she, lived; in other words what sort of community he belonged to. If he lived in a large town such as York or London that was run by a corporation, for most practical purposes he was answerable to the mayor and aldermen, sometimes acting in their own right, and sometimes by virtue of a royal commission. If he lived close to the Scottish Border he was in theory governed by the march warden (a royal official), but in practice largely by his clan (or kindred) chieftain. In the English–Welsh borderlands, the 'marches of Wales', a notoriously lawless area, he would have been answerable to the lord of that particular march, and was probably governed by Celtic law.

However, the vast majority of the people lived in the English shires under the common law. If such a person was guilty of a minor offence, such as pasturing his cattle in the wrong place, he might well be under the 'customary law' administered by the manorial court, presided over by the lord's steward; but for most offences he would be brought before a royal court: the ancient 'hundred' court (for small offences), the quarter sessions, or for serious offences such as murder or rape, the assizes (these issues are elaborated in Chapter 5). The days when the king's justice could be distorted or even frustrated, by the local influence of powerful lords (which had been frequent in the 1450s) were largely over by 1500. The key to much local government, administrative as well as judicial, lay in the royal commission—the delegation of the king's authority to groups of local men. The commission had both power and immediacy.

Alongside the king's authority lay that of the Church. A whole range of matters, including marriage, probate and contract, were deemed to be 'spiritual' and were adjudicated by the court of the bishop or archdeacon. There were spiritual offences as well as issues, and anyone refusing to accept communion or making rude remarks about the local saint—or even neglecting to pay his tithes —was liable to be hauled before an ecclesiastical court on the initiative of his incumbent or churchwarden.

In theory every aspect of a man's life was tightly controlled, by the king, the Church or his local trade guild, but in practice the inefficiency of all these agencies left most men a good deal of free-dom, especially if the community was indulgent, as it often was.

It goes without saying that all the offices of justice, from the highest to the lowest, were occupied by men. Women had very little control over their own lives, except what they could exert privately by dominating their menfolk. The law recognized and protected the interests of the *femme seule* (the unmarried woman or widow), but the *femme couverte* (married woman) had no legal existence apart from her husband. There were some women (usually widows) in crafts and trades, and some who owned land, but the only realistic options for a girl growing up about 1500 were marriage or the veil. A gentleman's honour was public, and might well be military; a lady's was private and sexual—and the same applied to her poorer sisters.

We now know that Henry VII brought the dynastic struggles of the Wars of the Roses to an end. But they did not know that in 1491, the year of Prince Henry's birth. Henry VII had made a good start by marrying Elizabeth of York, who had borne him two sons, but the challenge of the young Earl of Warwick remained, as did that of the Duke of Suffolk, to say nothing of anyone who felt like impersonating Richard of York, the younger of the 'Princes in the Tower'.[4] In fact Henry was little more than an adventurer, who by a mixture of good luck and good manage-ment had defeated (and more importantly, killed) Richard III on the battlefield at Bosworth in 1485. Richard had died childless, and his nephew and designated heir, the Earl of Lincoln, had died in 1487. However, it would have been a rash man who in 1491 would have pronounced that England had now entered upon a era of political stability. Even 15 years later, when some surmised what a good king the Duke of Buckingham would make, the suc-cession of his surviving son could not be taken for granted. 1485 is a date the significance of which is almost entirely retrospective, and it was only by getting his heir to the very threshold of manhood that the king could be assured of a peaceful succession.

Nor had Henry been in any real sense a 'new monarch'. He had used the traditional machinery of government with great care and efficiency, but he had innovated comparatively little. He had improved his revenues, but mostly in time-honoured ways; only in the exaction of large bonds for good behaviour did he exceed the customary use of the royal prerogative. He avoided war, securing his ends, on the whole, by diplomacy—but that was no more than good husbandry. Unlike Edward he did not govern through great nobles, but through servants of lesser rank directly dependent upon himself; but that again was a traditional style of kingship.

In short, Henry VII was a very conservative monarch. He understood the meaning of magnificence, and used it when necessary, but it was not natural to him, as it was to be to his son, because he had been brought up in exile and in comparative poverty. His piety was equally traditional. His relations with successive popes were good. He was swiftly recognized by the curia, the papal court, and he warmly supported the jubilee that Pope Alexander VI proclaimed in 1501. He hated the anti-clerical followers of John Wycliffe, the Lollards, and encouraged their persecution, but he saw no threat (apparently) in humanism, or the New Learning as it was pejoratively known, which he encouraged in a rather uncomprehending kind of way. Whether he was aware of the changes that were taking place in the Church is uncertain, but quite probably not, because they were not very visible in his lifetime. Fashions, however, change, in religion as in everything else.

Even before the Black Death the *opus dei*, that constant round of liturgical prayer and praise that sustained the monastic way of life, was losing its appeal. The great new foundations of the 12th and early 13th century were not repeated, and existing houses were having to make do with a lower level of benefaction. The plague by no means killed monastic vocations, but numbers recovered only very slowly and in some places not at all. The mendicant religious orders, on the other hand, who worked in the world, had come to be better regarded, and recovered strongly. There was also a major shift in benefactions, away from the regular orders altogether, and towards perpetual chantries (whereby the donor gave money for the singing of masses for his soul in perpetuity)—and educational foundations—colleges and schools. In other words withdrawal from the world was no longer seen as the Christian ideal, and prayer was not the only way to deal with social problems and inadequacies.

At the same time, certain areas of traditional piety were strengthened. The mass luxuriated in innumerable special forms, and devotion to the Eucharistic elements intensified.[5] This made the Lollards, who rejected transubstantiation, particularly unpopular, and helps to explain the king's hostility. Henry had no pretensions to intellectual or theological sophistication, and was probably closer to his people in this respect than in any other. At a time when there were anti-papal 'Gallican' murmurings in France, and when Savonarola was calling for bonfires of the vanities in Florence, and when various radicals in Germany like the so-called 'Drummer of Nickelhausen' were gathering popular support, England remained a jewel in the papal crown, and no royal family was more orthodox than the Tudors.

Henry used to be thought of as a great patron of merchants, who introduced clauses in favour of the Merchant Adventurers into his treaties with the Low Countries. He did indeed do that, but less out of affection for merchants than because he appreciated them as a source of wealth. The customs revenues of the port of London were worth almost as much as the rental from the royal estates, because there had been significant shifts in the pattern of trade over the previous half century. In the first place woven (but not finished) cloth had taken over from the trade in raw wool as the principle export commodity; and secondly that trade had become increasingly focused on London. As the demand for English cloth steadily increased, entrepreneurs established a widespread cottage industry, whereby middle men took up the wool where it was grown, farmed it out to the weavers, and then marketed their produce through London's Blackwall Hall. The wool merchants (or 'staplers') suffered, and ports such as Southampton and Kings Lynn suffered, but the Merchant Adventurers and the City of London flourished exceedingly. Hence the king's favour. It was probably because he was persuaded of the profitable possibility of selling English cloth to the Chinese that he invested in John Cabot's voyage from Bristol in 1496. When Cabot got no further than Newfoundland and no market was in prospect, the king's interest evaporated.

By 1509 Henry VII was rich, and widely respected, both at home and abroad, but seen from Venice, or even Bruges, England was an odd backwater, best known (apart from its cloth) for its piety and its xenophobia: 'The English think that there are no people like themselves,' wrote one Italian, 'and if they see a handsome foreigner they say he looks like an Englishman.'[6] But 1509 would be Henry's last year.

When Henry VII died, on 22 April 1509, the auguries for the new reign were good. The realm was at peace, as it had been through most of Henry's 24 years on the throne. Henry, Prince of Wales, was his father's only surviving son, and although there were still possible rivals to his claim in the form of the Yorkist de la Pole brothers (as we shall see later), they presented no real challenge: Edmund de la Pole, the self-styled Duke of Suffolk, was in the Tower, and his brother Richard was in the service of the king of France.

The fact that young Henry was a few weeks short of his 18th birthday was officially ignored. There was no question of even the briefest minority. Henry VIII was king, and both looked and acted the part. He was head and shoulders taller than the gentlemen of his court, and possessed of a magnificent physique. A skilled horseman, jouster, tennis player and dancer, he had also been provided by his perceptive parent with a first-class classical and theological education. Few kings can ever have come to a throne better equipped—except in one very important respect: he was absolutely inexperienced in the exercise of any public authority. According to the Count of Fuensalida, the Spanish ambassador (who arrived in England only in 1508), young Henry, when not at his exercise or his books, was kept in virtual seclusion 'like a young girl', always chaperoned and closely controlled.[7] Perhaps this was just a question of his youth; and there is more than a suggestion of exaggeration in the ambassador's report. Had the old king lived only a little longer, he might have inducted his son into some of the responsibilities to which he was heir. Or perhaps not. There is more than a suspicion that Henry VII feared this magnificent young man—not in the obvious sense that he suspected him of any disloyalty, but because he saw himself, an elderly and rather drab figure as he was well aware, completely eclipsed by the rising sun. So although young Henry had been through the *cursus honorem*, being first Duke of York and then Prince of Wales, he had in a sense been kept under wraps, and had never discharged any official royal duties. Expectations ran high, partly because no one had had any chance to detect potential weaknesses, or any reason to believe that this idol might have feet of clay—and perhaps that had also been part of his father's calculation.

Those who knew his tutors hailed him as a beacon of the New Learning, and Erasmus and his friends relished the prospect of a new era. As Lord Mountjoy commented:

O, MY ERASMUS, *if you could see how the world here is rejoicing in the possession of so great a prince … Avarice is expelled [from] the land, liberality scatters riches with a boun-teous hand, our king does not desire gold or silver, but virtue, glory, immortality. The other day he said to me 'I wish I were more learned than I am.' 'That is not what we expect of your grace,' I replied, 'but that you should foster and encourage learned men.' 'Yea, surely,' said he, 'for without them we should scarcely exist at all.' What more splendid saying could fall from the lips of a Prince?[8]*

It was later to transpire that the glory that Henry sought was not necessarily quite what Mountjoy had in mind, but his testimony was genuine enough. At the same time, in political terms, the transition was almost seamless. The chancellor and Archbishop of Canterbury (William Warham), the lord privy seal and Bishop of Winchester (Richard Fox) and the lord treasurer (the Earl of Surrey) all remained in office, and the same councillors who had guided Henry VII continued to serve his son.

Only in one respect was there an abrupt change of direction, and that may have owed at least as much to the old council as to the new king. Richard Empson and Edmund Dudley, the old king's financial enforcers, were arrested, accused of various malpractices, and eventually tried and executed. They had broken no law, but they had pushed the fiscal prerogative to extreme limits, exacting heavy fines for relatively trivial offences and imposing crippling 'recognizances' (bonds) upon those whom Henry VII had chosen to suspect. The old king's favour had protected them for years, but in April 1509 that favour was suddenly withdrawn. It is very unlikely that young Henry had any strong feelings about them one way or the other, but their sacrifice had one major advantage. It symbolized the new regime. Not only had the old drabness disappeared, the old tightfistedness had gone as well.

The new king was not only magnificent, he was also liberal. His nobles were his companions, whose language of chivalry he spoke, and whose games he was prepared to play. He was rich; generous to scholars and artists (hence the enthusiasm of Erasmus); forgiving of old debts; and anxious to cut a dash, not merely at home but also abroad. The sacrifice of Empson and Dudley, who represented the old regime, was therefore politically expedient. They had become almost as unpopular with the old councillors as they were with the nobility at large, so they were easy meat. Preachers denounced them, and they were whisked into the Tower within days of Henry's accession. Their subsequent condemnation and execution was not only unjust but also of dubious legality, being based upon allegations that they had assembled followers and conspired against the new king.[9] However, such chicanery seems to have troubled no one except their families. That this might also be a portent of things to come does not appear to have occurred to anyone in the general euphoria of the moment.

THE DOWNFALL OF EMPSON AND DUDLEY

... IN THE SAID proclamation was contained, that if any man had sustained injury, or loss of goods by the Commissioners [Empson and Dudley] before appointed, as appeareth in the xix year of King Henry the seventh, that he should make his humble supplication unto the king's grace, and therein express their grief, and he was ready, not only to hear them, but also to cause satisfaction to be made. When this proclamation was published and known abroad, all such from whom any thing had been exacted or taken, whether it were by right or wrong, speedily came unto the Court, and every man alleged and showed just occasion that they had for complaint. But the Council examined and tried their causes, and such as they found to be openly & manifestly injured, they made due restitution ... But the rage and cry of the people was so grievous against the commissioners, whose names were Richard Empson knight, and Edmund Dudley esquire, that the Council to cease and quiet the rage of the people, were forced to apprehend and commit to the Tower of London the aforesaid Empson and Dudley, and being called before the Council and other justices, where they (as Polydore [Vergil] saith), being both learned in the laws of England, pleaded for themselves, namely Sir Richard Empson, which was the elder, who said as followeth: I am sure, right honourable, you are not ignorant how expedient & profitable unto mans life be good and wholesome laws, without which neither private house may be maintained, nor public weal duly and orderly governed. Even those laws among us by the oversight and negligence of magistrates, partly were depraved, and now in some part abrogate and clean out of memory, the which

evil increasing daily more and more, king Henry the seventh
(now deceased) a most prudent and politic prince (as ye all know)
endeavoured to redress, who unto us committed the charge to see,
and provide that the common and accustomed laws might be
maintained and executed ... And that such persons as had
violated & transgressed any of them should suffer condign and
worthy punishment. We therefore as faithfully and uprightly as
we could have according to our commission executed our office truly
unto the great commodity of the public weal ...

These their sayings, unto many that were wise, virtuous and
discreet, seemed to be very good and right, but unto other, and
that unto the greatest number, who supposed that the examination
and execution of laws being done through avarice and covetousness
and for filthy desire of gain, they judged that even they by putting
in execution with extremity the laws to the loss of many an honest
man's goods, should now be recompensed with the loss of their
heads, who within three days after were beheaded at the Tower
Hill, but their bodies with their heads were buried ...

[Richard Grafton, *A Chronicle and mere history*, 1809 edition, pp. 235–6.]

The other thing that Henry VIII did almost immediately was to marry. Catherine, the youngest daughter of Ferdinand and Isabella of Spain, had been lurking unhappily in England since 1501. At the age of 17 she had been briefly married to Henry's elder brother, Arthur, at that time of course the Prince of Wales. The wedding had been the subject of great celebrations and triumphs; and it represented something of a coup for the parvenu Tudors that the ancient royal line of Trastamara was prepared to deploy one of its daughters in their interest.[10] However, the marriage had lasted only a matter of months before Arthur succumbed to pneumonia, and it was probably never consummated.

The widowed Catherine then remained in England for a number of reasons. In the first place both her father and her father-in-law wanted to maintain their relationship, and secondly Henry VII had no desire to return the substantial sum with which she had come endowed. There was immediately talk of her being transferred to Prince Henry. Both her parents were keen on the idea, and a dispensation for that purpose was obtained from the pope. This was necessary because the canon law forbade marriage between two persons so closely related.[11] Prince Henry, however, was only 11 years old. This would not have prevented a binding espousal, but it would have prevented cohabitation, and so a delay ensued.

Then in 1504 Isabella died, and the political landscape changed. Not only had she been enthusiastic to continue the English connection, she had also been queen of Castile in her own right. When she died her heir was not Ferdinand, who was king only of Aragon, but their elder surviving daughter, Juana, who was married to Philip, Duke of Burgundy, the son of the Emperor Maximilian. A number of Castilian nobles had no desire to see a foreigner like Philip holding the crown matrimonial, and Ferdinand began to work on that feeling in order to build up a position for himself. However, if Juana were to be rejected by the Castilians, the next heir was not the king of Aragon, but Catherine — currently unmarried.

It is therefore easy to see why Ferdinand wanted his younger daughter to stay in England. In Spain she would have been a complication of which he had no need. By 1506 Philip and Juana had made good their claim, and the king of Aragon had been forced out. Philip had also signed with Henry VII a treaty of friendship that effectively terminated the latter's relations with Ferdinand.[12] However, Philip then died and Juana became (it was conveniently claimed) deranged. This enabled Ferdinand to return, in theory as regent for his six-year-old grandson, Charles, but in effect as king until his own death ten years later. During the tense period while this *modus vivendi* was being worked out, Catherine's presence in Iberia was considered to be even less desirable.

Consequently Catherine had remained in limbo as the Dowager Princess of Wales, inadequately funded and not really welcome at court, as Henry VII had changed his mind about continuing his links with Ferdinand. In 1506, when Prince Henry reached the canonically significant age of 14, Henry VII caused his son to repudiate the match that had been previously agreed, and Catherine's future became increasingly murky.[13] She was still only 23, and apparently a political refugee. Then in 1507 her father came to the rescue by formally accrediting her as his ambassador. His existing representative, Dr De Puebla, was an old man and of lowly status, although of vast experience, and the idea was that he and Catherine should work together. Catherine threw herself into this role with enthusiasm, and her knowledge of the English language improved vastly in consequence.[14] Although now less isolated, she continued to seek solace in her devotions, and convinced herself that it was the will of God that she should marry the young Henry. This was no doubt a way of persuading herself to wait in patience, but when the older Henry died, she was suddenly and dramatically vindicated.

Whether the young king was really obeying his father's dying wish (as he claimed)[15] or following his own fancy scarcely matters.

THE KING'S MARRIAGE TO CATHERINE OF ARAGON

Henry VIII to Margaret of Savoy (regent of the Netherlands), 27 June 1509. (The source adopts the third-person form for Henry's voice.)

H E I S W R I T I N G *to the Emperor (Maximilian), who, in consideration of his love towards the late king his father, he makes the participator of his news. He was charged by Henry VII on his deathbed, among other good counsels, to fulfil the old treaty with Ferdinand and Isabella of Spain by taking their daughter Katherine in marriage; now that is of full age, he would not disobey, especially considering the great alliance between Aragon, the Emperor and the House of Burgundy by reason of the marriage concluded between the Prince of Spain and the king's sister Mary, and considering also the dispensation obtained from the Pope by Henry VII, the King of Aragon and the late Queen of Spain. Accordingly the espousals were made between him and*

Katherine on the 11th [of this month]. On St John the Baptist's
day (24th June) they were both crowned in Westminster Abbey in
the presence of all the nobility. The realm is in as good peace as in
the late king's time. Begs she will forward his letter to the Emperor,
and certify him frequently with news. Westminster, 27th June.
[signed]

[Taken from the *Letters and Papers ... of Henry VIII* (1862–1932), I, no.
84. The original, in French, is BL MS Add. 21404, f. 10.]

Henry VII was buried at Westminster on 10 May, and the new
king immediately announced to an astonished council that he
would marry his sister-in-law forthwith. All the doubts, over the
validity of the papal dispensation and about money (particularly
money), which had been used as pretexts for doing nothing, were
suddenly swept away. Whatever may have been the case with the
fate of Empson and Dudley, his marriage was the king's own will
and decision — as it was right that it should have been. The couple
were quietly wed at the friar's church in Greenwich towards the
end of June, and crowned together on Midsummer's Day. In spite
of the nine-year difference in their ages they made a splendid
couple, Catherine as handsome as Henry, and flushed with a triumph that would have rendered many a woman beautiful. During her entry into London before the coronation she was, we are
told, 'beautiful and goodly to behold'. It must have seemed to the
onlookers like a tale out of a romance. 'Our time is spent in continual festival,' she wrote to her father, who seems to have been as
surprised by the turn of events as anyone.[16]

All the evidence suggests that the couple were for some time
blissfully happy with each other, but there may have been more to
Henry's action than romantic impulse. The king wanted a war,
and his target was France. He was young, energetic, and anxious
to try out his carefully honed tiltyard skills in real combat. His
head was also full of the chivalric dreams that had been planted
there by his instructors in the arts of war, to the horror of his
humanist tutors. His hero was Henry V, and Henry V had won

glory against the French at Agincourt. The young king's ambition was 'to win our ancient right in France again', and this meant looking for aggressive pretexts. His councillors were deeply worried, but decisions of peace and war belonged to the king alone, and their attempts to dissuade him were in vain. However, Henry was not so out of touch with reality that he believed himself to be capable of fighting France alone; the ideal ally was Ferdinand of Aragon, who had been intermittently at war with France, first with Charles VIII and then with Louis XII, since 1494.

Catherine understandably shared the king's enthusiasm. She was anxious to bring her husband and her father closer together, and in her new-found fortune was more than willing to forgive the latter for his intermittent neglect. So although her ambassadorial credentials had officially come to an end with the old king's death, in effect Henry was sharing his bed with a woman who was still the Spanish ambassador.

There were also other aspects to the situation that made the king's attitude less quixotic than is sometimes claimed. Henry was not the only monarch in Western Europe who was prone to judge his colleagues by their performance on the field of battle. Chivalric values were deeply ingrained and widely shared, so there was some point in a young and untried king seeking to prove himself in this way if he wanted to be taken seriously on the political battlefields of the future. Moreover, his nobles were almost as irked by the long years of peace as they were by Henry VII's fiscal oppression. Most of them still saw their primary role as serving the king in war. They were his natural comrades in arms, and this role had been denied them by his parsimonious sire. It would be an exaggeration to say that they were on the verge of revolt, but they were not happy—particularly the younger ones—and a king who shared their values, and their own perception of their role, was a hugely welcome relief.

Finally, Henry could afford to go to war. Henry VII's avarice had been largely defensive: he had had no intention of waging war if he could avoid it, but he had known perfectly well that he might be given no choice. He had consequently built up a reserve that was effectively a war chest for an attack that never came. This was not the millions of pounds that Francis Bacon later imagined, but a comfortable cushion equivalent to two or three years revenue—perhaps £300,000.[17] Experience was to show that this would not go far, but it was enough for a few campaigns, and an irrefutable argument against those cautious old councillors who argued that the means were not available.

Catherine, meanwhile, had demonstrated both her happiness and her fertility by conceiving within a few weeks of her marriage. Henry's mother, Elizabeth of York, had done the same, and the prompt appearance of Prince Arthur had done much to strengthen his father's position, which had still been shaky in September 1486. In 1509 the young king had no such need—which was just as well because there was no such remedy. On 31 January 1510 the queen was delivered of a stillborn girl, many weeks premature.[18] In the light of subsequent developments this looks like an ominous portent, but at the time it was shrugged off, not without grief but without serious concern. Such things happened and both parties were young. Catherine was obviously doing her duty with noble persistence, because within about four months she had conceived again, and on New Year's Day 1511 gave birth to an apparently healthy boy.

The child was named Henry, and the sound of rejoicing echoed around the kingdom. The king jousted magnificently under the name of Coeur Loyale ('loyal heart'), and laid his trophies at his lady's feet, as all gallant knights were supposed to do.[19] Seven weeks later, disaster struck when the latest Henry Tudor died in his sumptuous cradle at Richmond. This time there was real heartache. Such a divine affliction could only be a punishment for sin, but whose sin, and what could it have been? The reactions of the royal couple were characteristic of their differences. Catherine retreated into prayer, and multiplied her devotions. Henry indulged in a brief but profound bout of self-doubt and self-pity, as he took issue with the Almighty for his unkindness.

Catherine took longer to recover. She was older and beginning to get anxious about her body. Henry also had an exciting war in prospect. The diplomatic path to that end had not been straightforward, because in 1509 the pope, the king of France and the Emperor were ostensibly allied in the League of Cambrai against the Republic of Venice. Henry could have allied with the Venetians, but that would have meant taking on the pope and the Emperor, which was no part of his plan. While Catherine and some of his council were moving towards an alliance with Spain, which was what the king wanted, other councillors were striving to retain the existing amity with France. The pro-French party were slightly ahead in this race, and early in 1510 persuaded Henry (by what means is not known), that he should renew his father's understanding with Louis XII.[20] It may be that the king had concluded that the League of Cambrai made any serious hostilities with France impossible for the time being, and he was creating a smokescreen. However, a month or so later the pro-Spanish party came up with what was to all intents a counter-plan, and offered a pact with Ferdinand that was clearly — although not immediately — aimed against France.

This was much more to Henry's taste, so by the summer of 1510 he found himself a party to what were effectively two incompatible treaties. However, events conspired to rescue him from any potential embarrassment, because by that time the League of Cambrai was breaking down, and Pope Julius II was trying to put together a Holy League to drive the French out of Italy. Italy was of no particular interest to the king of England, but the prospect of an anti-French coalition certainly was, especially when it became likely that Ferdinand would also be a member. Henry sent the strongly Francophobe Archbishop of York, Christopher Bainbridge, to Rome, and waited upon events.

As he recovered from the death of his son, Henry stuck his toe into the military ocean by sending a small force of archers to help the Emperor against the Duke of Guelders, a perennial rebel. It was a mere gesture, but his men acquitted themselves well. At the same time a 'volunteer' force under Lord Darcy went to Spain to accompany Ferdinand in an attack on Morocco. Not for the last time the king of Aragon changed his mind at the last moment, and Darcy's men returned home full of resentment. The frustrated Englishmen had brawled with their ostensible allies, and Ferdinand put on a convincing show of indignation.[21] However, by the time that this unsatisfactory conclusion had been reached, more important events were afoot. In October 1511 the Holy League was signed at Rome, and Henry (who had been taken by surprise and had failed to give Bainbridge adequate powers) joined a few weeks later. In November the Anglo-Spanish entente was carried a stage further when the allies agreed that their contribution to the League's strategy in the spring of 1512 would be an Anglo-Spanish attack on Aquitaine, to recover it for England.[22] It looked as though the first stage of Henry's dream was about to be realized.

Meanwhile, Louis' response to the likelihood of a hostile papal League had played into his enemies' hands. He convened a local council of the French Church. Relations between the French crown and the papacy were still governed by the Pragmatic Sanction of Bourges of 1438, which gave the French Church considerable autonomy and was advantageous to the king, but there were always those within the Gallican Church who believed that it did not go far enough in securing their independence.[23] These voices Louis now encouraged, and anti-papal sentiments were uttered.

Had he stopped at that, it would have been of little significance, but Pope Julius was not entirely master in his own house, and there were a number of cardinals sympathetic to France who disagreed with his policy. Louis now secured the backing of these cardinals, and with their support summoned a general council of the Church to meet at Pisa in May 1511, one of the aims of which was to displace Julius as pope.[24] This threatened schism on a large scale, and immediately gave the Holy League a credibility that it could not otherwise have enjoyed. Henry's self-righteousness knew no bounds. When he joined the League he not only had the perfect pretext for the attack on France, which he had wanted since his accession, but the blessing of the Church on his endeav-ours. Louis had overreached himself and was isolated in the face of the impending conflict.

A PROCLAMATION CONCERNING RETAINERS

Issued at Westminster, 3 July 1511.

WHEREAS THE KING *our sovereign lord, Henry by the grace of God King of England and of France, and lord of Ireland, for the defence of his most noble person, his realm, and his subjects, hath now lately, by the advice of his council, by his letters under his signet and sign manual, commanded all the lords, as also the substance of all the nobles of this his realm forthwith to prepare such and as many able men for the war, sufficiently harnessed, as they can and may prepare of their own servants and other inhabitants within their offices and rooms, and none other, as in the said letters is more plainly expressed and specified.*

Our said sovereign lord is now informed, to his great displeasure if it so be, that divers and many of the said lords and nobles … prepare for the war divers and many persons not being their own tenants nor inhabited within their offices and rooms, contrary to the king's said letters, but also retain diverse persons, wheresoever they may get them, some by promises and some by badges and cognizances, and some otherwise, contrary to the mind of our said sovereign lord and in laws in that case provided.⃰

Wherefore his highness straightly chargeth and commandeth that no manner of man, of what degree or condition he be, make no retainers otherwise than his laws will suffer, upon the dangers and perils of the same laws; nor no man bear or wear any man's badge or cognizance otherwise than the law will, upon the same peril; nor prepare no man for the war but only such as be his own servants or inhabited within his office or rooms, according to the said letters.

And that every man that hath otherwise ordered or demeaned him in that behalf forthwith purvey the remedy, so that his high-

*ness hereafter have no complaint thereof, at his uttermost peril,
and upon the king's great indignation and displeasure.*

[P.L. Hughes and J.F. Larkin, *Tudor Royal Proclamations* (1964), I,
no.62.]

* There were about ten statutes against retaining, going back to the Act
of 13 Richard II, st.3 of 1389.

Although not insignificant, the pope was not a major player in
military terms. However, he had other weapons at his disposal,
and in March 1512 he deployed some of them. In a brief dated 12
March, and couched in the florid language of the *plenitudo potestatis* (the fullness of the judicial and spiritual power of the papacy),
he deprived Louis of his kingdom of France and of his title of 'most
Christian king', and conferred both upon Henry of England.[25] In
a sense, Henry's ambition could go no further, but of course it
was one thing to receive titles and another to make them real.

The campaign in Aquitaine was a fiasco. Henry had formally
declared war on France in April 1512, using all the traditional
heraldic formalities, and the Marquis of Dorset duly landed his
force near San Sebastian in June. However, it soon became apparent that Ferdinand had no intention of providing the promised
collaboration, but was rather using the English force as a cover for
his own seizure of Navarre. When he invited Dorset to take part
in the Navarre campaign, Dorset refused and quarrels broke out.

While stranded and inactive, Dorset became ill and his troops
mutinied. At the end of August they commandeered ships and
returned to England, bearing their hapless commander with them.
Their return coincided with orders from Henry to the effect that
they should obey the orders of the king of Spain. Ferdinand, who
had a lot of experience in such tactics, milked this situation to his
own advantage, placing all the blame on Dorset. 'The king of
Aragon was sore discontent with their departing', as Edward Hall
later wrote, 'for they spent much money and substance of his
country, and said openly, that if they had tarried he would have
invaded Guyan …'.[26]

THE WAR WITH FRANCE (1512)

W HILE THIS WAS HAPPENING *in Italy, King Henry in the meantime had already prepared an army, the hand picked flower of men in their military prime, together with a fleet of sixty great ships, complete with armament and all other equipment necessary for warlike action. He appointed Thomas, Marquis of Dorset, as commander of the army and Sir Edward Howard as Admiral of the fleet; both men were well versed in the affairs of war. The king thereupon quickly sent Thomas and this fine army to Aquitaine about the 14th May (as had been agreed with the king's father in law, Ferdinand). Having embarked, Thomas was carried in a short term a little too far, and landed in Cantabria, which adjoins Aquitaine and today is called Biscay. He disembarked his troops at the seaport of the area, which is called Fuenterrabia in the vernacular, and is, both naturally and by human contrivance, a most well defended place. Here he encamped. The spot is eighteen miles from Bayonne, the nearest seaboard town in Aquitaine. High born gentlemen were sent by King Ferdinand to meet Thomas; they gave him a friendly welcome and informed him that the royal forces would be at the place very soon. This did not in fact happen, and hence nothing was done in those parts by the important English army. The English took this very badly …*

The king accordingly informed the Marquis promptly in writing and by envoys to join the Spanish army as quickly as possible. But by now winter had come and many Englishmen, unable to bear the sultry climate of the area, because they are unaccustomed to the greater heat of the sun, died of disease and fell seriously ill. The Marquis, not waiting for the king's orders, in the meantime returned home with his army, five months after he had first crossed over to the continent.

While the Marquis was immobilized in camp, Edward Howard, Admiral of the fleet, while patrolling off the French coast, turned by chance towards Brittany. Having disembarked a not very large force, he made a short incursion in full view of the

*French who were in garrison there; having burnt some houses, he
returned safely to his ships with booty. The French did not once
leave their stations ...*

[Polydore Vergil, *Anglica Historia*, 1534, edited by D. Hay, Camden Society, LXXIV, 1950, p. 175.]

Henry was furious and humiliated. However, he was not the only
loser, because during the same summer the French were driven
out of Italy, and with a little creative imagination the English could
persuade themselves that their presence on the southwestern
frontier had contributed to this outcome by diverting French
forces from Italy. The Spanish alliance survived, for the time being.

Catherine, meanwhile, had problems of her own. She had dismissed, in circumstances that are not entirely clear, one of her
Spanish ladies, Francesca de Cárceres. Francesca continued to lurk
around the court, and assiduously bent the ear of Ferdinand's official ambassador, by this time Don Luis Caroz. Caroz was soon
reporting that the queen's marriage was in difficulties. The gossip
focused on two married sisters of Edward Stafford, Duke of
Buckingham: Elizabeth Ratcliffe and Anne Hastings. Elizabeth
was a great favourite with Catherine, while Anne was being
courted by one of Henry's favourites, Sir William Compton,
groom of the stool, who, it was alleged, was a stalking horse for
the king. Elizabeth informed her brother, who then caught
Compton *in flagrante delicto*. The duke was furious, not only at the
behaviour but also at the disparagement. In his view, Stafford
ladies were no fit conquests for the likes of Compton—or even
Henry Tudor. The duke made a scene, and the king became
equally angry at the insult to his favourite, and by implication to
himself.[27] A major row ensued, one of the results of which was
that Catherine was forced to dismiss Elizabeth Ratcliffe, and a
sulky standoff between the royal couple then followed.

How much substance there was behind all this is a matter of
conjecture. Francesca had her own agenda, and Caroz was not
close enough to events to be able to check her stories. It is quite

possible that Henry took a fancy to Anne Hastings, and equally possible that the duke was angry. However, it may well have been that the whole storm arose from the mildest of flirtations, and was mainly devised as an explanation of the fact that Catherine did not become pregnant again until 1514. Henry and Catherine were still very much in love, and like all such relationships, theirs had its stormy moments, but he treated her with the greatest affection in public, and the claim that Anne Hastings was ever his mistress rests on no firm evidence whatsoever.

There was, however, a threat from a different direction. Caroz was no rival when it came to relations with Ferdinand, but Catherine was also a councillor in a more general sense. Henry was more disposed to listen to her than to the Archbishop of Canterbury or the Bishop of Winchester. But by 1512 a new influence was coming on the scene—the king's almoner (i.e. dispenser of alms), Thomas Wolsey. Wolsey was a cleric who had allegedly caught the old king's attention by the speed with which he was able to say mass, and had been made a royal chaplain. The younger Henry had also approved of him, hence his promotion as almoner. That was not in itself a position of much significance, but it did create opportunities for access to the king, and these Thomas began to exploit. He was already beginning to acquire a reputation for outstanding competence before a row over clerical privileges in 1512 gave him an additional opportunity. The Parliament of that year passed an act effectively abolishing benefit of clergy (the right to be tried in an ecclesiastical court) for those in minor orders. This was immediately attacked by conservative clergy as infringing the divine law, and Wolsey was given the task of defending what was effectively the king's position.[28] This he did with notable effectiveness, and the favour that resulted led to other employment in the quite unrelated field of military logistics.

In the latter role, Wolsey was largely responsible for setting forth Sir Edward Howard's fleet, which raided the coast of Brittany while the Marquis of Dorset was being made a fool of in Aquitaine.[29] Howard's campaign was not conspicuously successful either, resulting in the mutual destruction of the ships *Regent* and *Cordelière*, but insofar as it was a free-standing naval operation, not supporting a land army, it had some originality. Wolsey was not responsible for that strategy, which was conceived by Admiral Howard, but letters to and from him form our principal source of information about the campaign.[30] Wolsey did come under fire when the victuals ran out, but no blame for the military stalemate was attached to him, and by the autumn of 1512 he had become firmly entrenched as the king's man for the purpose of getting things done. He was only a step away from displacing Warham, Fox and Catherine as the king's most confidential adviser.

By the time Henry's reign entered its fourth year in April 1512, the king had imposed himself in a number of ways. Not only was he his father's heir, he was his mother's as well. For one thing, it was via her that he derived his imposing physique from his grandfather, Edward IV; for another, the Tudor rose was now for the first time both red and white. Henry VII had been (or so he claimed) the heir of Lancaster; Elizabeth was the heir of York. Their marriage had been successfully calculated to ensure that their children were the heirs to both. In Henry VIII, as his praise-singers pointed out, the long feud of the rival houses was finally brought to an end. The Wars of the Roses, which could still be perceived in the events of 1497, had finally come to an end in this magnificent young man. He had, through his own initiative, a beautiful, intelligent and fertile wife who would no doubt do her duty in due course, and he had established at least a foothold in the premier league of European diplomacy. He might still be a little green around the edges, as Ferdinand had demonstrated, but he was only 21. The best, surely, was yet to come.

§2 The King's Court

THE COURT WAS, of course, the king's immediate context. It was where he lived and where he conducted his business. Traditionally it was divided into two parts, the *domus providencie*, which was the household proper, and which provided for all the ordinary needs of the community—food, clothing, heating, transport and so on; and the *domus regie magnificencie*, or chamber, where the monarch himself was on display, and where public and ceremonial events took place.[1]

The household was divided into numerous functional departments, such as the kitchen, the scullery and the wood yard, and was controlled by a financial agency called variously the counting house or the board of greencloth. There the heads of the various departments met, determined policy and allocated funds. The counting house was presided over by a senior official called the controller of the household, and he was answerable in turn to the lord steward. The steward was appointed personally by the king, and had *ex officio* jurisdiction over the whole staff, and over all offences committed within the 'verge', which was the topographical limits laid down for the court, wherever it happened to be.[2] The household normally had about two hundred persons on the payroll, although shift work and the presence of numerous unpaid (and sometimes unacknowledged) hangers-on make an accurate head count difficult.

The whole organization was stable and strictly hierarchical, patronage within the various departments belonging by tradition to the sergeants (or departmental heads), and above that level to the lord steward. The king seldom interfered in the running of the household, which was self-contained and self-regulating.[3]

The chamber was quite different. Its staff was about 50 per cent aristocratic, ranging from the knights and esquires of the body to musicians and yeomen ushers, and it was much more directly controlled by the king. There were many forms of status within the chamber, but no hierarchy, and no set pattern of promotion. The lord chamberlain presided, and allocated duties, as well as being responsible for accommodation when the court was on progress (around the country), but unlike the steward he had no judicial authority. The chamber took its name from the fact that medieval kings, when they were not dining in public in the great hall, needed a retreat—somewhere for the council to meet, somewhere to receive ambassadors and suitors, somewhere to eat in what passed for privacy. The 'great chamber' was never a single room, but a set of rooms of increasing dignity as the king's person was approached.[4] By the latter part of his reign, Henry VII had retreated further, into a 'privy chamber' to which access was strictly controlled by servants who had no pretensions to being the king's companions. He emerged into the great chamber to dine in public and to conduct certain kinds of business; and it was in the great chamber that his household officers kept their tables, at which were fed those resident members of staff who were entitled to 'bouge of court', the right to eat at the king's expense.[5]

Henry VII's companions, in so far as he had any, were his councillors and the knights and esquires of the body. The latter performed the humble but honorific work of handing the king his shirt when he dressed in the morning, and of bearing the towels, etc., while his barber shaved him. The great chamber was all about display, and the king's orchestra, his jesters, his players, his wardrobe of the robes and his guard, were all members of the chamber staff, along with innumerable gentlemen waiters and ushers. At the beginning of Henry VIII's reign the chamber staff was about ninety, but here, even more than in the household, part-time and unpaid officers, who attended as required, make numbers hard to calculate.

EARLY FESTIVITIES AT COURT
1510

*T*HE KING *soon after came to Westminster with the Queen and all their train, and on a time being there, his grace, the earls of Essex, Wiltshire, and other noblemen to the number of twelve came suddenly on a morning into the queen's chamber all apparelled in short coats of Kentish Kendal, with hoods on their heads and hosen of the same, every one his bow and arrows and a sword and buckler, like outlaws or Robin Hoods, whereof the queen, the ladies and all other were abashed, as well for the strange sight as for their sudden coming, and after certain dances and pastime made, they departed. On Shrove Tuesday the same year the king prepared a goodly banquet in the Parliament chamber at Westminster for all the ambassadors which then were here out of diverse realms and countries. The banquet being ready, the king leading the queen, entered into the chamber, then the lords, ambassadors and other noblemen followed in order. The king caused the queen to keep the estate and then sat the ambassadors and lords as they were marshalled by the king, who would not sit but walked from place to place, making cheer to the queen and strangers.*

Suddenly the king was gone, and shortly after his grace, with the Earl of Essex came in apparelled after Turkey fashion, in long robes of bawderkin [a type of cloth] powdered with gold, hats on their heads of crimson velvet with great rolls of gold, girded with two swords called cimiteres [scimitars] hanging by great baldericks of gold. Next came the lord Henry, Earl of Wiltshire and the lord Fitzwalter in two long gowns of yellow satin, traversed with white satin, and in every ben[d] of white was a bend of crimson satin after the fashion of Russia or Russland, with fine hats of grey on their heads, either of them bearing an hatchet in their hands and boots with pikes turned up. And after them came Sir Edward Howard, then Admiral, and after him Sir Thomas Parre in doublets of crimson velvet, voided low on the back and before to the connel [breast] bone, laced on the breast with chains of silver, and over that short cloaks of crimson satin, and on their heads hats after dancers fashion, with pheasants feathers in them. They were apparelled after the fashion of Prussia or Spruce [i.e. also Prussia]. The torchbearers were apparelled in crimson satin and green, like Moriscos, their faces black. And the king brought in a mummery. After that the queen, the lords and ladies, such as would, had played, the said mummers departed and put off the same apparel, and soon after entered the chamber in their own apparel. And so the king made great cheer to the queen, ladies and ambassadors.

[Modernized from Edward Hall, *The Union of the two noble and illustrious houses of York and Lancaster*, 1550 edition, f. 5.]

The new king also had somewhat different requirements from his father. He had no use for privacy in the earlier sense; what he wanted was to be surrounded by congenial young aristocrats who would share his numerous pastimes — hunting, jousting and making music in particular. These boon companions were there from the beginning of the reign, but at first they lacked any organization or any recognized status. However, during the friendly contacts with France that at first followed the accession of Francis I in 1515, a privy chamber took shape on the French model.[6] Henry VIII kept his father's retreat with its menial servants, but added to them a new animal called a 'gentleman of the privy chamber'. These were people such as Charles Brandon, who became Duke of Suffolk, and William Compton, and their appointment belonged to the king alone. They were presided over by the most intimate and highly favoured of their number — the groom of the stool.[7] It became a matter of some contention whether they were in theory subject to the lord chamberlain, but in practice their loyalty was exclusively to the king, and successive lord chamberlains treated them with kid gloves.

The privy chamber in its new form was created between 1515 and 1518, and it was not long before its members were causing concern to the king's political advisers. They were perceived as being too intimate — 'playing light touches' — with the king, and as misbehaving themselves in public, thus bringing dishonour upon their master. In May 1519 Henry was persuaded to dismiss four of them and to draft in four knights of the body (perceived as older and more responsible men) to take their places. It used to be thought that Thomas Wolsey was responsible for this purge, but it now appears that the whole council was involved, and it may well have been this unanimity that persuaded Henry that he must act.[8]

Both the size and the nature of the privy chamber changed as the king got older. It showed an inexorable tendency to inflate in numbers, and every so often the brakes had to be applied, but the average number through the reign was about twenty. By the 1530s the jousters and 'wild boys' had disappeared, and the appointments look more political in nature. Because they had unsupervised access to the king, his gentlemen were much sought after as patrons and promoters of causes, and Thomas Cromwell, in particular, was careful to secure places for some of his own friends and supporters. They could be positions of danger as well as honour. Ease of access might embrace the queen as well as the king, and both Henry's queens who were accused of adultery—Anne Boleyn and Catherine Howard—brought down members of the privy chamber with them. The king used his gentlemen as private messengers, and was in the habit of entrusting delicate missions to them, both at home and abroad. Wolsey is alleged to have surrendered the Great Seal to the Duke of Norfolk only when he noticed that he was accompanied by a gentleman of the privy chamber, thereby demonstrating that his mission was really from the king.[9] As we have seen, Henry was also suspected of wooing Anne Hastings by proxy, in that case using Sir William Compton.

Because of its intimate nature, and because the king was the centre of all politics, the privy chamber inevitably became a centre of pressure. Between 1529 and 1533 it was purged of supporters of the cast-off Catherine of Aragon; and in 1536 of the Boleyns and their clients at Anne Boleyn's fall from grace.[10] However, no such purge followed the fall of Thomas Cromwell in 1540, so from then until the end of the reign, the privy chamber formed a sort of 'alternative council', often giving the king contradictory advice to that which was being handed down by the council proper. The latter was under conservative control by then, while the former retained many of Cromwell's men. This could only have happened because Henry so willed it, and if he took privy chamber advice from the likes of Sir Anthony Denny, it was because his mind was moving in that direction. In the political and religious conflicts of the last decade of the reign, the privy chamber was an active player.

The rise of the privy chamber was probably the most important change to occur in Henry's court, but it was not the only one. From 1509 to 1537, from 1540 to 1541, and again from 1543 to 1547 there were separate establishments for Henry's successive queens. In each case the consort chose her own intimate servants, and had at least some say in the appointment of her household officers. In Catherine of Aragon's case this meant the employment of a fair number of Spaniards and Italians; thereafter the queens usually appointed their own kindred, both male and female. Each consort was given a substantial endowment in land, from the proceeds of which she was expected to keep up her own residences and pay their staff, but those who attended her at court were paid by the king.[11] The royal children that Henry would beget—Mary, Elizabeth and Edward (all three of them future sovereigns)—were also given their own establishments, which fluctuated in size with the status of the child, and hence with the politics of the reign. These were all paid for from the chamber accounts, and while Mary was in Wales from 1525 to 1529, she was costing her father £4,000 a year.

The other main change to the court during Henry's reign was structural, but it is arguable as to how much difference it made. Thomas Cromwell, like Wolsey, became worried about how much the household was costing, and rightly believed that this was largely due to the existence of large numbers of traditional perks. He therefore decided to abolish both the chief offices, the lord chamberlain and the lord steward, replacing them with a single

'lord great master'. Like the privy chamber this office was modelled on the French system, and was intended to improve efficiency by unifying control.[12] Ironically, Cromwell's changes were
implemented in the very year of his fall, 1540. The king must have
consented to them, but he had no will to persist. As early as 1543
he had appointed a new lord chamberlain, and the lord great master thereafter became little more than the lord steward under
another name until the whole traditional structure was restored
in 1553.

A COURTIER'S CAREER—SIR WILLIAM PAULET

(i) January 1531

SIR WILLIAM PAULET *to be Surveyor General in
England, Wales, and Calais of all possessions in the King's
hands by minority of heirs, according to the act of 14 & 15 Henry
VIII, c.15. Also to be Surveyor of the King's widows, and
Governor of all idiots and naturals in the King's hands. Vice
Thomas Magnus* [*Archdeacon of the east Riding of
York*]. *Westminster, 14th January.*

[*Letters and Papers*, V. 80. Patent 22 Henry VIII, pt. 1, mem. 32.]

(ii) January 1531

SIR WILLIAM PAULET, *Master of the King's Wards.
Licence to build walls and towers within and around, and to
fortify the manor of Basing, and to empark 300 acres of land and
20 acres of woods in and about the said manor. Westminster,
30th January.*

[*Letters and Papers*, V. 80. Patent 22 Henry VIII, pt. 1, mem. 34.]

(iii) 9 March 1539

AN ACCOUNT *of the creation of Sir William Paulet* [as]
Lord St John, Sir John Russell [*as*] *Lord Russell, and
Mr William Parr* [*as*] *Lord Parr, 9th March 30 Henry VIII.
The three barons were created at Westminster after the sacring*

[*consecration of the elements*] *of the King's High Mass. Garter*
[*King of Arms*] *bore their Letters Patent before them from the*
pages' chamber. Lord Clinton followed Lord St John, bearing his
robe, he being led between Lord Cobham and Lord Dacre of the
South. Then Clarenceaux [*the herald*] *bearing the robe of Lord*
Russell, who was led between Lord Sturton and Lord Windsor.
The Norroy [*the pursuivant, i.e. the rank below herald*] *in*
default of a baron, bore the robe of Lord Parr, led by Lord Went-
worth. They then proceeded to the Chamber of Presence, where
they were commanded to put on their robes, and from that in due
order to the King and received their Patents not read. Their styles
were proclaimed afterwards, at the second course as they sat at
dinner. Fees to heralds given.

[*Letters and Papers*, XIV, I, 477. BL Harley MS 6074, f.56.]

The court was constantly on the move. This was partly to enable
the king to show himself to his people, but more because contemporary hygiene was primitive, and after several weeks of residence by 200–300 people even the most commodious palace
became insalubrious. Henry went on progress every so often, most
notably to York in 1541, but most of his migrations were simply
from one to another of his own residences in the Home Counties.
He had nearly sixty houses by the 1540s, some as far away as Lud-
low (Shropshire) and Newcastle upon Tyne, but seldom visited
more than about six or eight of those within easy reach.[13] Greenwich, Westminster and Windsor were his early favourites, but
once he had acquired Hampton Court from Wolsey in 1525 that
became the most favoured of all. The great new palace that he
built at Nonsuch was visited from time to time to oversee work in
progress, but it was never finished in his lifetime.

When not in use, these palaces were on a care and maintenance basis, with a skeleton staff in each, because most of the furni-
ture and fittings required when the court was in residence arrived
in an enormous baggage train a few days before the king himself.
As a result last minute changes of plan were extremely unpopular

with the marshals and harbingers (those officials sent on ahead) who had to organize the transit.

Particularly in his younger days, Henry was also in the habit of going off hunting. He had a number of hunting lodges within easy reach of London, of which Oatlands in Surrey was probably his favourite. Such visits were usually small scale (twenty or thirty people) and of relatively short duration. If the king's intentions were known in advance, some servants would be sent down from the court to look after him and his party, but if they were not, a scratch staff would be recruited locally, and those living close to the more popular lodges became accustomed to such demands.

How much all this cost is very difficult to ascertain, because a number of separate accounts were involved. In 1531–2, for example, the 'cofferer', who paid wages and oversaw staff, accounted for £27,947, but that was just on the household, and the chamber accounts are confused by the fact that the treasury of the chamber was also a public-spending department and was used for many other things apart from the chamber wages.[14] At this time the chamber proper was probably costing about £20,000 a year, which was to rise to £25,300 by the last year of the reign. If we assume that the average cost of the whole court between 1530 and 1547 was £45,000–50,000 a year, that would probably not be far out. At the same time the ordinary revenue of the crown, exclusive of direct taxation and windfalls like monastic lands, was about £130,000.[15]

The king always had his own privy purse, which was administered by the groom of the stool, and for which he accounted to nobody. This was used for such matters as gambling debts, special rewards, unscheduled alms and the occasional purchase. It amounted to about £3,000 or £4,000 a year, and was replenished from such windfalls as the French pension, paid by Francis I (when there was no war, and when he felt like it) in accordance with the terms of the treaty of 1514; and also from the sale of lands or the produce of estates. During the last decade of the reign there was also another office, called the king's coffers. At the end this was held by Sir Anthony Denny in his capacity as keeper of the Palace of Westminster.[16] Denny eventually accounted for over £100,000, spread over several years, when it was noted that £11,350 in cash had been secreted in the Jewel House at the time of Henry's death. This money seems to have come mainly from the activities of the Court of Augmentations, which administered the proceeds of the dissolution of the monasteries, but it also absorbed all the other casual sources, and the privy purse drew on it. It was also used rather as the treasury of the chamber had once been used, for state purposes, particularly diplomatic, but also occasionally military. In addition the king used it to fund his building projects. The treasury of the chamber had been returned to its earlier function when the financial administration was reorganized in the 1530s, and the king's coffers seems to have taken its place—except that it was subjected to no regular accounting procedure. When Denny eventually accounted in 1548, it was before a special commission.[17]

There were thus no clear distinctions drawn between the king's private expenditure and the expenditure of the state. In a sense the court was the government, or at least the political end of it. The administration and judiciary had long ago gone 'out of court', as it was significantly expressed, so the chancery and the Court of King's Bench no longer functioned within the verge, but in every other sense the court was central, and the tendency to financial confusion reflects that.

A PAGE OF HENRY VIII'S PRIVY PURSE EXPENSES
1530

Item the xix day paid to my lord of Norfolk for so much
    money by him lent to the king's grace in play xxvii li.
    in Angels in sterling   *xxx li viis vid.*
Item the same day paid to master Bryan for so much money
    by him lent unto the king's grace in play which was
                                C crowns xviii li vis viiid

Item the same day to Will[ia]m Crane for the wages of
Will[ia]m pury for one quarter ended now at Michaelmas
                                                        xliiiis viiid
Item the same day paid to Wa[l]ter Walshe for so much money
by him paid to my lord of Rocheford for shooting at Hunsdon
                                                        xxiis vid
Item the last day paed to Ch[rist]ofer Myllon for edges of gold
weighing ii ounces and iii quarters and iiis at xi crowns the oz.
                                                        vi li xixs vid
Item the same day to the keeper of Richmond in Reward   vis viiid
Item the same day to the ferryman in Reward   vis viiid

S[u]m[a] part[es]   *lxiiii li xiis ixd.*
S[u]m[a] to[talis] solc' hui mensis Septembris   CCCix li ixs xid

   [signed] Henricus R

[*The Privy Purse Expenses of King Henry the Eighth from 1529 to 1532*, ed.
N.H. Nicolas (1827), p. 76.]

Security, as that is understood in the modern world, was almost
non-existent at court. Henry VII had established, soon after his
accession, a bodyguard of two hundred (or so) archers, known as
the yeomen of the guard. At the time this was a sensible protection against the most obvious kind of threat, a physical attack
upon the court, which was a real possibility, particularly on progress. However, by the time that his son was settled on the throne,
the yeomen served mainly ceremonial purposes. There were always
some of them on duty, but they are not known to have been
called upon in earnest until the time of the Wyatt rebellion during Mary's reign, in 1554.[18]

   Henry VIII, as we have seen, loved military display, and in 1511
attempted to set up a new ceremonial guard, of higher social status, known as 'the spears'. For some reason or other this was a
short-lived experiment, and it was not until 1539 that such a group
became established. It was then known as 'the gentlemen pensioners', the idea being to provide honourable employment for

old soldiers, as well as to safeguard the king. The gentlemen pensioners numbered 50, had their own officers, and were paid at the dignified rate of £50 a year.[19] Members of the band served in shifts, and usually had other occupations, sometimes also around the court. These gentlemen guarded the privy chamber, and would no doubt have been reasonably effective if they had ever been called upon. The privy chamber (again a suite of rooms, not a single one) was the one part of the court to which access was tightly controlled. Elsewhere the public came and went, almost at will. It was said that all you needed to get past the porters on the gate was a presentable appearance and a little money to pay an inducement. The merest pretext of legitimate business (plus further inducements) would have enabled the interloper to pass various doors in the chamber, theoretically guarded by yeomen or gentlemen ushers.

When a tournament or some other display was in hand, the gates were in any case open to all, who were invited to come and be overawed by the royal splendour. In spite of his controversial policies and opinions, no one (as far as we know) ever made an attempt upon Henry's life—or on those of any of his courtiers. The courtiers themselves probably constituted a greater danger, to each other and to the king, for at this time it was common for a gentleman to wear a sword, and honour was sensitive and tempers short.[20] Nevertheless, an absolute ban on weapons in the privy chamber and the most draconian penalties for bloodshed in the royal presence seems to have kept the problem under control.

Henry liked receiving petitions: it added to his sense of being respected, and he deliberately made himself available to receive them from time to time, usually when he was on his way to the Chapel Royal, or off hunting. Petitions could be presented at other times, but only through the mediation of a well-placed courtier, who was likely to charge heavily for his assistance. Successive queens were also energetic petitioners, and their ladies developed a clientele of their own for a similar purpose.[21]

The more general security of the household at large was even less strict. One of the main problems was that the king's lavish lifestyle (necessary for his honour) meant that a great deal more food was cooked than was consumed. Some of this was distributed to the normal servants by way of perquisites, and some was regularly distributed in alms, but much was up for grabs by anyone who could infiltrate the kitchen or the scullery. Consequently, there were always a lot of unauthorized extra hands in those departments. If they did not fight, or make nuisances of themselves, the sergeants tended to turn a blind eye, and sometimes, if there was a push on, it was useful to have their labour. Every so often the senior officers conducted a purge of these undesirables, but they always came back.[22]

The other problem was caused by the fact that there was a chronic shortage of women. Even in the chamber the queen's ladies and their female servants constituted only a small minority; in the household it was much worse. Apart from the laundresses (an indeterminate number and not a department), there were none in legitimate service. As a result, whichever palace the court was in was besieged by the local prostitutes, who did a roaring trade. Again the departmental officers tended to turn a blind eye: undesirable as they might be, these women performed a necessary function, and in any case their activities were preferable to encouraging the 'detestable sin of buggery', which was the realistic alternative.[23] Only a small minority of the more established servants were married and lived in, or nearby, with their wives and children. As with the 'vagabonds and boys', the prostitutes were periodically driven away by the senior officers, but nothing could deter them for long. Rather surprisingly, given this ease of access, there were no recorded riots in the lower reaches of the court, and no one tried to poison the king's soup. Venereal disease was probably a different matter, but no statistics were kept.

As the court surrounded the king, and the council always met within the verge, in a sense all the politics of the realm was also the politics of the court. However, it is unrealistic to treat most of the problems of government in that way. The most obvious point of contact between court and politics was the king's sex life. Insofar as this constituted successive marriages and the question of getting an heir, this will be dealt with in later chapters. But there was always rather more to it than that. One might have expected a young man like Henry, who prided himself on his virility, to have run a series of mistresses alongside his legitimate wives. However, Henry did this only to a very limited extent, and the fact may be that he was never as good in bed as he liked to think he was.

As we have seen, his relationship with Anne Hastings was simply a matter of rumour and speculation, and for about the first four or five years of his marriage to Catherine of Aragon he was probably (more or less) faithful to her. However, that relationship, after a few years, began to have its ups and downs. Henry was furious with Ferdinand for betraying their alliance in 1514, and some of his indignation rubbed off on his wife. Her pregnancy of that year also seems to have ended in a miscarriage, which did not help. However by the autumn of 1515 she was pregnant again, and in February 1516 bore a healthy daughter, Mary, who lived and thrived. Both partners were hugely relieved, and relations between them visibly improved, although both were equally aware that their task, dynastically speaking, was only half done.

Ironically, it was at this same time, probably during his wife's pregnancy, that Henry took his first identifiable mistress. This was Elizabeth Blount, the 16-year-old daughter of John Blount of Kinlet, a family that has been described as 'county rather than court', although Elizabeth herself had probably been placed in Catherine's entourage by her kinsman, Walter Blount, Lord Mountjoy—a man who was definitely of the court.[24] The attraction appears to have been purely physical; Elizabeth was a pretty, vivacious blonde, and not so well brought up that she would have spurned the king's advances. Henry seems to have run her alongside Catherine for about three years. The latter must have been well aware of this, but was too well disciplined to protest.

However, in 1518 the fortunes of the two women dramatically overlapped. In the summer of that year Catherine was delivered of a stillborn daughter, which turned out to be her last confinement, and in the autumn Elizabeth fell pregnant. In June 1519 she was delivered of a son, whom the king immediately acknowledged and named Henry FitzRoy. Young Henry was not brought up at court, perhaps to avoid affront to the queen, but he was well provided for.[25] By the end of the year his mother had been married to Gilbert Tailboys, and her relationship with the king seems to have ended. In a sense she had served her purpose, in demonstrating that Henry was capable of getting a healthy son (and that therefore his dynastic problem was all Catherine's fault), but the real reason for Henry's abrupt change of direction seems to have been that his attention had been diverted elsewhere. Knowing what was good for her, Elizabeth went quietly. Kings were like that.

HENRY FITZROY, THE ILLEGITIMATE SON

YOU SHALL UNDERSTAND *that the king in his fresh youth was in the chains of love, with a fair damsel called Elizabeth Blunt, daughter to Sir John Blunt, knight, which damsel in singing, dancing, and in all goodly pastimes, exceeded all other, by which goodly pastimes she won the king's heart: and she again shewed him such favour that by him she bore a goodly man child, of beauty like to the father and mother. This child was well brought up like a Prince child, and when he was six years of age, the king made him knight, and called him Lord Henry FitzRoy, and on Sunday being the xviii day of June [1525], at the manor or place of Bridewell, the said Lord, led by two Earls, was created Earl of Nottingham, and then he was brought back again by the said two Earls; then the Dukes of Norfolk and Suffolk led him into the great chamber again, and the King created him Duke of Richmond and Somerset ...*

[Taken from Richard Grafton, *A Chronicle and mere history*, 1809 edition, pp. 382–3.]

Henry's new love was Mary Boleyn, the elder daughter of Sir Thomas Boleyn, and a young lady of both breeding and lineage.

Exactly when this relationship began, and how long it lasted, we do not know. The king probably became interested during Elizabeth's pregnancy, although he had by no means given up on Catherine at that point, and Mary was married to George Carey before Henry became seriously involved with her younger sister Anne in about 1527. Mary quickly became pregnant by her husband, but never seems to have been so by the king, and certainly bore him no child, which raises questions about Henry that cannot now be answered. Mary, like Elizabeth, went quietly, but Anne was a quite different proposition, and her liaison with the king would become the matter of high politics for which it is famous.

It all began with the well-known pastime known as 'courtly love'. These games were essentially charades, in which the gallants of the court pretended to be passionately enamoured of their female counterparts. Moves and evasions were carefully plotted, tokens exchanged, trophies offered, and dramatic scenes of passion, disdain and reconciliation played out.[26] The winners were those who kept up the pretence longest and most convincingly. All these encounters were supposed to be platonic, but human nature being what it is, they very often turned into real affairs— and sometimes into scandals. Henry was a skilful and enthusiastic player, and one much in demand, so that many of the rumours of his 'amours', which become increasingly frequent after about 1518, can be traced to this source and need not be taken seriously. However, Anne, who was a feisty and talented flirt rather than a great beauty, found that she had—perhaps inadvertently—hooked the biggest fish of all.

A LETTER FROM HENRY TO ANNE BOLEYN
Undated, but probably 1528

To my Mistress

B ECAUSE THE TIME *seems very long since I heard concerning your health and you, the great affection I have for you has induced me to send you this bearer, to be better informed*

of your health and pleasure, and because since my parting from
you I have been told that the opinion in which I left you is totally
changed and that you would not come to court either with your
mother, if you could, or in any other manner. Which report, if
true, I cannot sufficiently marvel at, because I am sure that I have
since never done anything to offend you, and it seems a very poor
return for the great love which I bear you to keep me at a distance
both from the speech and the person of the woman I esteem most
in the world. And if you love me with as much affection as I hope
you do, I am sure that the distance of our two persons would be a
little irksome to you, though this does not belong so much to the
mistress as to the servant.

Consider well, my mistress, that absence from you grieves me
sorely, hoping that it is not your will that it should be so. But if I
knew for certain that you voluntarily desired it I could do no other
than mourn my ill fortune, and by degrees abate my great folly.
And so for lack of time I make an end of this rude letter,
beseeching you to give credence to the bearer in all that he will tell
you from me.

Written by the hand of your entire servant   HR

[The originals of these letters are lost. Italian translations remain in the
Vatican archives, and this retranslation into English is taken from an
edition by V. and H. Trovillion, privately printed in the United States
in 1936.]

There is no doubt that by 1528 Henry was passionately in love
with Anne, and thoughts of a second marriage were certainly in
his mind.[27] It is at that point that the politics become important,
because Catherine was past the age of child-bearing, and the king
needed an heir. The traditional story is that Anne held out on
him, demanding marriage as the price of her compliance, and
that it was this resistance that forced him into the path he would
follow. However, that story was circulated by Anne's supporters,
particularly Protestants of the next generation who were anxious
to present her as promoter of godliness. Her honour needed

safeguarding, particularly in view of her eventual fate. However, the king needed a marriage just as much as she did. Another Henry FitzRoy would not solve his succession problem, and since he had decided not later than the summer of 1529 that Anne would be his next wife when (and if) he managed to get rid of Catherine, it is quite possible that it was he who was holding back.[28] He could hardly marry a mistress who had already presented him with a child, no matter how much he might love her. He was perfectly well aware that Anne was unpopular, and was getting the blame for Henry's estrangement from his wife, and that her supporters formed a political party at daggers drawn with Catherine's adherents.

The politics of all this is discussed in later chapters, but it was no accident that it was only after Archbishop Warham's death in August 1532, when Henry could see a way out of the impasse over his marriage, that he eventually slept with Anne, and she almost immediately became pregnant. When that pregnancy was discovered in January 1533, events had to move fast. Thomas Cranmer was summoned back from a diplomatic mission to Germany and made Archbishop of Canterbury on the clear understanding that he would solve the problem of Catherine. With that in prospect, Henry and Anne were secretly married, and Cranmer duly pronounced the king's first union null and void. This was done in direct defiance of a papal prohibition, and signalled the real point of rupture between the two jurisdictions. The king then had to rally his court to put on a convincing show of rejoicing and solidarity in the face of a sceptical, and often hostile, world.

That was the point of the splendid coronation with which she was provided on 8 June 1533, an account of which was published almost at once (see Chapter 4).[29] The latter was a pure propaganda exercise, with the praise for the king and his new queen heavily emphasized, and a lot of names dropped to indicate support. What were not, of course, mentioned, were the names of those who had conspicuously absented themselves—the Imperial ambassador, the Duchess of Suffolk (Henry's sister) and the king's

17-year-old daughter Mary. Anne's triumph split the court, and caused quite a few of Catherine's supporters to withdraw altogether, considering that the king had been dishonoured by his actions. When Elizabeth was born in September, there was much hilarity, heavily suppressed in London, but less so in Edinburgh or Brussels (effectively the Imperial capital). Henry had got himself excommunicated and driven his Church into schism, for the sake of another daughter.

Nevertheless, there was no sign of estrangement between the royal couple, and the Boleyn party remained dominant at court. Anne's father, Sir Thomas, had been created Earl of Wiltshire in 1529, and his son George was a member of the privy chamber. Such change as took place was scarcely visible to the outside world, but it was important. So accustomed to being the coquettish mistress, Anne did not adapt very readily to the role of wife; there were scenes, tantrums and passionate reconciliations, and the conventionally minded king became disillusioned. A wife should be dutiful and submissive, and Anne was neither of those things. So their relationship became fragile. Anne did not conceive again until the summer of 1535, and then in February 1536 was delivered of a stillborn son. Henry's demons returned. Someone had offended God, and it could not have been him.[30]

At the end of April, and using evidence that was either circumstantial or spurious, the queen's enemies at court succeeded in convincing Henry that Anne had been guilty of grievous sexual misconduct. Catherine had died in January, so there was no longer any risk of his being forced to take her back, and the temptation to wipe the slate clean and start again became irresistible. Anne had not helped her own cause by making some ill-considered gestures to male companions; two members of the privy chamber, Sir Henry Norris and her own brother, George, were identified among her 'paramours', and shared her fate. The wife for whom Henry had paid such a high price was executed on 19 May 1536.

There were political as well as personal reasons for this, as we

shall see, and one of the consequences was that Catherine's former supporters now looked to the reinstatement of the Princess
Mary, and she herself expected no less. The expedient alliance
that had brought down Anne quickly dissolved, and a sharp tussle
ensued between the principal secretary, Thomas Cromwell (now
Henry's closest advisor), and Mary's adherents, which resulted in
several of the latter being rusticated, sent from court to their estates,
and one or two imprisoned. At the end of June the princess herself capitulated to her father's demand that she acknowledge his
ecclesiastical supremacy (and her own bastardy), and a degree of
harmony returned to the court.[31]

THE SURRENDER OF PRINCESS MARY

Imperial ambassador Eustace Chapuys to the Emperor Charles, 1
July 1536.

WHEN THE PRINCESS, *having written several good letters
to the King her father, and to this Queen [Jane Seymour],
expected to be out of trouble, trusting to the hope held out to her,
she found herself in the most extreme perplexity and danger that
she had ever been in, and not only herself but also her principal
friends. The King ... took a fancy to insist that the princess
should consent to his statutes, or he would proceed by rigour of
law against her, and to induce her to yield sent to her the Duke
of Norfolk, the Earl of Sussex, the bishop of [Chi]chester, and
certain others, whom she confounded with her wise and prudent
answers, till they, seeing that they could not conquer her by
argument, told her that since she was so unnatural as to oppose
the king's will so obstinately ... she was a traitress and should
be punished ... Nevertheless the said princess found means to
send me immediate information of everything, begging me not to
leave her without counsel in her extreme necessity. On this I wrote
to her very fully, telling her among other things that she must
make up her mind if the king persisted in his obstinacy, or she
found evidence that her life was in danger ... to consent to her
father's wish, assuring her that such was your advice, that to save*

*her life, on which depended the peace of the realm and the redress
of the great disorders which prevail here, she must do everything
and dissemble for some time ...*

*Cromwell, for having communicated with me upon the affairs
of the princess, and showing himself rather favourable, was not free
from suspicion, or without danger of being put to death, and as he
has since told me, he remained for four or five days considering
himself a lost man and dead ... I have been informed from more
than one source, that the king had sworn in a great passion, that
not only the Princess should suffer, but also the Marquis [of
Exeter], Cromwell and several others. Now I hear that the judges,
in spite of threats, refused to decide and advised that a writing
should be sent to the Princess, and that if she refused to sign it,
they should proceed against her. The Princess, being informed from
various quarters of how matters stood, signed the document without reading it. For her better excuse I had previously sent her the
form of protestation which she must make apart. I had also warned
her that she must in the first place endeavour to secure the king's
pardon ... As soon as news arrived of her subscription, incredible
joy was shown in all the court ... Innumerable persons sent to me
to congratulate me on the reconciliation of the King and the
Princess ...*

[Taken from *Letters and Papers*, XI, 7. The original, in French, is in the
Vienna Staatsarchiv.]

Henry swiftly married Jane Seymour, a move that seems to have
had general support, and a new group of kinsmen came to the
fore, notably Jane's brother, Sir Edward Seymour, created Earl of
Hertford on 18 October 1537. Jane succeeded where her predecessors had failed, and presented Henry with his long-desired
son, Edward, born on 12 October 1537. Unfortunately she died of
the effects, and this rather plain, amiable and innocuous young
woman passed from the scene as quickly as she had burst upon it.
Henry was genuinely distressed. His only illegitimate son, Henry
FitzRoy, had died during the previous summer, but Edward

flourished. The king now had one legitimate son and two illegitimate daughters, and although his anxiety was diminished, it had not entirely gone away.

For over two years the king remained unmarried, and the marriage with Anne of Cleves, which then ensued, does not belong here. A household was created for her at court, but it was of such short endurance that it scarcely impacted.[32] His fifth marriage, however, to Catherine Howard, was very much a court affair. It came about (allegedly) because the Duke of Norfolk deliberately dangled his nubile niece before the king's nose in the hope of establishing a family ascendancy in the interests of conservative politics. Whether that was the case or not, the 50-year-old king quickly became infatuated with this attractive young woman. They were married on (or about) 28 July 1540,[33] and for a few months Henry appeared to enjoy a return to the amorous and athletic enthusiasm of his youth. Unfortunately, he had no idea what kind of a woman he had taken on.

Brought up in the ill-regulated household of the Dowager Duchess of Norfolk, Catherine had acquired a lot of sexual experience, and developed a healthy appetite. She was by no means the innocent bride that the king thought she was, and Henry's elderly and erratic performance came nowhere near to satisfying her. As early as 12 July 1540, when the well-informed already knew which way the wind was blowing, one of her former 'bedfellows' demanded and obtained a place at court as the price of her silence,[34] and during the spring of 1541 Catherine renewed a relationship with one of her previous partners, Thomas Culpepper, now a junior member of the privy chamber. While the court was on progress in the north in the summer of 1541, the queen, with the connivance of her chief gentlewoman, Jane Rochford, indulged in what can only be described as a bedroom farce, involving Culpepper and another former lover, Francis Dereham. At the time, Henry was blissfully unaware of all this, but there was no such thing as privacy at court: a servant, or servants, somewhere always knew what was going on.

As a person, Catherine was too insignificant to have enemies, but her family and the interests that they represented certainly had. Among these enemies was one John Lascelles, whose sister had been in the service of the dowager duchess. This sister, Mary Hall, knew the whole story, and on 1 November 1541 Lascelles passed circumstantial details to the Archbishop of Canterbury.[35] Cranmer broke the news to the king as gently as he could, and Henry's first reaction was one of outright denial—the whole story was mere slander. However, he ordered an investigation, and before long a tearful and distraught Catherine had confessed to everything.

It is a desperately sad story, and one that touches the very heart of the court. The queen was little more than a wayward child, who had no notion of how to behave. However, she was the king's consort, and she was guilty of adultery. By the same token her paramours and their facilitator, Jane Rochford, were guilty of treason. By the terms of the act of 1534, anyone who should 'by craft imagine, invent, practice or attempt any bodily harm to be done or committed to the king's most royal person, the Queen's or their heir apparent's ...' was so guilty, irrespective of what those crafty imaginings had actually achieved. In fact there is some doubt as to how far Catherine's amours had actually gone, but there is no doubt that the intention was there—and that was sufficient.

Francis Dereham and Thomas Culpepper were tried and convicted on 1 December, and subsequently executed on the 10th. Catherine herself and Jane Rochford were condemned by act of attainder, and beheaded on 13 February 1542.[36] Henry had been deeply humiliated by the conduct of his once-adored wife, and was vindictive in his anger. If ever a butterfly was broken on the wheel, it was Catherine Howard.

The king was probably redeemed from an orgy of self-pity by the demands of diplomacy and war, but Howard influence was for the time being completely destroyed. Apart from the duke himself, who tactfully withdrew to his estates, the whole family stood accused of 'misprision' (not disclosing knowledge of treasonable

activities), and could have forfeited everything that they possessed. It did not come to that, because they were eventually pardoned, but the balance of power within the court was seriously
disturbed. Cromwell's former supporters were now in the ascendant, and that ascendancy was reinforced by the king's last marriage, on 12 July 1543, to Catherine, the recently widowed Lady
Latimer—better known by her maiden name of Catherine Parr.

Catherine was a benign presence rather than a power.[37] She
was a little over 30, and was already well known at court. As
queen she was a caring stepmother to Edward and Elizabeth, a
friend to Mary, and a nurse and companion to her increasingly
ailing and irascible spouse. As was normal, her kindred were promoted, particularly her brother William, who became Earl of
Essex, and the ladies of her privy chamber were of a distinctly
humanist or 'evangelical' persuasion. This last factor spelt danger,
because although the conservatives in the council were on the
defensive, they were still capable of counterattack, and there is an
unsubstantiated story that Gardiner and Wriothesley, the lord
chancellor, attempted to remove the queen by playing on Henry's
dislike of heretics—and his dislike of being lectured.[38] The story
is plausible, and no doubt based on the known sympathy of some
of her ladies for the aggressively heretical Anne Askew, but it
hinges upon the improbable accident of Catherine finding out
what was afoot. It is then alleged that by humbling herself before
the king, and disavowing all pretensions to knowledge, she turned
aside the wrath to come, and effected 'a perfect reconciliation'.
Collapse of reactionary party.

Whether this story is basically true or not, it points to one
undoubted fact. The politics of the court always depended, ultimately, upon the will (or whim) of the king. Factions, in the sense
of groups of like-minded individuals sharing a common goal,
certainly existed, and Henry's successive consorts, although not
necessarily leaders, were often the symbols of these factions. This
was most obviously the case with the Boleyns, who with their
supporters constituted an anti-papal and pro-French pressure

group for about ten years, from 1526 to 1536. In that case Anne was the real leader as well as the figurehead, but both their success and ultimate failure depended upon Henry and the nature of her influence over him. Catherine of Aragon and the Princess Mary were not leaders in the same sense, but they were equally the centre of a contrary faction, which fought tooth and nail to resist Boleyn influence.

Catherine was no match for Anne as a king-pleaser, but after her death, when the boundaries shifted somewhat, Catherine's pro-papal, pro-Imperial faction also enjoyed their moment of success—because the king changed his mind about Anne and her circle. Mary's surrender, though, destroyed her mother's supporters after 1536 because they no longer had a focus, and the princess refused to be used as a pressure point against her father. Jane Seymour played no such part, and the rise of her kindred cannot be associated with any cause, but the Howards were another family based faction, who, during Catherine's brief ascendancy, undoubtedly influenced the king. However, the total eclipse that they suffered as a result of her indiscretions should warn us against supposing that they had any control over Henry.

It would also be a mistake to think of the religious conservatives after 1540 as having any kind of coherence, even after the rehabilitation of the Howards. They were, perhaps, a group of factions. Their rivals, the 'evangelicals', certainly shared the common aim of securing influence and resisting their rivals, and they certainly used Queen Catherine Parr as a rallying point, but they also were a miscellaneous bunch, and whether Catherine was a real leader is still an open question. At an earlier date, the Duke of Buckingham had been brought down by the king's suspicions, and by his own stupidity, not by factional rivals, and although Wolsey had many enemies, they had no consistent purpose beyond discrediting him. It is slightly more realistic to see Anne Boleyn and Thomas Cromwell as victims of faction; certainly, their enemies were organized, but in both cases those enemies' efforts would have come to nothing if they had failed to convince the king.[39]

The point is emphasized, not only by the survival of Catherine Parr, but even more by the survival of Thomas Cranmer, who was the target of factional hostility on at least two occasions.

Henry was always the master in his own house, although he did not always appear to be. For a variety of reasons, commentators—both contemporary and historical—have often sought to explain his apparently abrupt changes of favour and direction in terms of who had the king's ear—it was all the fault of these 'evil counsellors', who included unsympathetic consorts. The king was not immune to influence, even pressure, but his erratic behaviour sprang from deep roots within himself. His concentration span was limited, particularly in his younger days, and on some occasions he may simply not have been paying attention to what he was told. In later life he acquired a range of prejudices and dislikes, which his courtiers and advisers simply had to take account of, and steer around—unless, like Catherine Howard, they were too stupid. Henry's successive marriages, and the rise and fall of his consorts' kindred, tell us a great deal about the sensitivities of the court environment. His first, second and fourth marriages all had international implications, which will be dealt with elsewhere, but the Seymour, Howard and Parr unions raised only domestic issues. Each in turn refocused the court, readjusted its personnel, and to some extent altered its climate. But the man who had to be satisfied, pleased and humoured was always the king.

§3 The King at War

WAR FOR HENRY was simply a political option. It was also in a sense the sport of kings, in which their subjects participated rather like pieces on a chess board. In spite of the influence that his tutors and humanist friends exercised on him in other ways, he never shared their moral revulsion against violence, nor objected particularly to Christians fighting among themselves. In spite of the provocative policies that he followed, Henry was never the object of attacks by others, and although his strategy from 1535 onwards could be described as broadly defensive, he was actually the aggressor in all the wars he undertook. He spent vast sums of money on military campaigns, fortifications and the navy, and that expenditure influenced his domestic policies profoundly and in many ways.

Just as his tournaments imitated the chivalric culture of 15th-century Burgundy, so he seems to have perceived very little difference between gallant gentlemen fighting 'at the barriers', on foot in tournaments, and those same gentlemen on the field of battle. Protected as he was from many of its grimmer realities, the young Henry looked on war rather as the public-school 'bloods' used to regard a game of rugby—a manly exercise, not without its dangers, but carrying a high reward in terms of glory and reputation. Even to the ageing Henry of the 1540s, whose jousting days were long since past, it was essential to take to the field in person if he was to preserve his self-respect and justify his place among the great princes of Europe.

As we have seen, Henry attacked France in 1512 because he

wanted to, and because it seemed the right thing for a young and virile king to do. The war lasted about two years, and in the course of it Henry was taught some very salutary lessons. In spite of the initial humiliation in Aquitaine, he continued to trust Ferdinand, and in December 1512 put forward a new suggestion for the forthcoming season. He would pay the Spaniards a large subsidy and leave the southwestern campaign to them. He preferred to attack from the north, through Picardy, taking advantage of the friendly (or at least acquiescent) attitude of the Emperor Maximilian.[1] This plan had two big advantages from Henry's point of view: he would not be dependent on Ferdinand's support, which seemed to be so vulnerable to misunderstandings; and he would be able to campaign in person. The fact that it was also likely to be enormously expensive did not at this stage worry him. Although his reserves were disappearing at an alarming rate, Parliament was cooperative and voted him a war subsidy. It had been a long time since it had been asked for such support.[2]

Henry also achieved what appeared to be a major diplomatic coup, by reforming and expanding the Holy League to include the Emperor, an agreement signed at Malines on 5 April 1513. However, no sooner had this been achieved than Ferdinand signed a one-year truce with Louis, and thus opted out of any forthcoming campaign. This time Henry was seriously annoyed, and all the more so when Ferdinand accused him of bullying his ambassador into endorsing the Malines agreement.[3] Nevertheless, Henry pressed on with his own plans, and landed with a massive army at Calais on 30 June. It is easy to see why he was not to be deterred. Both his fleet and his entourage had been in preparation for months, and the military pageantry that accompanied his arrival was worthy of an emperor setting out to conquer the world. So impressive was his display that the real Emperor did not attempt to compete, offering only the most modest support in discharge of his treaty obligations.

Inevitably the campaign itself failed to live up to the preliminaries. It was successful enough, but hardly on the grand scale.

Siege was laid to the small fortress of Therouanne, and on 16 August an enemy relief force that had miscalculated the scale of its task was put to flight, a skirmish magnified by Henry's praise-singers into the Battle of the Spurs. A few days later, on 24 August, the town fell, and was promptly handed over to Maximilian, who razed it. A month later the more substantial city of Tournai was taken after an eight-day siege, and was to remain in English hands for several years.[4] Henry convinced himself that this was a glorious triumph, and celebrated on a lavish scale with jousts and pageants, but in truth it was almost irrelevant in terms of his war aims.

The king sent his trophies from Tournai to lay at the feet of his queen in the best chivalric tradition, but Catherine, as his governor in England for the duration of his absence, had in fact won a far more significant victory than anything he had achieved. James IV had been at peace with England since the Treaty of Ayton in 1503, when he had married Henry's sister, Margaret, and had no good reason to break that peace now. Nevertheless he did so, motivated partly by the ancient alliance of the Scots with the French, and partly by the thought that Henry's involvement in France created an opportunity that was too good to miss. He sent a formal defiance to the English king on 11 August 1513, and few days later crossed the Tweed at the head of a large army. If he thought that his enemies would be unprepared, he miscalculated disastrously. Confronted by the Earl of Surrey at Flodden on 9 September, his army was routed, and James himself, together with 12 earls and three bishops was killed in the battle.[5] His son and heir was fifteen months old, and Scotland was taken out for the foreseeable future.

THE BATTLE OF FLODDEN
1513

T HEN THE ENGLISH *men removed their field on the water of Tyll [Till], and so forth over many hills and straits, marching towards the Scots on another side, and in their sight the Scots burned certain poor Villages on the other side of the*

Marishe [*marsh, bog*].

The English men always leaving the Scottish army on the left hand, took their field under a wood side, called Barmer wood, two miles from the Scots, and between the two armies was the river of *Tyll*, and there was a little hill that saved the English men from the gunshot, on which hill the Lord Admiral perfectly saw and discovered them all …

The king of Scots perceiving the Englishmen, marching toward Scotland, thought that they would have entered into Scotland, and burn and foray the plentiful country called the March, for so he was made to believe by an Englishman named *Gyles Musgrave* which was familiar with the king of Scots, and did it for a policy to cause him to come down from the hill …

Then the Lord Admiral perceived four great battles of the Scots all on foot with long spears like moorish pikes: which Scots furnished them warlike, and bent them to the forward, which was conducted by the Lord Admiral, which perceiving that, sent to his father the Earl of Surrey his agnus dei that hung at his breast that in all haste he would join battle even with the brunt or breast of the vanguard: for the forward alone was not able to encounter the whole battle of the Scots, the Earl perceiving well the saying of his son, and seeing the Scots ready to descend the hill advanced himself and his people forward and brought the[m] equal in ground with the forward on the left hand, even at the brunt or breast of the same at the foot of the hill called Bramston [*Branxton*], the English army stretched East and West, and their backs North, and the Scots in the South before them on the foresaid hill called Bramston. Then out burst the ordnance on both sides with fire, flame and hideous noise, and the master Gunner of the English part slew the master Gunner of Scotland, and beat all his men from their ordnance, so that the Scottish ordnance did no harm to the Englishmen, but the Englishmen's artillery shot into the midst of the kings battle [*formation of troops*] and slew many persons, which seeing, the king of Scots and his noble men made the more haste to come to joining, & so all the four battles in

manner descended the hill at once. After that the shot was done,
which they defended with pavises [shields], they came to
handstrokes, and were encountered severally ...

All these four battles in manner fought at one time, and were
determined in effect, little in distance of the beginning and ending
of any of them one before the other, saving that Sir Edward
Stanley, which was the last that fought, for he came up to the top
of the hill, and there fought with the Scots valiantly, and chased
them down the hill over that place, where the kings battle joined.
Beside these four Battles of the Scots were two other battles, which
never came to hand strokes.

Thus through the power of God on Friday, being the ix day of
September, in the year of our Lord 1513 was James the fourth king
of Scots slain at Bramstone (chiefly by the power of the Earl of
Surrey, Lieutenant for king Henry the eight, King of England,
(which then lay at the siege before Tournai) and with the said
king were slain[:]

The Archbishop of saint Andrews, the kings Bastard son ...
[there then follows a list of 44 bishops, lairds and knights slain;
Scots losses in total have been estimated at 10,000–12,000.]

[Richard Grafton, *A Chronicle at large and meere History of the affayres of*
England, 1568. Taken from the edition by Henry Ellis, 1809, pp. 274–6.]

Although he had secured no conquests in either Aquitaine or
Normandy, in a way Henry had got what he wanted out of his
first war. He had blooded himself, tasting battle and the hardships
of campaigning. He had won towns and taken prisoners; and
most importantly he had laid down markers. Both Maximilian
and Ferdinand now knew that they had to take this young man
seriously. The Emperor appeared to be enthusiastic for a new
campaign in 1514, and promised to wed his 14-year-old grandson,
Charles, to Henry's 18-year-old sister, Mary.

Before the new season could open, however, the king of England had changed his mind. His coffers were empty, and it was
beginning to dawn upon him that everybody was taking his

subsidies and giving him nothing in return. Maximilian professed friendship, but he had done very little to support the Tournai campaign, certainly not the full participation that he had promised, so why should his new undertakings be trusted? Ferdinand had betrayed him not once but twice. That hurt Henry's vanity more than his tangible interests, but a king's vanity was an important political fact and as 1514 advanced the desire for revenge upon his father-in-law was growing.

There were also other considerations. Pope Julius II, on whose behalf Henry was theoretically making war, had died on 21 February 1513, and his successor, Leo X, wanted peace. Thomas Wolsey, rapidly emerging as the king's chief adviser, was inclined to follow the papal lead, and was also somewhat favourable to France.[6] Some preparations for renewed hostilities were made, but they were half-hearted, and in May Leo sent Henry a 'sword and cap of maintenance', ceremonial symbols of approval, as sweeteners for his peace campaign. During the summer embassies were exchanged, and in August a treaty of peace was signed, one of the conditions of which was that young Mary was transferred from the even younger Charles to the distinctly elderly Louis. It is alleged that Henry won her consent to this unsatisfactory match with the promise that she should have the man of her choice the next time around. In October 1514 Mary was married and crowned queen of France. At the same time Henry made overtures to his new brother-in-law for joint actions against Ferdinand—perhaps the recovery of Navarre would have sufficient appeal?

A TOURNAMENT FOR THE MARRIAGE OF THE KING'S SISTER, MARY
1514

THEN THE DAUPHIN *of France … for the more honour of the marriage, before the Englishmen departed from Abbeville, caused a solemn Justs [jousting] to be proclaimed, which should be kept at Paris in the month of November next ensuing … When this proclamation was reported in England*

by the noblemen that returned from the marriage: the Duke of
Suffolk, the Marquis Dorset and his four brethren, the Lord
Clinton, Sir Edward Neville, Sir Giles Capel, Thomas Cheney
and others, sued to the king to be at the challenge, which request
he graciously granted …

The Dauphin desired the Duke of Suffolk and the Lord
Marquis Dorset, whose activity he knew well by report, to be
two of his immediate aids, which thereto assented. Therefore was
erected an arch of wideness at the Tournels [a place name] beside
the street on St Anthony, directly before the Bastille, on the which
were set four targets or scutchions [emblazoned shields], the one
silver, and he that set his name under that shield, to run at the tilt
according to the articles; he that put his name under the golden
target should run with the sharp spears and fight with sharp
swords; they that put their names to the black shield should fight
afoot with spears and swords for the one hand. And he that
touched the tawny shield should cast a spear on foot with a target
on his arm, and after to fight with a two hand sword … While all
these things were preparing, the lady Mary of England, the fifth
day of November being Sunday, was with great solemnity crowned
Queen of France in the monastery of St Denis …

[Richard Grafton, *A Chronicle at large and meere history of the affayres of*
England (1568), edition of 1809, p. 283.]

Nothing came of this initiative, but the treaty that was signed in
August 1514 lasted for nearly eight years: a very long time in an
age when the average duration of a 'perpetual' alliance was about
three years. During that time the political landscape changed a
great deal. Within three months of his marriage, the 52-year-old
Louis was dead; danced to death, it was said, by his youthful bride.
Mary then married, with a haste indicative of desperation, her
brother's boon companion, Charles Brandon, Duke of Suffolk,
who had been sent over to retrieve her from the French court.
Since it was concluded without Henry's specific consent, this
marriage landed them both in a lot of trouble.[7]

Louis was succeeded by his 20-year-old cousin, Francis, the Duke of Valois, and the king of England found himself confronted by a monarch even younger than himself, equally chivalric, equally warlike and with vastly greater resources. Within months of his accession, Francis had won, at Marignano in Italy, a great victory over the Emperor—the kind of victory that Henry could only dream about.

As the two young men eyed each other warily, other changes were also taking place. In 1516 Ferdinand, by this time the *bête noir* of both of them, died in Estramaduras, and was succeeded by his grandson, Charles of Ghent, who at 16 was even younger than Francis. In 1518 Thomas Wolsey, now cardinal and chancellor of England, was able to take advantage of this situation to further the papal aim of peace, and persuaded Henry to host what would much later be called a 'summit conference' with the aim of establishing a binding amity between these three volatile young men in the face of the growing menace of the Ottomans. Wolsey's complex and protracted diplomacy was strikingly successful, and resulted in the Treaty of London, intended to put an end to the internecine squabbles of Christendom.[8]

Alas for good intentions! The ink was scarcely dry on the treaty when the Emperor Maximilian also died, and all three of the young monarchs entered the lists to succeed him. Because the Holy Roman Empire was an elective monarchy, any one of them —or even the elector of Saxony—could have been successful. But Charles was not only Maximilian's grandson, he also had the backing of the Fuggers, the leading Augsburg bankers, and their pockets were even deeper than those of the king of France. So in 1519 Charles I of Spain became the Emperor Charles V. His sprawling territories now surrounded France on every side, and it was only a matter of time before Francis would feel the need to break out of this encirclement.

In this impending confrontation, England enjoyed a strategic importance that was new, and to Henry exciting. According to the balance-of-power principle, which was fashionable with contemporary strategic thinkers, he should have allied with France as a counterpoise to the Emperor's overwhelming superiority. On the other hand, if he really wanted to defeat Francis and help himself to a piece of his kingdom, an Imperial alliance was the obvious answer. There was also the serious consideration that Charles controlled the Low Countries, which were England's main trading partners. Wolsey favoured France, and the preservation of the status quo, but Wolsey, for all his prestige, was only a councillor. He did not make such decisions. He could, and did, persuade Henry to honour his long-standing commitment to meet Francis, but he could not persuade him to renew the Treaty of London.

This was partly because Henry and Francis were too much alike to be friends. Both showed their competitive edge when they met in June 1520 at the magnificent charade that was the Field of the Cloth of Gold, and each was jealous of the other.[9] In fact the king of England met the Emperor twice, both before and after his encounter with Francis, and found he had far more rapport with the undersized and rather lugubrious Habsburg. Nevertheless, and in contrast with the situation ten years earlier, this time Henry was in no hurry to embark on hostilities. Even when the inevitable conflict broke out in 1521, at first he offered to mediate. However by August of that year he had determined to side with the Emperor, and justified his stand by convincing himself that Francis had been the aggressor. His primary motive was probably the same as it had been before, to recover some of the lands lost to France in the middle of the previous century, but this time there was also the more constructive intention of rebuilding Edward IV's Burgundian alliance, and of making himself a valued ally to the most powerful prince in Christendom.

In the event Henry achieved neither. Partly because of anxieties about a renewed threat from Scotland, and partly through sheer poverty, nothing was accomplished in 1522. Wolsey was also still seeking a diplomatic solution, and that may have contributed to the delay, but perhaps the most compelling reason was the potential defection of the Duke of Bourbon, a high-ranking nobleman and the constable of France. For what were essentially private reasons, Bourbon had fallen out with Francis and was negotiating with the Emperor.[10] By the late summer of 1523 a strategy was in place that called for a three-pronged thrust against France. Imperial troops would invade from the south, the English would once again land in Picardy, and Bourbon would mobilize his own retinue on the eastern border. The English, led by the Duke of Suffolk, duly set out from Calais at the end of August, but the rest of the strategy collapsed in fiasco. The Spaniards retreated after a brief and pointless incursion, and the Duke of Bourbon left Besançon only to flee to Genoa. Suffolk was left stranded in northern France, with the winter closing in, and could do nothing but retreat into such quarters as he could find.

At first Henry's new-found belligerency was unaffected by these setbacks. At Christmas he was still talking of marching on Paris, but this was largely bluster. If Charles and Bourbon could mount realistic attacks, he would play his part, otherwise he would seek a separate peace. Two-faced negotiations continued through the early part of 1524, and what was left of Suffolk's army was retrieved. Then in the summer, Bourbon began to make progress and Henry's interest in peace waned. However, Bourbon was holding out for a substantial subsidy, and that the king had neither the will nor the means to grant. At the end of August the siege of Marseilles collapsed, and peace was back on the agenda. It looked as though the whole coalition plan had run into the sand.

Francis did not know when he was well off. Re-entering Italy at the beginning of 1525, he was shatteringly defeated at Pavia on 14 February. His army was destroyed and he himself captured. Henry received the news with unseemly glee, and promptly sent envoys to the victorious Emperor proposing a division of the conquered kingdom.[11] Never had the opportunity been so good. Charles, however, was not interested. For him this unexpected triumph had been a last throw of the dice. He was virtually bankrupt, and had Francis in a position where he could impose terms.

In spite of its losses, France was not defenceless, and further expensive campaigning was not on the Emperor's agenda. If Henry wanted a slice of France, he would have to take it for himself. Charles convinced himself, rather unfairly, that Henry had not pulled his weight over the last three years, and saw no reason why he should share his success. Consequently he snubbed Henry's enthusiastic messengers. In fact he was ready to break with England, having decided that he was no longer prepared to wait for the Princess Mary (whom he had undertaken to marry in 1521) to grow up. He declared himself free and wed the 22-year-old Isabella of Portugal. Meanwhile Henry was hamstrung by the fact that the failure of Wolsey's so-called 'Amicable Grant', an attempted extra-parliamentary tax ruse of 1525, had left him without the resources to do anything of significance. Disillusioned, he cut his losses and signed the Treaty of the More (The More being the royal house in Hertfordshire where it was signed) with the interim government of Louise of Savoy on 30 August, thereby getting one ahead of the Emperor—the much more significant Treaty of Madrid not following until January 1526.[12]

THE FAILURE OF THE AMICABLE GRANT
Paraphrase of a letter from Archbishop Warham to Cardinal Wolsey, 5 April 1525.

At THE SITTING *of the commissioners at Otford, March 30th [he] obtained from the contributors the names and sums enclosed. It will be hard to raise the money, especially as other parliamentary grants are now payable. Reports for the secret ear of the Cardinal the dissatisfaction prevailing.*

1. The people speak cursedly, saying they shall never have rest of payments as long as some [i.e. Wolsey] liveth.

2. That some of the commissioners, through fear of the people, will only announce the king's command, without pressing it further, leaving the obnoxious portion to the Archbishop.

3. That complaint is made that the loan is not repaid, nor will this grant be.

4. They would give, but cannot; and will not at any other than the king's appointment.

5. That too much coin of the realm is exported already into Flanders.

6. That it would be the greatest means of enriching France to have all his money spent there, out of the realm; and if the king win France, he will be obliged to spend his time and revenues there.

7. They are sorry, rather than otherwise, at the captivity of Francis I.

8. That all the sums already spent on the invasion of France have not gained the king a foot more land in it than his father had, which lacked no riches or wisdom to win the kingdom of France, if he had thought it expedient.

[He] would have been glad if the time had allowed, that this practising with the people for so great sums might have been spared to the cuckoo time, and that the hot weather (at which time mad brains be most busy) had been passed. Otford, 5th April.

[Paraphrase taken from *Letters and Papers*, IV, no. 1243. Original BL Cotton MS Cleopatra F. vi, f.339.]

Henry's first French war could be described as adolescent posturing. This second one was pure Renaissance politics, an affair of short-term advantages and rapidly shifting diplomacy. The first had been successful up to a point, the second was an unmitigated failure, because by the end of it the king had lost the alliance by which he appeared to set so much store and had effectively changed sides, having secured no advantage against anyone. Moreover he had alienated the Emperor even to the point of being notionally at war against him in 1528–9. This was a 'phoney war', but it did mean that Charles was his enemy at precisely the time when Henry was seeking to annul his marriage with the Emperor's aunt —and Charles had a stranglehold on Pope Clement VII who would have to grant the annulment.[13]

For the next ten years or so, Henry's foreign policy was dictated by the needs of the domestic crisis that he had stirred up by his urgent need to change his wife. As he moved his Church into schism, and toyed somewhat selectively with heresy, his relations with the ultra-orthodox Emperor varied from the frosty to the downright hostile. In so far as Henry had a friend in Europe during these years, it was Francis I, but the main effect of this was not so much to mitigate the hostility of the papacy as to blunt the Emperor's enthusiasm for turning his hostility into action. Charles's numerous territories each carried their own burdens and commitments, and he was overstretched. The Ottomans threatened what was left of Hungary, the Lutheran princes threatened to disrupt Germany, and Francis threatened to secure control over northern Italy. The last thing Charles needed was to add Henry to his growing list of enemies, so although he seriously considered supporting the Kildare revolt in Ireland (see Chapter 8), and rather less seriously toyed with the idea of backing the Pilgrimage of Grace (see Chapter 7), in the end he did nothing.[14]

Nevertheless, Henry remained apprehensive, and when Francis and Charles signed a peace treaty at Toledo on 12 January 1539, he became almost paranoid. One of the reasons for this was that he had too much information, most of it of dubious value. Thomas Cromwell, who had become his chief adviser in 1532, was a spymaster. His agents both at home and abroad supplied him with a vast amount of 'intelligence', much of it completely undigested. Consequently he knew of every hostile plot against England (real and imaginary), but had few means of assessing how dangerous they were.

FEAR OF ATTACK FROM THE CONTINENT
Thomas Cromwell to Christopher Munt (representative in Germany), 1539.

ALSO YOU SHALL *show to Burgnatus, or some trusty friend by whom it may come to the Duke or Landgrave's ears that the King has heard that the Bishop of Rome and his adherents have taken counsel together how utterly to abolish the maintenance of Christ's word, but that for diversity of opinion they could not resolve how to bring their purpose to pass … And specially such* as were induced [by the] traitor Pole, Cardinal [Reginald Pole, in exile since 1532], were of the opinion [that] forasmuch as the king's highness of England, being one of the three principal princes, and [who] had most openly rejected the Bishop of Rome's usurped authority and abolished it in his realm, and by whose means others might take example, as following his title of Defender of the Faith—and besides that because they esteem his majesty of such strength, that if they could overthrow him, the rest of the Evangelical princes would yield at the Bishop of Rome's pleasure. To set forth their malice against him, they have grounded a bull upon the divorce, which is now of a long season out of question, the abolition of his usurped authority, and the execution of Fisher, the Cardinal of St Vitale, as they call him [sometime] Bishop of Rochester, their champion, containing fulminations and censures against the king and his subjects. They are looking for an opportunity to set upon one or the other, and study to keep the princes of their allegiance at peace between themselves, and with the Turks and other. What they mean against the princes of Almain [Germany], deeds do show, and what they intended against the king has been rumoured, but as yet the princes words purport rather the contrary, that they will not meddle with his majesty, but rather keep their treaties, for otherwise they would be likely to have the worst end of the staff.

The bruit [rumour] has been very sore that the Emperor will attack the King, and the French King also, at the Bishop of Rome's intercession, for no cause but for mesprising and avoiding of his abuses and maintaining the Word of God … for the papists malice against the King is grounded only on their envy of the religion common to the princes of Almain and him …

[signed]

[Extracts and paraphrase taken from *Letters and Papers*, XIV, no. 580. Original BL Cotton MS Vitellius B. xxi, f. 147.]

As a result, Henry became convinced during the summer of 1539 that his realm was about to be subjected to a joint invasion by the

French and the Germans. Musters were held, and huge sums of money spent on coastal defences. Ironically, it was the very policy that created the danger which also provided the means to meet it. The dissolution of the monasteries had brought the king the kind of wealth that, had it been available fifteen years earlier, would have sent a grand army sailing into France. Now this new-found wealth paid for a string of forts along the south coast (see plate 11), strengthened the navy, and left enough in reserve to contemplate a defensive war, should one arise.

By 1540 the danger was passed—if it had ever existed—as Francis and Charles showed signs of squaring up to each other again. Henry's passing enthusiasm for the Schmalkaldic League of Protestant princes evaporated and his foreign policy returned to neutral.[15] Meanwhile Charles was also reassessing his priorities. Henry might be an incorrigible schismatic, but he was a strong prince and his bad relations with the papacy might also have advantages. Moreover, the Emperor's aunt, Catherine of Aragon, whose fate had done so much to damage relations between them, had died in January 1536 and her *bête noire*, Anne Boleyn, had followed her a few months later. Had he wished, the Emperor could always have used the papal sentence against Henry as an excuse to break off diplomatic relations, or even to attack, but he did not so choose, and when the king began to put out feelers for a renewal of their old friendship, he responded positively. Negotiations began about the end of 1541, and by the summer of 1542 had been successfully concluded. Charles and Francis were again at war, and Henry would support his ally with an invasion of France in 1543.[16]

However, there was a little local difficulty to be tidied away first. Henry had been trying for several years to persuade his cousin James V of Scotland to follow his lead against the pope—a course that James had no intention of following. While Henry had been on progress in the north of England in 1541, he thought he had persuaded James to meet him at York. The king of Scots had no intention of doing that either, but the illusion persisted and when James failed to turn up Henry was extremely angry.

Armed with a sense of grievance, and remembering how James IV had served him thirty years before, the king decide to neutralize Scotland before embarking upon any Continental campaign. By causing his Border commissioners to make excessive demands, and then by launching a gratuitous raid into southern Scotland, he provoked James into sending an army into the debatable land north of Carlisle. It was a trap, and the Scots army was caught and defeated at Solway Moss on 23 November 1542. James, who was not with his army, died a few days later of a long-standing illness, and the circumstances of 1513 were recreated.[17]

Solway Moss was not a shattering defeat like Flodden, but it did leave many Scottish nobles as prisoners in Henry's hands, and quite fortuitously again left the Scottish crown in the hands of a child. Only this time the child was female—James's week-old daughter, Mary. This presented the English king with an opportunity (as he thought) to solve the Scottish problem once and for all. If Mary were married to his own six-year-old son Edward, the crowns would in due course become united—to England's advantage. Henry began to deploy his diplomatic strength to that end, and made his prisoners swear to further the cause as a condition for their release. The Earl of Arran, the Scottish regent, stalled as best he could, because the union was about as popular in Scotland as the winter weather. A treaty was eventually signed at Greenwich on 1 July 1543, which ostensibly gave Henry what he wanted, but it was subsequently repudiated by the Scottish Parliament, and its most immediate effect was a dramatic surge by the pro-French party in Scotland, which the regent was soon to join.

It soon transpired that the temporary ascendancy created by the victory at Solway Moss had been dissipated, and that Henry had seriously annoyed the Emperor by failing to produce his European campaign while he strove to secure his position in the north. However, in another sense the victory was not wasted, because however strong the pro-French sentiment among the governors of Scotland might have been by 1544, no attempt was made to enter the war on the French side. The Scots had no desire to risk another Flodden, and Cardinal Beaton, Primate of Scotland, was content to have frustrated the marriage plan. It was to be another five years, after the deaths of both Henry and Beaton, before Mary was betrothed to the French dauphin and English plans finally frustrated.

Meanwhile Henry had followed up his understanding with the Emperor by signing a new treaty on 11 February 1543.[18] This was before it had become apparent that he would do nothing during that campaigning season, but Charles was already beginning to have doubts about his ally, and limited his obligations under the treaty. In the event it was June 1544 before the English 'Army Royal' landed at Calais and the now portly and irascible king prepared to take the field in person for the last time. There was supposed to be a joint strategy, but Henry ignored it, concentrating his forces on the sieges first of Montreuil and then of Boulogne. The latter was his real objective, and he led his army with the boundless enthusiasm of renewed youth. Excellent as this was from his point of view, he got in everyone's way and succeeded in annoying the Emperor still further. When Boulogne eventually fell on 18 September, he entered in state and spent two weeks arranging for its fortification and garrisoning. He then returned to England and made it clear that as far as he was concerned, the campaigning season was over.

THE SIEGE OF BOULOGNE
Extracts from a report dated 12 October 1544.

I N THE YEAR *of our Lord 1544, 11th July, (all his majesty's captains and army sent before to Montreuil and Boulogne) the king took his journey from Westminster … the 14th he took shipping and arrived at Calais at 9 p.m., being met by Lord Cobham … On Saturday, the 19th [the Duke of] Suffolk removed the camp to Boulogne, and certain of our arquebusiers approached the wall and skirmished, and divers were slain on both sides. Forthwith our artillery was bent upon the town and removed daily approaching nearer. [On] Monday, 21st July …*

Bas Boulogne was taken and the Frenchmen driven into the high town before they could harm Bas Boulogne, where they left much salt, pitch, tar and other merchandise, but carried more away in boats and ships for lack of our ships being at the haven's mouth. That day much cattle was taken by our horsemen, who killed and drove into the sea many Frenchmen on the far side of the haven. Tuesday 22nd July, a cannon was taken to shoot at the watch tower, which thereupon surrendered ...

On the 26th the King marched to Boulogne, being met and accompanied by Sir Ralf Ellerker and a great many light horsemen, and received by Suffolk. He camped on the north side of the town, near the sea ... Friday, 8th August, our men gave the town alarm at 1 a.m. Tuesday, 12th came captain Taphorne with 500 Flemings and one Lyghmaker with 100 Clevois horsemen. On the 13th August three ensigns of Almain, well horsed, arrived, one ensign being gunners and the rest light horse ... William Burgat, surveyor of Calais, was slain in the trenches. The Earl of Hertford came to the King ...

Tuesday 19th August a hundred or more picked men of France would have entered the town, whereof 65 were slain, and some entered the town. They came from Hedyng, guided by a priest, who forsook them at their most need, but was taken, with all their horses, which were very simple. Our scout, a northern man, was hanged for not watching ... Tuesday, 2nd September, our men in the trench and braye [earthworks] gave the castle alarm and also false alarm, and broke certain doors into the castle; but were met with such hailshot, storm and fire that they were bound to recoil. Many were burnt and hurt, among whom Woodall was burnt and Sir Richard Long's captain and Sir Richard Cromwell's captains [Spencer and Humbart] were sore hurt with many other of our men ...

Thursday, 11th September the Earl of Surrey and Lord William Howard came from Montreuil to the King and (the train of powder being set to the castle) accompanied the king to his standing to see the castle fall; at which fall many of our men were

hurt with flying stones. Our men assaulted the Flemings Tower,
and other places of the town, and many were slain of both parts
… On the 14th September M. de As returned to M. de
Santblemont, and both dined with the Lord Marshall, the earl of
Arundel, and then went to the king and made the rendition …

On Thursday, 18th September, the king at afternoon,
accompanied by the Duke of Albuquerque and others made his
entry into Boulogne, and there lay, fortifying it and gathering his
artillery, and viewing what work he would have done, until his
departure into England …

[Taken from *Letters and Papers*, XIX, ii, no.424. Original BL Cotton
MS Caligula E. IV, f. 57.]

The Emperor was furious. His own campaign was bogged down
and getting nowhere, so on the same day that Henry returned to
England, 30 September, Charles signed the Truce of Crespy with
Francis. If Henry wanted to fight the French on his own, the
Emperor would be happy to watch. In fact the king of England
was also thinking about peace, but the Emperor got his retaliation
in first, and, as Boulogne was non-negotiable, discussions with the
French got nowhere either. Consequently, as 1545 opened, Henry
was in the unusual predicament of confronting the French, and
possibly the Scots, without allies. As in 1539, England was gripped
by the fear of invasion—and with good reason, because Francis
was determined this time to take the war to the English. He prepared an invasion fleet of over two hundred vessels, which entered
the Solent on 19 July and landed troops on the Isle of Wight.[19]

However, as was so often the case with 16th-century warfare,
the result was little short of a fiasco. The English fleet, inevitably,
blocked the invaders' path. The winds were fitful and neither side
could manoeuvre properly, so after an inconclusive exchange of
gunfire, the French withdrew, taking what was left of the Isle of
Wight landing party with them. It was probably the French admiral's intention to try again in a less-protected spot, but even as he
backed off plague broke out among his ships, and after sailing a

few miles down the coast, he returned to Rouen and disbanded. Not for the first (or the last) time a massive and expensive preparation had come to nothing.

Buoyed by this success, and determined to retain Boulogne, Henry endeavoured to ignore the fact that he was bankrupt. It was not until the following spring that the awful reality of his financial situation, together with signs of flexibility on the French side, persuaded him to change his mind. The 1544 campaign alone had cost over £650,000, about two-thirds of his total income from the sale of Church lands. When he learned that Francis was willing to do a deal over Boulogne, he decided to settle, and the Treaty of Camp was signed on 6 June 1546.[20]

Boulogne was his for eight years—or longer if the French could not raise 2 million crowns (about £750,000) to ransom it. Scotland was not included in the treaty, and it was an open question whether a state of war existed in the north or not. Henry was determined to insist upon the Treaty of Greenwich, and the Scots would have none of it. That situation remained unresolved on the king's death about six months later. Henry therefore died in possession of a small part of France. It was strategically of little use, and enormously expensive to maintain, but at least it represented success of a sort.

Henry had spent between 8 and 9 years of his 38-year reign at war, and spent not only the whole of his father's legacy, but the whole of the proceeds from the sale of monastic land. As an aspect of policy, these years are normally described as wasteful and futile; a mere expression of the king's egotism, without any constructive result. However, they have to be seen in the context of an aristocratic culture that was still predominantly military. A king's honour, like a nobleman's, was most conspicuously fulfilled on the field of battle, and it was a wise ruler who periodically gave his lords and captains something suitable to do.

The king, moreover, was highly successful in one respect. He was taken seriously both as an ally and as an antagonist by his much more powerful neighbours. Both Francis and Charles deployed many times his resources, but they treated him as an equal. His court (as we saw in Chapter 2) was the equal of the French and more attractive than that of the Emperor. This was not only because of the king's prowess on the field and in the tilt-yard, but those qualities helped. A Renaissance prince needed to be magnificent, and warfare was as much about pomp and show as it was about fighting. Henry did not live his dream, and on his last campaign was more than a little ridiculous, but by fighting abroad he periodically rallied his people and defused tensions at home. His real achievements were domestic, and were deeply divisive, but war and the danger of war helped to overcome these divisions. If ever a king 'busied giddy minds with foreign wars', it was surely Henry VIII.

In the end, war was the sharp end of a foreign policy that was endlessly complicated in detail, but fairly straightforward in outline. Henry wanted three things: glory, security and a piece of France. His realm was never successfully invaded, and he was accepted in Europe as a serious warrior. He even died in posses-sion of a very small part of his neighbour's kingdom—so any ver-dict of futility needs to be revised. Even his debts were appreciably smaller than those of Charles or Francis.

War, however, was also a profession. Kings might ride magnifi-cent horses, wear gilded armour and display their lavish heraldry, but there were also mundane matters such as weaponry, logistics, recruitment and victualling; and kings who aspired to lead armies needed expertise in at least some of these areas. Henry loved big guns. This was partly a childlike delight in the noise they made, and partly a shrewd appreciation of their destructive potential.[21] His father had imported French gunfounders to establish a works at Buxted, south of Ashdown Forest, as early as 1490. This made the guns that were used in the Scottish war of 1496, but Henry VII was not particularly innovative, and all these weapons appear to have been wrought-iron breach loaders.

Henry VIII established a second foundry at Hounsditch in 1511. This made cast-bronze cannons, but its output seems not to have been large, and the king imported most of the guns he needed from the Low Countries. However. a major breakthrough was achieved in 1543 when an Englishman, William Livet, succeeded in casting a large gun in iron. In 1545 Henry ordered 200 of these, but in spite of a further foundry being opened in 1546, the order was still incomplete when he died.[22] In the event the king's artillery was used in anger only three or four times in his entire reign, and his interest in ballistics did not really justify the outlay.

In one respect Henry was both original and influential, and that was in the deployment of guns on ships. The Portuguese had used a few large guns on their big carracks in the Indian Ocean during the late 15th century. In contrast, big English warships, such as the *Regent*, mounted large numbers of relatively small guns called serpentines.[23] The appearance of big guns, mounted to fire through specially constructed ports on the main deck, can be dated to 1510 and the construction of the *Mary Rose*. The king was deeply interested in ship design as well as guns, and although it cannot be proved that he had any hand in this design revolution, the coincidence is extraordinarily tempting. We know that most of the 200 cast-iron guns ordered in 1545 were destined for the navy, and it seems that the interest ran right through his life.

Whether Henry made any contribution to the design of these early ships in other respects, we do not know, but he did remain extraordinarily interested in the fortunes of the *Mary Rose* throughout her career, and he was devastated when she sank before his eyes in 1545. His interest in oared ships is better documented, and the *Great Galley* (which was a galleass—a ship propelled by both oar and sail—rather than a true galley), launched in 1515, is known to have been partly his work. In 1541, when the king was contemplating the building of some new galleasses, the Imperial ambassador Chapuys wrote:

T HE KING *has likewise sent to Italy for three shipwrights experienced in the art of constructing galleys; but I fancy that he will not make much use of their science, as for some time back*

*he has been building ships with oars, according to a model of which
he himself is the inventor.*

The very small galleys, known as rowbarges (15–20 tons), of
which a number were built for the navy during the final French
war, were particular favourites of Henry's, and were, reputedly,
his own idea. The fact that they were sold off shortly after his
death would appear to confirm that.

The king's real contribution to the development of the navy,
however, did not lie in the design of ships or the deployment of
guns, but in its new scale and organization. It had been normal,
even in time of war, for English kings to own very few ships of
their own. A 'Navy Royal' was assembled by requisitioning merchant ships and converting them on a short-term basis. By the
15th century ship service in the old quasi-feudal sense was obsolete, and the ships that served in the brief campaigns of Edward IV
and Henry VII were 'taken up' for the purpose. Only Henry V
had had, briefly, a war fleet of his own, numbering some thirty
ships, but that had been disposed of as soon as the campaigns were
over.[24] Things changed in 1514, when Henry VIII, who also had
about thirty ships at that point, decided to retain them, mostly on
a care-and-maintenance basis. This meant more dockyards and
anchorages, greatly increased expenditure, and two further officers to supplement the existing clerk of the ships. It also marked
the true origin of the Royal Navy as a standing force.

Sir Edward Howard had apparently made up his tactics as he
went along during 1512 and 1513, because traditionally ships had
been used only in support of field armies, but as lord admiral during those years Howard had deployed his ships independently, not
only in raiding the Breton coast, but in bringing the French fleet
to battle. In doing so he lost his life, but his point about the use of
the navy had been well and truly made, and it may well have been
for that reason that the king decided to keep his fleet in being.[25]
He neither wanted nor expected long years of peace. For centuries naval battle orders (such as they were) had always been of

the 'grapple and board' variety, in which individual ships, locked together, fought what were essentially land battles. That was still true as late as 1530, but by 1545 Spanish influence and the deployment of large guns had wrought a major change. Lord Lisle's orders of that year show a fleet intending to fight in coordinated squadrons, using their guns to sink or disable their opponents instead of coming to close quarters.[26]

A tactical corner had been turned that was to dominate naval thinking until the days of Nelson. Unfortunately we do not know to what extent (if at all) the king contributed to this development, but we know that he was interested in such matters and that it took place during his reign. Such tactics were not an English invention, but by the middle of the 16th century the use of medium-range gunnery in sea fighting was beginning to be noticed as a characteristic of the way the English used their ships. It was even recalled by Spanish officers at the time of the Armada.

A much larger standing navy, which had risen to 50 ships by 1544, necessitated a new administrative structure. Until about 1540 the three officers who were responsible for the care and maintenance of the ships had been controlled directly by the king's chief minister—first Wolsey, and then Cromwell. But the fall of the latter, and the sheer scale of the navy by 1543, required new thinking if the whole programme was not to fall apart. At some time between 1544 and 1546—the exact timing is uncertain —a new department was created called the 'council for marine causes'. This consisted of the existing three officers, plus four others, a vice admiral, a surveyor and rigger, a master of naval ordnance, and a treasurer. There was by this time no chief minister, and the council for marine causes was answerable directly to the king via the privy council.

It immediately assumed responsibility for all routine naval administration: the control of the dockyards, care and maintenance, and the deployment of all ships during peacetime. All accounts were to be passed through the treasurer.[27] The lord admiral would retain control of naval operations, and would account separately for expenditure during wartime. This was the origin of the later admiralty, and gave Henry, during the last months of his life, the most effective and sophisticated system of naval management in Western Europe—or probably anywhere. It took a long time to turn the king's interest in ships and guns into a naval revolution, but it did happen in his lifetime. Only the finishing touches remained to be applied. In 1550 the office of 'surveyor general of victuals for the sea' was created and added to the council, and in 1557 a budget or of £14,000 a year was decreed. Elizabeth thus took over her famous navy fully formed.

By 1547 this navy had earned the healthy respect of England's neighbours. Her field army was less well thought of, not because the English were not good fighting men—even the Scots admitted that—but because Henry was always playing 'catch up' in terms of equipment and logistics. The only standing forces were the garrisons of Calais and Berwick, and the English had relatively little experience of professional military service. For general defensive purposes there were the county militias. Theoretically every able-bodied male between the ages of 16 and 60 was liable to serve, and was expected to provide his own equipment. Musters were called at times of national danger, and some training provided, but the result was ramshackle and the weapons primitive and obsolete, only the formidable archers providing a partial exception.

For serious fighting, particularly overseas campaigns, the king issued 'commissions of array' to selected nobles and captains, authorizing them to raise and equip so many soldiers at his expense.[28] These men were clad, armed and fed by their leaders, and formed coherent fighting units, known as 'retinues'. Since the king of England, unlike the king of France, could not afford a standing field army, there was little alternative to this semi-private system, and it had been in use for several generations. However, Henry was not entirely happy with the extent to which it left him dependent on the nobility, an increasing number of whom had no military training or experience. He began to experiment with the (strictly illegal) use of men drawn from the militias in foreign campaigns. They were not better soldiers, but they were more amenable to direct control.

As we have seen, by the end of Henry's reign the English were making good iron and bronze guns, but the manufacture of armour and other weapons lagged far behind, and one of the main functions of the king's agents in the Low Countries was the purchase of such supplies. As the longbow began to become obsolete, and to be replaced with the much more expensive arquebus, the cost of equipping a field army steadily rose. The military revolution, which in Europe produced the Swiss pikemen and the Spanish *tercios* (trios of a pikeman, arquebusier and swordsman), was not reflected in England, and although Henry did enjoy some success against the French, it was usually when their attention was distracted, and his main successes were against the Scots, who again tended to be good fighting men, but were even more poorly equipped than the English. England had its military revolution at sea, and that was not equalled anywhere else. English ships were no better than those of the French, the Spaniards or the Flemings, but their guns (and gunners) were. Success bred prestige, and in spite of the chivalric culture that lingered so strongly at Henry's court, service at sea had become as worthy of recognition as service on land.

The king's preoccupation with things military also had other consequences. Through the need to survey and develop harbours he became interested in hydrography, and even appointed a hydrographer royal.[29] A concern about coastal defence also involved him in the arts of fortification. High medieval walls invited demolition by the large guns in use by the 1530s, so Henry hired French and Flemish engineers to design such places as Camber Castle, which were essentially artillery bastions.[30] By the end of his life the French style was already being overtaken by the Italian, which involved sloping, earth-faced bulwarks, but Henry did not build in that style and it was not until a decade later that Berwick began to be protected in that manner, a task not completed until well into the reign of Elizabeth.

In fact Henry's attitude, as opposed to his technology, was distinctly old fashioned. His tournaments, to which a number of references have been made, belonged to the world of fantasy rather than warfare, and yet they were hugely important. Masques and jousts in which favoured knights competed for their ladies' favours, were an essential part of the military culture. The imagery and language were drawn more from the *Morte d'Arthur* than from the stricken fields of France, but they symbolized a world of honour in which noblemen were those who fought, as distinct from those who worked or prayed. In a world where real noblemen were increasingly civil servants, these fictions had their place. The king himself gave up jousting in the 1520s, but every great event at court continued to be celebrated with a tournament, and the tradition was to be revived in the Accession Day tilts of Elizabeth's reign. By then, of course, real warfare was even more remote, and it was the capricious lady who mattered rather than the embattled knight.

§4 The King's Great Matter

THE KING'S 'Great Matter' was a phrase used at the time, and since, to describe Henry's struggle to secure an annulment of his first marriage—or, to put it another way, the king's desire to swap Catherine of Aragon for another wife. The Great Issue, though, was neither Catherine nor Anne Boleyn, but the succession. By 1527 Catherine was 42, and her childbearing years were over: she had not conceived since 1518, and had probably passed the menopause by 1525 at the latest. They had a daughter, Mary, then aged 11, and Henry had an illegitimate son, Henry FitzRoy, Duke of Richmond, aged 8. Both of these were possible successors, but neither was an attractive prospect.

There was no law in England, as there was in France (the Salic law), to bar a female from the throne, but England had never had a ruling queen and nobody knew what such an eventuality would imply.[1] Mary would, of course, marry, and her husband would become king by virtue of that fact. Because of the dangers of 'disparagement' (marrying beneath herself) and faction if she were to marry an Englishman, she would almost inevitably choose a husband from one of the royal houses of Western Europe—and this would mean a foreign king, and probably his equally foreign servants in positions of authority. The thought was deeply distasteful, not only to Henry but to most of his nobility, who saw themselves being displaced from favour.

On the other hand, for Henry FitzRoy to succeed, he would have to be legitimated. The easy route to this, through the subsequent marriage of his parents, was not an available option; so such a process would have to depend on the special intervention of the pope. Even if the incumbent at the time was willing to oblige, such a course was fraught with danger. Could such a dispensation be valid? The chances of a successful challenge were high, and since the stakes would also be high, arguably a risk too great to take.[2]

Realistically, Henry faced three options. The last, legitimation, was the least attractive. He could seek to marry off his daughter as quickly and as innocuously as possible, in the hope that she would bear a son in his lifetime, to whom the crown could pass direct on his death. Not only would that mean gambling on his own longevity, it would also depend on Mary achieving a prompt puberty —and as she was an undersized child the prospects were not good.[3] The third alternative, which became increasingly attractive with every month that passed, was to get rid of Catherine and start again.

HENRY'S SCRUPLE OF CONSCIENCE

WHEREFORE HE [*Henry*] *like a prudent prince and circumspect doer in all his affairs, and willing all men to know his intent and purpose, caused all his nobility, judges and councillors, with divers other persons, to come to his palace of Bridewell on Sunday the 8th of November* [*1528*] *at afternoon in his great chamber, and there to them said as near as my* [*a reference to Edward Hall, the basis of Grafton's version*] *wit could bear away, these words following.*

'Our trusty and well-beloved subjects, both you of the nobility and you of the meaner sort, it is not unknown to you that we, both by God's provision and true and lawful inheritance have reigned over this realm of England almost the term of xx years. During which time we have so ordered us, thanked be God, that no outward enemy hath oppressed you nor take anything from us, nor we have invaded no realm but we have had victory and honour, so that we think that you, nor none of your predecessors never lived more quietly, more wealthily, nor in more estimation under any of our noble progenitors. But when we remember our

mortality, and that we must die, then we think that all our doings
in our life time are clearly defaced, and worthy of no memory, if we
leave you in trouble at the time of our death. For if our true heir
be not known at the time of our death, see what mischief and
trouble shall succeed to you and your children ... And although it
has pleased Almighty God to send us a fair daughter of a noble
woman and me begotten to our great comfort and joy, yet it hath
been told us by several great clerks, that neither she is our lawful
daughter, nor her mother our lawful wife, but that we live together
abominably and detestably in open adultery ... For this only cause
I protest before God & in the word of a prince, I have asked council
of the greatest clerks in Christendom, and for this cause I have
sent for this Legate [Cardinal Campeggio] as a man indifferent
only to know the truth and to settle my conscience, and for none
other cause as God can judge. And as touching the Queen, if
it be adjudged by the law of God that she is my lawful wife,
there was never thing more pleasant, nor more acceptable to me
in my life, both for the discharge and clearing of my conscience,
and also for the good qualities and conditions which I know to
be in her ...'

   To see what countenance was made amongst the hearers of this
oration, it was a strange sight, for some sighed and said nothing,
others were sorry to hear the king so troubled in his conscience.
Others that favoured the Queen much sorrowed that this matter
was now opened, and so every man spoke as his heart served him,
but the king ever laboured to know the truth for the discharge of
his conscience.

   Shortly after this the two Legates [Wolsey and Campeggio]
came to the Queen at the same place of Bridewell and declared to
her how they were deputed judges indifferent between the king
and her, to hear and determine whether the marriage between
them stood with God's law or not. When she heard the cause of
their coming, no marvel though she were astonished, for it touched
her very near. And when she had pause a while she answered.
Alas my lords, is it now a question of whether I be the king's

*lawful wife or no? When I have been married to him almost xx
years, and in the mean season never question was raised before? ...*

[Taken from Richard Grafton, *A Chronicle and mere history ...*, 1809
edition, pp. 415–16.]

Henry's conscience was a convenient instrument, and by the
summer of 1527 he had convinced himself that his marriage was
unlawful in the sight of God. The grounds for this were the Old
Testament prohibition against a man taking his brother's wife, the
penalty for which was childlessness (Leviticus 20:21). Henry and
Catherine were not actually childless, but the king allowed himself to be convinced that the original Hebrew had said 'without
sons'.[4] Something, after all, must have caused the queen's constant
and futile efforts to bear a son; miscarriages, cot deaths and still
births had followed each other relentlessly. In the absence of much
in the way of gynaecological knowledge, the only possible explanation was the wrath of God. In his enthusiasm to marry in 1509
Henry had overlooked this vital impediment, and now the consequences had caught up with him. No further attempts were possible, and the issue had to be faced.

Exactly what brought Henry to this state of mind is uncertain.
Catherine blamed Wolsey for sowing the seeds of doubt, and that
is possible. It is also possible, as was claimed later, that French ambassadors negotiating a marriage for Mary had raised the question
of her legal status.[5] The scruple certainly arose before the king's
infatuation with Anne Boleyn began (or at least before it was
known), because Wolsey was already discussing the possibilities of
a second marriage for Henry before he realized that the king had
already made his choice. Wolsey was not pleased, but had to
adjust, as did most of the court.

The one person who could not be expected to adjust was
Catherine. The king's doubts, and his relationship with Anne, were
apparently both well advanced before she discovered something
of what was afoot. Had the matter been tactfully handled, and an
appeal made both to her own conscience and to her powerful

piety, the matter could have been resolved. She knew, after all, that the king needed the son that she would never now be able to bear him. She also knew that if she withdrew gracefully into a nunnery, the legitimacy of her first marriage need never be called in question. Both her own conviction of divine dispensation and the rights of her daughter would be protected, and the king would be free to marry again, as he clearly wished. This did not happen, partly because of Henry's clumsiness, and partly because the queen found out about Anne. In the summer of 1527 the king baldly confronted his wife with a prepared statement to the effect that they were not, and never had been, married.[6] The shock produced a storm, and the storm resulted in an implacable resolution never to be set aside—least of all for 'that whore, Nan Bullen'.

The battle lines that were consequently drawn up had serious international implications, because the queen's first reaction was to appeal to her nephew, the Holy Roman Emperor. At the time Henry's relations with Charles V were already strained to breaking point, so the chance to use his aunt to embarrass the king of England was too good for Charles to miss. To be fair to Charles, he also seems to have been genuinely outraged by what Henry was proposing to do. Moreover, as fate would have it, he had Pope Clement VII at his mercy. In May 1527 a mutinous army, operating ostensibly in the name of the Emperor, had sacked Rome and confined the pontiff in the Castel Sant'Angelo.[7] Had Henry been in a position to offer Clement effective diplomatic and financial aid at this point, he might have won his case, but he was not, and the opportunity passed. The pope emerged from captivity, but, as he put it himself 'determined to live and die an Imperialist'. For nearly five years Henry was to batter away at the walls of the pope's obstinacy, and achieve precisely nothing.

In 1529 Henry thought that he had made a breakthrough, when Wolsey obtained a legatine commission (i.e. permission to act on the pope's behalf) to hear the case in England. However, the success was illusory. The commission, which opened on 18 June, was subject to appeal, and since Catherine had already made it clear that she *would* appeal if the decision went against her, it was so much waste of time. In addition, there were already those emerging, such as John Fisher, Bishop of Rochester, whose position of publicly defending the marriage was hardening.

BISHOP FISHER DEFENDS THE ROYAL MARRIAGE

(i)

'WHEREIN AFTER *I* (Henry) *once perceived my conscience wounded with the doubtful case herein, I moved first this matter in confession to you my Lord of Lincoln [John Longland] my ghostly father. And forasmuch as then yourself were in some doubt to give me counsel, moved me to ask further counsel of all you, my Lords, wherein I moved you first, my Lord of Canterbury [William Warham], asking your licence, for as much as you were our metropolitan, to put this matter in question. And so I did of you all, my Lords, to the which ye have all granted by writing under your seals, the which I have here to be showed.'*

'That is truth, if it please your highness' quod [said] the Bishop of Canterbury, 'I doubt not but that all my brethren here present will affirm the same'. 'No Sir, not I' quod the Bishop of Rochester, 'ye have not my consent therto'. 'No hath?' quod the king, 'look here upon this, is not this your hand and seal?' And showed him the instrument, with seals. 'No forsooth, Sir' quod the Bishop of Rochester, 'it is not my hand or seal'. To that quod the king to my Lord of Canterbury, 'How say you, is not this his hand and seal?' 'Yes, Sir' quod he. 'That is not so', quod the Bishop of Rochester, 'for indeed you were in hand with me to have both my hand and seal, as other of my Lords hath already done, but then I said to you that I would never consent to no such act, for it were against my conscience, nor my hand and seal should never be seen at any such instrument (God willing) with much more matter touching the same communication between us.'

'You say the truth' quod the Bishop of Canterbury, 'such words ye

had unto me, but at the last ye were fully persuaded that I should
for you subscribe your name, and put to a seal myself, and ye
would allow the same'. 'All which words and matter', quod the
Bishop of Rochester, 'under your correction my Lord, and
supportation of this noble audience, there is nothing more untrue'.
'Well, well,' quod the king, 'it shall make no matter. We will not
stand on argument herein, for you are but one man.'

[Taken from 'The Life and Death of Cardinal Wolsey,' by George
Cavendish, in *Two Early Tudor Lives*, ed. R.S. Sylvester and D.P. Harding,
1962, p. 87. These words were spoken in the context of the legatine
court. For the likely document under discussion here, see plate 5.]

(ii)

Cardinal Campeggio to Bernard Salviati, prior of St John at Rome,
and nephew of Pope Clement VII, 29 June 1529.

Y ESTERDAY *the fifth audience was given. While the*
proceedings were going on as usual, owing to the Queen's
contumacy [non-appearance, 'contempt of court'], *the Bishop*
of Rochester made his appearance, and said, in an appropriate
speech, that in a former audience he had heard his majesty discuss
the cause, and testify before all that his only intention was to get
justice done, and to relieve himself of the scruple which he had in
his conscience, inviting both the judges and everyone else to throw
some light on the investigation of the cause, because on this
account he found his mind much distressed and perplexed. If,
on this offer and command of the king, he [Fisher] *did not come*
forward in public and manifest what he had discovered in this
matter after two years of most diligent study,—and therefore … *
both in order not to procure the damnation of his soul, and in
order not to be unfaithful to the king, or to fail in doing the duty
which he owed to the truth, in a matter of such great importance,
he presented himself before their reverend lordships, to declare, to
affirm, and with forcible reasons to demonstrate to them that this
marriage of the King and Queen, can be dissolved by no power,
human or divine; and for this opinion he declared that he would

even lay down his life …

The affair of Rochester was unforeseen, and consequently has kept everyone in wonder. What he will do we shall see when the day comes. You already know what sort of a man he is, and may imagine what is likely to happen. But as the messenger will not stop and I am much occupied, I will write no more.

[Taken from *Letters and Papers*, IV, iii, 5732. The original, in Italian, is in the Vatican Archive.]

* There appears to be a break in the sense here, which was noted by the translator.

When Wolsey's colleague, Lorenzo Campeggio, acting on papal orders, adjourned the case on 31 July with nothing decided, he ruined Wolsey and left the king in a blind fury.[8] The English cardinal had failed in a task that only an English cardinal could perform: to influence papal policy in his master's favour.

By the end of 1529 a political stalemate had been reached. Neither the king nor the queen were prepared to make any concessions, and the pope was nailed down, partly by his dependence on the Emperor, but also by his unwillingness to have papal authority called into question by overturning the dispensation granted by Julius II in 1503. The problem was exacerbated by the fact that Henry *did* have a case, although neither Catherine nor her supporters would admit it. It was at least arguable that a scriptural prohibition had the force of divine law, and that the pope could not dispense it.[9] Moreover (his feelings for Anne Boleyn set aside) Henry was manifestly acting in the best interests of his realm in seeking to father a legitimate heir. The queen, on the other hand, while behaving with great moral and legal rectitude, was not acting reasonably, and had got herself into a position where victory would be meaningless and defeat unacceptable.

Henry was forced to seek an alternative policy, and with Wolsey in disgrace the king's links with Rome were extremely tenuous. For about two years Henry tried blackmail, charging first Wolsey and then the whole English clergy with praemunire

—that is, exercising ecclesiastical jurisdiction without royal assent
—in the hope that the pope would buy him off with concessions.
When that failed, he set his servants to find evidence that histori-
cally the English crown was not subject to Rome in a number of
regular causes (including matrimony). They found nothing relevant, but he made the assertion anyway, provoking suppressed
mirth in the curia, the papal court.[10]

By the end of 1529 there was a curious *ménage à trois* at the
English court. Catherine was still the queen, and occasionally
appeared as such on formal occasions. Henry no longer slept with
her, but they dined together from time to time. Anne, meanwhile, had moved in. She was the king's constant companion, and
her political influence, and that of her family, was growing steadily.
It would be hard to say which of the three was the most frustrated,
but it was Anne, characteristically, who gave vent to her feelings.
She stormed at Henry:

D ID I NOT TELL YOU *that when you disputed with the
Queen she was sure to have the upper hand? I see that some
fine morning you will succumb to her reasoning, and that you will
cast me off. I have been waiting long, and might in the meantime
have contracted some advantageous marriage … But alas!
Farewell to my youth and time spent to no purpose at all …*[11]

Perhaps the king found such spirited performances attractive. His
reaction on this occasion is not recorded, but they did the relationship no harm at all. However, Anne was right. Such a psy-
chologically stressful situation could not be allowed to endure. By
July 1531 Henry seems to have made up his mind. A final attempt
was made on his behalf at the end of May to persuade Catherine
to accept the annulment upon which he was determined. She
merely replied that she would abide by the decision of the papal
court. Slow as that was for a number of reasons, she knew perfectly well that it would be in her favour. Henry set off with Anne
to Woodstock, in Oxfordshire, leaving the queen at Windsor, and

then sent a message dismissing her from the court. He never, he declared harshly, wanted to see her again.[12]

Anne had now got rid of her rival, and put an end to any reports of a reconciliation, but she had not altered the legal situation. Whatever her position in the king's favour, Catherine was still the queen. However, under the pressure of circumstances, Henry's extremely conservative mind was beginning to take on some radical notions. Under the influence of such advisers as Thomas Cranmer, Edward Foxe and Nicholas del Burgo, he was beginning to convince himself that the pope had no right to interfere in England at all. In ancient times, before the popes had become worldly and pretentious, his ancestors had run the Church to suit themselves. All the jurisdictional claims of contemporary Rome were just so many human inventions, designed to fill the coffers and flatter the egos of successive pontiffs. He, Henry, would reassert his ancient rights—and solve his current problem into the bargain.[13]

The problem was, how to go about it? Ideally, and little as he might like the notion, Henry needed support, and not simply the support of Anne and her friends at court. He needed to be able to demonstrate to the world that he had the English Church, and better still the whole realm, behind him. There was a pause of several months, not because the king did not know what he wanted, but because he was unsure how to proceed. Then in August 1532 his old and loyal servant William Warham, the Archbishop of Canterbury, died. Warham had become distinctly uncooperative over the previous two or three years, and certainly could not have been relied upon to provide the leadership that Henry required. Now he was gone. Henry's phoney war with the Emperor had come to an end at Cambrai in 1529, but because of Catherine, relations between the two monarchs continued to be chilly to the point of hostility, and Charles's ambassador in England, Eustace Chapuys, could hardly have been more unflattering in his accounts of the court to which he was accredited.

However, the Emperor's enmity warmed relations with France,

and Anne, who had been brought up in the French court, was strongly Francophile. Francis was not much interested in Henry's matrimonial antics, but offered some diplomatic support, mainly to countermine Imperial influence, and the two kings agreed to meet near Calais in the autumn of 1532. It was to grace that occasion that Anne was created Marquis of Pembroke on 1 September, with which rank she accompanied the king to France. Under pressure from his own womenfolk, Francis avoided meeting her, but the event was redeemed from Anne's point of view by the fact that it was almost certainly while stormbound in Calais on the way back that Henry and Anne slept together for the first time.[14]

In January 1533, when Anne was found to be pregnant, the issues that had hung fire for so long were forced—as had no doubt been the hope. Thomas Cranmer, Archdeacon of Taunton and a leading member of Henry's think-tank, was summoned back from a diplomatic mission in Germany, and was appointed to the vacant archbishopric on 21 February, by which time the king was already secretly married to Anne—exactly when, and by whom, we do not know. Cranmer's first task was therefore obvious: he would pronounce Henry's earlier marriage null and void.

Whether the pope understood anything of this agenda is uncertain, although he knew about Cranmer's attachment to the king. Nevertheless Clement granted the pallium, the symbolic vestment of an archbishop, immediately and Cranmer was duly consecrated on 30 March. On 5 April the convocation of the ecclesiastical province of Canterbury conveniently ruled that the impediment of divine law could not be dispensed—in other words, it could not be nullified by the pope—and on 10 May Cranmer opened his special court at Dunstable. The location was chosen to be convenient for Catherine, but she declined to recognize the court, and refused to appear either in person or by proxy. On 23 May the archbishop solemnly found against her (see plate 8). From the queen's point of view this was a waste of breath, as she had already appealed to the curia. But to Henry it was critical. His second marriage was now lawful in the sight of God, and the child that Anne was carrying would be legitimate—at least within England and by English law.

THE CORONATION OF ANNE BOLEYN
June 1533

THE SUNDAY [1 June], in the morning, at eight o'clock, the Queen's Grace, with noble ladies in their robes of estate, assembled with all the nobles apparelled in Parliament robes, as Dukes, Earls, Archbishops and Bishops, with Barons and the Barons of the Five [Cinq] Ports; with the Mayor of the City and the Aldermen in their robes, as mantles of scarlet.

The Barons of the Five Ports bare a rich canopy of cloth of gold, with staves of gold, and four bells of silver and gilt. The Abbot Westminster with his [regalia] came into the hall in pontificalibus, with his monks in their best copes; the [members of] the King's chapel in their best copes: with the Bishops richly adorned in pontificalibus.

And the blue ray cloth spread from the high [dais] of the King's Bench unto the high altar of Westminster.

And so every man proceeding to the Minster in the best order, every man after his degree appointed to his order and office as appertaineth; came unto the place appointed: where her Grace received her crown, with all the ceremonies thereof, as thereunto belongeth. And so all ceremonies done, with the solemn Mass: they departed home in their best orders; every man to the Hall of Westminster: where the Queen's Grace withdrew for a time into her chamber appointed.

And so after a certain space, Her Grace came into the Hall. Then ye should have seen every nobleman doing their service to them appointed, in the best manner that hath been seen in any such ceremony.

The Queen's Grace washed. The Archbishop of Canterbury said grace. Then the nobles were set to the table. Therewith came the Queen's service with the service of the Archbishop. A certain space, three men with the Queen's Grace's service.

Before the said service, came the Duke of Suffolk (High Constable that day, and Steward of the feast) on horseback, and marvellously trapped in apparel with richesse. Then with him came the Lord William Howard, as deputy to the Duke of Norfolk, in the room of the Marshall of England, on horseback.

The Earl of Essex, Carver. The Earl of Sussex, Sewer. The Earl of Derby, Cupbearer. The Earl of Arundel, Butler. The Viscount Lisle, Panterer. The Lord Braye, Almoner.

These noble men did their service in such humble sort and fashion, as it was a wonder to see the pain and diligence of them: being such noble personages.

The service borne by Knights, which were to me too long to tell in order: the goodly service of kinds of meat; with their devices from the highest unto the lowest; there have not been seen a more goodly nor more honourably done in no man's days.

There were four tables in the great Hall, along the said hall.

The noblewomen, one table: sitting all on that one side.

The noblemen another table.

The mayor of London another table, with his brethren.

The Barons of the [Cinq] Ports, with the Master of the Chancery, the fourth table.

And thus all things nobly and triumphantly done at her Coronation; her Grace returned to White Hall with great joy and solemnity.

And on the morrow, there were great justs [jousts] at the tilt done by eighteen Lords and Knights, where were broken many spears valiantly; and some of their horses would not come at their pleasure, near unto the tilt; which was displeasure to some that there did run.

[*The Noble Triumphant Coronation of Queen Anne, wife unto the most noble King Henry the VIIIth, 1533.* Taken from A.F. Pollard, *Tudor Tracts*, 1903, pp. 18–19.]

A rupture of some kind with the papacy was inevitable, and a sentence of excommunication highly likely, so the king needed to broaden the basis of principle upon which he had now taken his stand. He needed also to spread the load, so that his action looked less like that of a whimsical tyrant determined to change his wife, and more like that of a godly prince recognizing his responsibilities. This he achieved by resorting to Parliament.

There was nothing particularly revolutionary about this as an idea. Parliament was a high court, and it could also claim to represent the consent of the realm. Lay peers and bishops were present in person, abbots and the commons by delegates. No institution was better qualified to speak for the whole kingdom, and it had assisted English monarchs in previous fallings out with the papacy —most notably over issues of papal appointments in England without royal consent, in the late 14th century, and the acts of 'provisors and praemunire' that pertained to these still remained on the statute books in spite of persistent campaigns from Rome to have them removed.[15] Henry had already given notice of intent by appealing to the statute of praemunire against first Wolsey, and then the whole clergy. As early as 1529 the House of Commons had been stimulated into making anticlerical noises over probate and mortuary fees, and in 1532 presented a 'supplication against the ordinaries' (a petition against ecclesiastical jurisdiction), which Henry was able to use to accuse his bishops of double allegiance.[16] Under intense pressure, the bishops surrendered their right to make independent canons, and agreed to submit future legislation for the king's approval.

Seeing which way the wind was blowing, Thomas More resigned the chancellorship, symbolizing the rift that had developed at the highest level. John Fisher, the scholarly and highly respected Bishop of Rochester, had already declared himself an unequivocal supporter of the queen, but most of his colleagues, uncertain of their ground and mindful of their allegiance, had been reluctant to make a similar stand. The king was therefore already half way to declaring his ecclesiastical independence before Warham died. For the time being he hoped against hope that such a declaration would not be necessary, but his conscience was already working upon that problem, as it had worked upon his marriage. By the time that he married Anne Boleyn, Henry was just as convinced that his first marriage had broken the law of God as Catherine was adamant that it had done no such thing. Similarly, by the time that a raft of legislation had culminated in the Act of Supremacy in 1534, and all traces of the papal primacy had been removed, the king believed with every fibre of his being that the pope was a usurping intruder, and that God's intention was that the Church in every realm should be ruled and led by its chief secular magistrate, be he king, or prince, duke or doge.

The political fallout from this situation was immense. More and Fisher were the most notable (and Fisher the most outspoken) opponents of the king's proceedings, but they were by no means the only ones. The Princess Mary absolutely refused to accept either her own or her mother's diminished status, and she had many sympathizers, particularly among the ladies of the aristocracy, to whom the name of Anne Boleyn was manure.[17] The Emperor was more alienated than before, and permitted his ambassador to intrigue vigorously with Henry's opponents, threatening an intervention that he never seriously intended. Chapuys consistently refused to recognize Anne as Queen, referring to her as 'the concubine', and his presence at court was deliberately corrosive.

More positively, the jurisdiction of Parliament was greatly enhanced. The statutes of 1533 and 1534 had ventured into territory where the Lords and Commons had never previously claimed competence, and although there were some who muttered that they were acting *ultra vires* (beyond their powers), nobody said so openly, and thanks to Thomas Cromwell's skilful draftsmanship and still more skilful management, the way was opened to solve other problems by statute. The most obvious example of this was the Act of Succession of 1534.[18] By sheer misfortune, Henry now had two daughters by different marriages, and it was necessary to lay down some principles. So it was declared that in the event of the king's death, the crown was to pass to any son who might be born to Queen Anne, or, failing that, to Elizabeth, the daughter who had resulted from her first pregnancy. Mary, as the king's 'natural' (i.e now illegitimate) daughter, had no claim. When the Lords of the Parliament had been appealed to in 1460 to resolve a rather similar problem, they had declared that they had no competence in so high a mystery. What a difference the creative use of circumstances can make!

It was one thing to declare the succession by statute, and quite another to beget a legitimate son. The latter feat continued to elude the king. That in itself would not have been sufficient to bring about the dramatic reversal of Anne's fortunes that occurred in 1536, but it probably contributed. The main causes were that she fell out with Thomas Cromwell, and that she became expendable after the death of Catherine in January. Cromwell was trying very hard to mend fences with the Emperor after Catherine died, and he realized that the defence of the royal supremacy (to which Henry was totally committed) no longer necessitated supporting Anne. Moreover, she and her family were strongly Francophile, and influenced the king as much as they could in that direction. So for a few short weeks the powerful secretary aligned himself with Anne's perpetual adversaries, the so-called 'Aragonese faction', and brought about her downfall.[19] If Henry's relations with his wife had not become volatile for other reasons, the improbable charges of adultery (with various men at court), incest (with her brother, Lord Rochford) and suggestions of witchcraft that brought her down might never have stuck. But stick they did, and by implicating her brother, they effectively destroyed the influence of the Boleyn family as well as bringing about the execution of the queen.

THE EXECUTION OF ANNE BOLEYN
1536 (translation)

THE COUNT *of Rochford, brother to the Queen (unjustly so called), Anne Boleyn, was beheaded with an axe upon a scaffold before the Tower of London. He made a very catholic address to the people, saying he had not come hither to preach, but*

to serve as a mirror and example, acknowledging his sins against
God and the King, declaring he need not recite the causes why he
was condemned, as it would give no pleasure to hear them. He first
desired mercy and pardon of God, and afterwards of the King and
all others whom he might have offended and hoped that they would
not follow the vanities of the world and the flatterers of the court,
which had brought him to that shameful end. He said that if he
had followed the teachings of the Gospel, which he had often
read, he would not have fallen into this danger, for good doer was
far better than a good reader. In the end he pardoned those who
had condemned him to death, and asked the people to pray for his
soul. After him Norris was beheaded, then Weston and Brereton
and Mark [Smeaton], the player on the spinet, who said scarcely
anything except to cry mercy of God and the King, and to beg
people to pray for their souls. Brereton and Mark were afterwards
quartered.

The said Queen (unjustly called) finally was beheaded upon
a scaffold within the Tower, with the gates open. She was brought
by the captain upon the said scaffold, and four young ladies
followed her. She looked frequently behind her and when she got
upon the scaffold was very much exhausted and amazed. She
begged leave to speak to the people, promising to say nothing but
what was good. The captain gave her leave, and she began to raise
her eyes to heaven, and to cry mercy to God and to the King for
the offence she had done, desiring the people always to pray to
God for the king, for he was a good, gentle, gracious and amiable
prince. She was then stripped of her short mantle furred with
ermine, and afterwards took off her hood, which was of English
make, herself. A young lady presented her with a linen cap with
which she covered her hair, and she knelt down, fastening her
clothes about her feet, and one of the said ladies bandaged her eyes.

Immediately the executioner did his office, and when her head
was off it was taken by a young lady and covered with a white cloth …

[Taken from *Letters and Papers*, X, no. 911. The original MS, in
Spanish, is in the Vienna Staatsarchiv.]

By the end of June, though, the temporary alliance that had destroyed Anne had fallen apart, and although Cromwell played a leading role in rescuing Mary from her self-delusions about her own restoration, it was only at the price of that young lady's total surrender to her father's demands, which took her off the scene as a political factor for the remainder of the reign.[20]

Meanwhile, the 'King's Great Matter' was unresolved, and Henry was 46, on the threshold of old age by the standards of the time. Within a matter of days after Anne's execution, on 30 May, he married Jane Seymour. She had been attached to the court for some time, and the king must have known her, but whether he had been 'enamoured' of her for nearly a year, and whether that fact had contributed to Anne's downfall, remain matters for speculation.[21] This marriage had no political significance, beyond the fact that it brought another consort's kindred to the fore. Jane was not known to be either pro- or antipapal, and had no factional baggage. Mary's friends regarded her as an ally, but in fact she seems to have been genuinely neutral. A peaceful, good-natured soul, she was not unintelligent, but was not in the least proactive, in marked contrast to her predecessor. She was no great beauty; her attractive qualities for Henry were, on the one hand, her quiet acquiescence, and, on the other hand, that she came from a proven breeding stock. Sir John Seymour had extensive progeny, and it may have been the consequent overstretching of his financial resources that had left Jane unwed at the mature age of 27.

What was important about her was that she was neither a French nor an Imperial princess, and the king's third marriage, it soon transpired, was not going to lead to any rethinking of the schism. This was important, because it was widely assumed, not least by Pope Paul III, that the rejection and death of Anne would lead to a new direction in English policy. He even put out feelers, indicating a willingness to lift sanctions in return for a formal submission. Henry was not interested.[22] The royal supremacy was now an integral part of his prerogative, and was not negotiable. Ironically, given her placidity, Jane Seymour was a symbol of that continued defiance.

Unlike either of her predecessors, Jane seems to have had no enemies. Even those (and there were many) who looked askance at the speed with which the king had married her, did not blame Jane. She was a good friend to the newly rehabilitated—and very deflated—Mary, who was now 20, and much in need of an elder sister. In an indulgent moment Henry referred to her as his first true wife, and if by that he meant the first who submitted to his will and kept her counsel, it was an accurate description. She was not, however, his wife at all in the eyes of Catholic Europe, because the realm was in schism and no valid marriages could be celebrated. The implications of this for English people at large were so enormous that they had every incentive to ignore it, and support for the royal supremacy increased. The second Act of Succession, of 1536, dutifully confirmed the annulment of the Boleyn marriage, bastardized Elizabeth and settled the succession on any child born to Queen Jane.[23]

In the circumstances it could have done no less, but there was still no male heir. It was therefore a huge relief when Henry's new-found domestic harmony was reflected in the fact that Jane conceived in about February 1537. The queen was sumptuously provided for, cosseted and protected, and the magnificent coronation that the king had been intending was quietly put on hold. Jane's pregnancy advanced normally and without alarms, but Henry became understandably nervous as time went by, and cancelled his intended progress on 12 June. Jane was in no fit state to travel, and he wanted to be close to her. She retreated into the customary seclusion at Hampton Court at the end of September, and went into labour on 9 October. After an easy pregnancy, the birth was a protracted and bitter one. Two days and three nights later, on 12 October, the long-anticipated prince finally appeared:

O N *St Edward's even was born ... the noble imp Prince Edward ... at the birth of this noble prince was great fires made through the whole realm, and great joy made with thanks-*

giving to almighty God which hath sent so noble a prince to
succeed to the crown of this realm.[24]

Jane was exhausted, but appeared at first no worse than was to be expected. Edward was christened on 15 October, and Jane was well enough to receive the congratulations that came flooding in. However, three days later she developed puerperal fever, a condition for which 16th-century medicine had no effective remedy, and late on the night of 24 October she died. The king was deeply and genuinely distressed; but he now had his son, and the child, guarded with neurotic care, lived and flourished.

In a sense, the King's Great Matter came to an end with the birth of Edward. A struggle that had lasted ten years, and cost three wives, had finally been brought to a successful conclusion. But in another sense it continued almost as long as Henry lived. A single life was no adequate protection for a Renaissance throne. Elizabeth of York had borne Henry VII three sons, but only one lived beyond adolescence; and Henry VIII had lost his first legitimate son, by Catherine, in infancy and his illegitimate son, Henry FitzRoy, at the age of 17. Even with the best care of which contemporary skill was capable, there was no guarantee that Edward would live, and indeed, although he survived long enough to succeed his father, he too died unmarried some two months short of his 16th birthday.[25]

A second son was eminently desirable, and while the king struggled with his emotions, his council addressed the issue as best they could. While there would be obvious advantages in finding another Jane—a docile young gentlewoman with no intellectual or political pretensions—at the beginning of 1539 the international situation turned their thoughts in a different direction. Francis and Charles, whose perpetual antagonism had hitherto given Henry a degree of protection, had met at Nice in June 1538 and had subsequently signed the Treaty of Toledo, professing the warmest friendship. Now thoroughly disillusioned with his attempts to negotiate with England, by December 1538 Paul III was preparing to promulgate his long delayed bull of excommunication against Henry, and had dispatched Cardinal Reginald Pole, by now the king's bitter enemy (see Chapter 7), to the north of England to foment discontent there and help persuade Charles and Francis to take joint action against the schismatic. Ideally, they should launch a joint invasion, but at very least withdraw their diplomatic representatives and impose trade sanctions. Faced with political isolation and the threat of war, Henry needed to use his widowerhood as a diplomatic weapon.

The result, largely negotiated by Thomas Cromwell, was the Cleves marriage. The duchy of Cleves was a strategically placed collection of territories on the lower Rhine, and its ruler, although traditionally hostile to the Emperor, was not a Lutheran nor a member of the Schmalkaldic League of German Protestant princes and cities. The possibility of such a union had been raised as early as June 1538, when the threat to England appeared to be mounting steadily. By the time that the negotiation was successfully completed late in 1539, the situation had changed, but there seemed no good reason to withdraw. Pole's mission had come to nothing. Neither Francis nor Charles withdrew their diplomats, and by the summer of 1539 these temporary friends were drifting apart again. The Scots, who might have been willing to intervene, were not strong enough to do so on their own, and the main consequence of the threat was that Henry had greatly strengthened his defences, and that the country had rallied behind him as never before.

The king (or rather Cromwell) had his spies in the court of Cleves, and Hans Holbein was sent over to paint the portrait of the lady in question, who was Anne, Duke William's sister. The information thus derived suggested a young woman of quiet dignity, good looking and sensible rather than exciting; but then the king was not looking for excitement—what he needed was another son. However, when Anne and her entourage reached England at the end of December, Henry quickly decided that he had been misled. With a flash of his old quixotic gallantry he intercepted her incognito at Rochester, and the result was a fiasco.

Her servants had had no chance to warn her of what was about to happen, and, speaking no English, she was totally confused and upset. If Henry was expecting the kind of improvised and witty response that he would have got from either Catherine or Anne, then he was immediately disappointed.[26]

When Henry met her properly a few days later, he was thus disposed to be highly critical. Although the courtesies demanded by protocol were strictly observed, the wedding night was a disaster. Anne, it quickly transpired, and been brought up in a kind of Teutonic seclusion. She had no language other than German, and none of the courtly graces in which her namesake had excelled. Worse still, she was so ignorant of the facts of life that she had no idea what was supposed to happen on a wedding night, and was not even disappointed when Henry failed to consummate their union. 'At this rate,' one of her ladies is alleged to have remarked, 'it will be a long time before we see a Duke of York.'[27]

The king had come to the same conclusion, and shortly after caused their marriage to be annulled on the grounds of non-consummation. His own account of this situation leaves little to the imagination, and it is obvious that there would have been no point in persevering. Anne, who may have been innocent but was not stupid, accepted her dismissal with good grace, and with it a generous financial settlement. Interestingly, she showed no desire to return to Cleves, or to marry, and lived in graceful retirement on the fringes of the English court for nearly twenty years, until her death in 1557.[28] Duke William was offended, but not mortally so, and in any case there was little that he could have done about it. No adjustments were made to the succession in anticipation of any offspring by Anne, and that was probably just as well, but more interestingly the same is true of his fifth marriage, to Catherine Howard.

Catherine was nothing if not sexually exciting, and just the tonic that Henry needed in that respect. To judge from the outcome, however, it would appear that his performance was not greatly superior to that with which he had addressed Anne, and his frustrated lady was quick to seek refuge in other beds, with disastrous consequences both for her herself and her husband. By 1542 Henry was 51, an old man and not in the best of health. He was devastated, as much by his own failure as by Catherine's desperate and irresponsible response. He recovered, after a fashion, and married again in the summer of 1543, but although there continued to be brave talk of children by his new queen, Catherine Parr, it is probable that no one, least of all Henry, now believed that such was a genuine possibility.

That thought lies behind his third and last Act of Succession, that of 1544.[29] The ostensible reason for this act was that the king was going on campaign to France, and thus hazarding his life. The act started conventionally by declaring that Prince Edward, now aged six, was his father's heir, ahead of any son that might be born to Henry by his present wife. It then departed from custom entirely, because by the normally accepted rules of primogeniture, if both Henry and Edward should die without further male heirs, the succession should have passed to the descendants of Henry's elder sister, Margaret. In 1544 that line was represented by her granddaughter Mary, the child of the recently deceased James V of Scotland. However, Mary was at that time betrothed by the Treaty of Greenwich to Prince Edward. Should that marriage take place, recognizing her as the next heir would complicate the situation intolerably, and if it did not take place, then she would be an alien born, and possibly an enemy.

The act consequently ignored the Scottish claim entirely, passing instead to the king's illegitimate daughters, Mary and Elizabeth. After Edward, they were declared to be second and third in line, in each case conditional upon their having married with the consent of the privy council. This was quite extraordinary. Not only had both girls been declared illegitimate by statutes that had not been repealed, but by no recognized criteria could both have been born in lawful wedlock. By the canon law of the Church, Mary was indeed legitimate, and should have been named first, because Jane Seymour's marriage was not recognized, but by no recognized standard (except that of English statute law at the time) could Elizabeth be so placed. Even more than the acts establishing the royal supremacy, which could be (and were) represented as fulfilling the law of God, this statute was a declaration that Parliament was a law unto itself, and that King, Lords and Commons in collusion could enact whatever they pleased.[30]

Having placed both the king's natural daughters in the succession, without any attempt to legitimate either of them, the Act of Succession then proceeded to name the children of Henry's second sister, Mary, the Duchess of Suffolk, in preference to the Scots. Mary had died in 1536, and her daughter, Frances, was married to Henry Grey, Marquis of Dorset. The act then proceeded to empower Henry either to confirm or alter these arrangements by his own last will and testament 'signed with his most gracious hand'.

By this time, the king was a corpulent invalid, and although he enjoyed himself hugely during the Boulogne campaign—most of all when he entered the town in triumph—it is by no means certain that he ever consummated his final marriage. The legacy of his Great Matter was to be a nine-year-old son and an act of Parliament of quite extraordinary pretentiousness. His will eventually confirmed the provisions of the act, so no issue arose between those two statements of intent, and together they were to determine the succession down to 1558. When the issue arose again, in the 1590s, the act of 1544 (which was never repealed) could be quietly forgotten. The Scottish line, in the person of James VI, succeeded almost without challenge, and the Suffolk line, represented by Edward Seymour, Earl of Hertford, never raised its head.

There were two other aspects of English politics that could be represented as legacies of the Great Matter, and each was to prove of more enduring importance. The first was the royal supremacy, under which the English Church was converted into that Protestant mode that was to be such an enduring part of the nation's identity. The second was the effective sovereignty of Parliament. Each constitutes an important aspect of the reign that is better considered as part of the king's government (see Chapter 6).

§5 The King's Laws

JUSTICE was one of the king's primary responsibilities. At his coronation he took an oath 'to make to be done after your strength and power, equal and rightful justice in all your dooms and judgements and discretion, with mercy and truth', and good justice was always held to be a benchmark of the strength of royal government. It had been one of the clearest signs of the disintegration of the king's authority in the latter years of King Henry VI that good justice had not been done. It was not that the courts had ceased to function (although that did happen from time to time and in some places), as that they ceased to be impartial between party and party. Instead of rising above the endemic local conflicts that were such a feature of the period, they sank beneath them. Process was distorted and juries rigged in the interest of the stronger party, and irrespective of the merits of the case. 'The law is used for nought else but to do wrong,' as Jack Cade's rebel followers complained in 1450. That attempts should be made to use the law as a weapon in factional conflict should surprise no one, but that the perpetrators should have got away with it was a damning indictment of the king.

Both Edward IV and Henry VII had been strong kings, and in general this kind of manipulation of the laws was ancient history by 1509. However, such lapses live long in the memory. There were still peers in Henry VIII's reign (and later) who behaved as though the ordinary laws did not apply to them, and it took the hanging of someone like Lord Dacre of the South to remind them that all were equally the king's subjects. Apart from anything else, peers and gentlemen were supposed to be the king's allies in the enforcement of justice, and were expected to set an example of exemplary obedience. As his reign progressed and its politics became more controversial, Henry himself sometimes used the law as a weapon, but he was always a stickler for 'due process'. To put it crudely, he frequently altered the law to suit himself before using it against his opponents. This made him, in his own eyes, an upright justiciar, but it is only fair to add that in suits between party and party, the council did maintain a tight supervision, which was part and parcel of the general effectiveness of Henry's government.

The common law of England was the king's law only insofar as it was administered in his name. He had not created it.[1] But it was the only law administered by the king's courts. It was amended as necessary, not at first by legislation, but by judicial interpretation —what became known later as 'case law'. The edicts issued by kings from time to time had to fit within this judicial framework, and were not seen as new law. The only constraint under which kings and judges operated was that the common law was supposed to be consistent with divine law—as laid down in the Scriptures and as interpreted by the Church.

It was recognized from an early date that the most authoritative interpreter of the law was the high court of Parliament, and that the will of the king, Lords and Commons reflected in an act had the force of law. By the 15th century the distinction between interpretation and the creation of new law had become blurred, so that Parliament had become in effect a legislature.[2] This meant that statute could amend and extend the law, introduce new penalties and create new offences. What it could not do was to legislate contrary to the spirit of the existing law, or contrary to the law of God.

As we shall see, these limitations were to be challenged in the course of Henry's reign. What is important to realize for the moment is that all serious offences—murder, rape, robbery and affray, were 'pleas of the crown', answerable by the common law in the king's courts, because they were deemed to be offences against the king's peace. Originally only free men (and women) could plead in, or be impleaded (sued) in, the king's courts, which had restricted access very considerably. Bondmen were answerable only in their lord's courts, although again normally under the common law. However, by the 16th century 'bondmen of condition', or villeins, were rare in England, and the great majority of criminal cases were heard before justices who derived their powers from the crown.[3]

Other laws still existed. The commonest form was 'custom of the manor', which varied from place to place and dealt with issues of land use, and minor offences such as straying beasts and moving boundary stones. Such cases were heard in manorial or 'honour' courts, presided over by the lord's steward, and could not be taken to the king's courts on appeal. The only appeal from such decisions lay through an expensive process in chancery, and given the nature of the litigants that was seldom resorted to.[4]

Early in Henry's reign there were also a number of areas—'liberties' or 'franchises'—where the king's writ did not run, and all proceedings were conducted in the name of the franchise holder. However by the 16th century the franchise holder was very often the king, as was the case in the duchies of Cornwall and Lancaster, and the law administered was usually the common law. The only exceptions were some of the franchises in the marches of Wales, where the law administered was Gaelic custom, even if the franchise holder was the king.[5]

AN ACT FOR FELONIES IN THE MARCHES OF WALES

AN ACT *that murders and felonies done or committed within any lordship marcher in Wales shall be enquired of at the sessions holden within the shire ground next adjoining.*

Forasmuch as the people of Wales and the marches of the same, not dreading the good and wholesome laws and statutes of this realm, have of long time continued and persevered in perpetration

*and commission of divers and manifold thefts, murders, rebellions,
wilful burning of houses and other scelerous deeds and abominable
malefacts, to the high displeasure of God, inquietation of the
king's well disposed subjects and disturbance of the public weal;
which malefacts and scelerous deeds be so rooted and fixed in
the same people that they be not like to cease unless some sharp
correction and punishment for redress and amputation of the
premises be provided according to the demerits of the offenders …*

*… And for the punishment and speedy trials … of all and
singular felonies [etc.] … committed within any lordship marches
of Wales, Be it enacted by authority aforesaid that the justices of
gaol delivery and of the peace and every of them for the time being,
in the shire or shires … next adjoining to the same lordship
marcher or other place in Wales … shall from henceforth have full
power and authority … to enquire by verdict of twelve men of the
same shire … to cause all such counterfeiters, washers, clippers of
money, felons, murderers and accessories to the same to be indicted
according to the laws of the land …*

[Statute 26 Henry VIII, c.6 (1534). *Statutes of the Realm*, III, 500–3.
Taken from G.R. Elton, *The Tudor Constitution*, 1982, pp. 215–16.]

The effect of all this is that in the mid-16th century, apart from
certain areas of the Welsh marches, most English men and women
were living under *two* systems of justice. The public justice, which
derived directly from the king, and the private justice, which was
exercised locally by a lord or charter holder. A lord's authority
was deemed to be 'natural', in that it was derived from his status as
a lord.[6] In this sense the head of a household was the 'lord' in his
own house, and his family and servants were subject to him, but
only on domestic issues, not on anything that might be deemed
subject to the king's laws. The same applied to a master's authority over his pupils. In the case of a chartered company, or town,
such as a London livery company or a parliamentary borough,
jurisdictional authority derived from the charter, which conferred certain defined rights of justice upon the holders. Some

boroughs were still seigneurial, that is their charters were issued by private lords, but most derived from the king.[7] By the reign of Henry VIII, manorial courts were largely relevant only to issues of land use and tenancy,[8] while boroughs had effective jurisdiction over trading matters, such as the regulation of markets. At the end of the day, all issues of customary or 'natural' law were amenable to control by Parliament, so there was no conflict, real or potential, between the two systems of justice.

The courts, however, were quite distinct, and no one involved in litigation would have been in any doubt as to which system he was involved with.[9] No customary court could touch life or limb, nor could it confiscate real property. Such courts could imprison offenders for limited periods, but the usual penalty was a fine or an order of restitution. Very often customary courts acted more like modern tribunals, and arbitrated disputes rather than imposing sanctions.

Royal courts, on the other hand, had a national structure, at the head of which stood the Westminster Courts of Common Pleas, which dealt with property issues, and King's Bench, which dealt with criminal pleas.[10] It was the delegated jurisdiction of these courts that the king's judges of assize took with them when they went on circuit in the counties. The assize judges had full powers, but if for any reason a case had to be called back to Westminster, that was done by a writ of *certiorari*, certifying it had not been heard in another court, and issued from the chancery. The assizes handed down capital and corporal punishments, as well as using fines or imprisonment. Appeal could be made to the central courts, although that was seldom done.[11] Usually the only remedy against a capital sentence was an appeal for clemency, directed to the king or the privy council, and that had nothing to do with the judicial structure.

The other main way in which royal justice was administered was by commission, that is when the king's judicial function was delegated to a group of local gentlemen and lawyers—usually stiffened with a few privy councillors and judges. There were many different kinds of commission, but two are relevant in this context: *oyer et terminer* and the 'peace'. A commission of *oyer et terminer* was usually issued to deal with a specific situation, such as the treason resulting from a rebellion, and its decisions could not be appealed within the system. Commissions of the peace were issued regularly to every shire in the realm.[12] The commissioners might number anything from twenty to fifty, according to the county and the date. Commissions tended to grow steadily in size, because membership, although unpaid, carried authority and status within the gentry community, and places were sought after.[13] The commissioners (or most of them) met four times a year, hence the term 'quarter sessions', and dealt, broadly speaking, with minor felonies and major misdemeanours. The quarter sessions hanged thieves and rioters, but usually referred such matters as treason to the assizes. The justices of the peace (JPs) also exercised a wide variety of administrative functions, usually determined by statute, took oaths and enforced proclamations—the latter not being laws but royal edicts.[14]

Both assizes and quarter sessions operated by indictment. That is, if a person was accused of felony, a jury of twelve local men had to decide whether a *prima facie* case existed. If it did, they found a 'true bill' and the person was indicted. It was indictment rather than accusation that brought the offender within the jurisdiction of the court. If he then pleaded 'not guilty', a trial jury (which was quite distinct from the jury of indictment) had to be recruited to adjudicate the facts of the case. These juries were gathered by the senior royal official in every county, that is the sheriff.

Originally the sheriff had been a powerful figure, who had commanded the shire levies and accounted to the exchequer for royal lands within his county. By the 16th century, however, the job was an expensive chore that local gentlemen did their best to avoid. Apart from recruiting juries, he presided at the shire court, which was an obsolete royal court whose only function by this time was the election of MPs.[15] He was also responsible for the pursuit and arrest of indicted offenders, and for distraining (seizing) the goods of those who could not be found. Most of his discretionary functions had been taken over by the JPs, and his financial functions by the receivers of the various revenue courts. Sheriffs were appointed by the lord chancellor, acting on the advice of the local assize judges, and even the most important gentlemen were anxious not to serve more than once. Justices of the peace were noblemen and gentlemen with land in the relevant county, but in the case of cities that were also counties—such as London—the mayor for the time being and his aldermen served *ex officio*. There were also commissions of the peace in the franchises of Chester, Cornwall and Durham, but there they were issued by the franchise holder rather than by the crown.[16]

So how did the ordinary citizen in Henry's kingdom tangle with this judicial system? The initiation of issues at common law was virtually confined to the well-to-do. A person charged with a crime or serious misdemeanour would be arrested by the parish constable or town bailiff, usually acting on the authority of a justice of the peace. A JP also had the authority to bail an offender if he thought it appropriate, which usually depended upon the nature (and plausibility) of the alleged offence.[17] If a person so arrested was subsequently indicted, then he would be tried and punished, which in the case of a felony might well mean hanging. Misdemeanours were normally punished by the justices without indictment. Many such cases, however, came to nothing, either because the offender had escaped and could not be found, or because evidence was lacking, or the accuser withdrew. No one could be tried *in absentia*. Escape was relatively easy, because of the way that jurisdiction was compartmentalized. All a fugitive had to do was to cross the county boundary, and the search had to begin all over again in the new county.[18] Distraint –technically, the seizure of assets to a certain limit—was effective only against those with substantial moveable goods; it was useless against the poor, who constituted the majority of offenders.

The lowest level of enforcement officer was the parish constable, usually a yeoman or tradesman, who was elected by the men of the parish on an annual basis. Such work was unpaid (although not unrewarded), and was often evaded by those eligible to serve because it carried implications of bad neighbourliness. The high constable of the 'hundred', that ancient division of a county, or the bailiff of a town, was the next rank up. They were similarly elected, and were expected to work closely with the justices. If there were tensions between the different levels of enforcement officers—as was to happen in 1549—there could be a serious breakdown of order, but normally they collaborated well enough. Both, after all, had property interests to defend against the depredations of the criminal—or the desperate.

Justice, however, was not only a question of law. Henry as king also wielded various powers, which pass under the general heading of 'equity'.[19] He could suspend particular laws, usually statutes, or dispense individuals from their provisions. This was really a political prerogative, although the beneficiaries were not always of high status, and the prerogative was not used in normal common-law cases. In those cases the only prerogative was that of mercy— the king could pardon any offence whatsoever once the judicial process was complete. Equity was also systematized as a quasi-judicial process. The king's council heard cases, originally between those who were deemed too powerful for the assizes to handle— particularly cases of unlawful retaining, maintaining a retinue of armed followers—but later between parties whose disputes were not covered by the common law.[20]

Cardinal Wolsey as chancellor deliberately encouraged this, because equity was the chancellor's preserve. He was the 'keeper of the king's conscience'. At the higher level the king's council sitting as a court was called the 'Council in the Star Chamber', and dealt, mainly, with cases involving the rich or exalted.[21] However, another conciliar court, called the Court of Requests, dealt with what were officially called 'poor men's causes', and was open to all. Equity procedure was cheap, conducted in English, usually in writing, and relatively speedy. Its main drawback was that its decisions did not have coercive force. For that reason cases often came back to Star Chamber and Requests over and over again; and were sometimes pursued simultaneously through the common law.[22] The regional councils, in the north and in the marches of Wales, also exercised equity jurisdiction within their areas—and, incidentally, also held standing commissions of *oyer et terminer*.

As we have seen, manorial courts might also act as tribunals of arbitration, but probably the commonest way of settling disputes was by appeal to informal intervention. This often involved the parish priest as arbitrator, but the essential ingredient was the consent of the parties. Two parties at odds would agree upon a person or persons to adjudicate their dispute, and would normally take an oath to abide by the arbitration. This might be called the lowest form of equity, and must have been very frequently resorted to, although records only survive where the decision for some reason was not adhered to and the case ended up in court anyway.[23]

There was also another system of jurisdiction that affected everyone, and that was the Church. Before 1533 the canon law was entirely independent of the crown, and dealt with a wide range of issues concerning discipline and the faith, very broadly defined. Every type of offence, from holding erroneous convictions about the Eucharist to pissing in the churchyard, was liable to land the offender before a Church court. Other matters, which were not in any sense criminal, also came under ecclesiastical scrutiny, because they were deemed to have a spiritual dimension. Examples included marriage cases, because matrimony was a sacrament; and contract, because contracts involved oaths that were taken upon the Holy Evangelists. Such cases, and particularly the latter, spread the tentacles of ecclesiastical jurisdiction well beyond what would normally be thought of as sacred issues.

The lowest level of enforcement officer in the Church structure was the churchwarden, who was responsible for the discipline and conduct of the parish, and who was roughly equivalent of the parish constable. He was of similar social status and was elected in the same way. The churchwardens were responsible for making presentations, either to the archdeacon, who was the bishop's enforcement officer, or to the 'visitors' when the church was inspected—which happened every so often.[24] Bishops also had minor officers, such as summoners and pardoners, to pursue those who might have eluded the churchwardens. Very minor disputes might be dealt with by the 'parochiani', that is the elders of the parish, but the normal court of first resort was the archdeacon's consistory. Beyond that, appeal could lie to the bishop's consistory or to the archbishop's Court of Arches—although only the most exalted litigants, or the most acrimonious disputes, ever got that far. In theory, appeal beyond the Arches could lie to the curia in Rome, but that was a route only for the very wealthy. It was, notoriously, the route chosen by Catherine of Aragon.

Unlike the common law, the canon law was a written code, consisting of the decrees and decisions of successive popes and general councils, and based generally upon the code of Justinian.[25] Local decrees were made from time to time by the convocations of York and Canterbury. There was, again before 1533, no such thing as a unified English Church, but rather the separate York and Canterbury provinces of the Universal Church. Papal legates interfered from time to time. Wolsey was a legate *a latere*, with enhanced powers, but that served mainly as a protection against interference from Rome.

Because the Church was heavily endowed with lands, and because all issues involving real estate belonged to the common law, border skirmishes between the two systems were endemic, and common and canon lawyers were in a perpetual state of feud.[26] There was an unwholesome tendency for some clergy, cornered in legal disputes before a secular court, to seek an escape by excommunicating their opponents, or even resorting to charges of heresy. Such tactics were bitterly resented and produced a few high-profile cases, of which that involving Richard Hunne is the best known.[27]

Over both clergy and laity, Church courts exercised extensive powers. A priest could be suspended or deprived of his living, imprisoned, fined, penanced or excommunicated, according to the nature of his offence. In an extreme case, such as unrepentant heresy, once convicted, he could be handed over to the secular authorities to be executed under a statute of 1414.[28] A layman could also be fined, penanced or excommunicated, but neither his livelihood nor his real property could be touched. Convicted of heresy, and unrepentant or relapsed, he shared the same fate as his clerical counterpart, because the Church courts could not inflict the death penalty.

The Church affected ordinary people in scores of ways, most of them positive. The sacraments provided both sociability and spiritual consolation; guilds and fraternities provided social-welfare benefits; and worship was a natural reaction to many of the problems and afflictions of life. The clergy were guides, confessors and counsellors, as well as arbitrators. Although all sorts of eccentric beliefs seem to have flourished below the surface of parish life, only the wildest, or the most unpopular, were ever presented before the courts. There was jurisdictional friction, and perpetual disputes over tithe payments, but of anti-clericalism in the German sense there is very little sign[29]—except, that is, where it mattered most, in London and in Parliament.

After 1533 and the break with Rome, the situation changed in various subtle but important ways. The end of appeals to Rome made no difference to the man or woman in the pew, and the removal of the pope's name from the intercessions affected him only marginally. If his local priest did what he was supposed to do, and preached every quarter against the usurped authority of Rome, he probably listened dutifully and shrugged his shoulders. However, after a while the fact that there was now one English Church, and that the king was its head, did begin to make a difference. Royal injunctions, enforced by visitation in 1536 and 1537, drastically curtailed the number of holidays, forbade them during harvest, and decreed that festivals of patron saints were all to be held on the same Sunday in October.[30] These were hardly revolutionary changes, but they did make a difference.

So, too, did the disappearance of the local friary or monastery, which had been part of the landscape for as long as anyone could remember. The monks and friars were soon absorbed into the parochial ministry, but many of them took a sense of grievance with them, which was particularly infectious in conservative communities. English bibles appeared, and men were exhorted to read them, an act that would not long since have been an infallible test of heresy. All this was ordered by the king, whose long arm now began to be felt even in the most remote parish. Even the conformist Christopher Trykhay, vicar of Morebath, digested his indignation and did as he was told.[31] It may be doubted whether the withdrawal of monastic hospitality made much difference in most places, although much was to be made of it, and fine tuning the use of images and the intercessory prayers for the deceased would hardly have been noticed by most laymen. The Latin rite, and the administration of the sacraments, remained untouched, and that was what mattered to lay people.

The clergy, some at least of whom were better educated, had rather a different perspective. Up to a point they sympathized with what the king was trying to do. The Church needed reform, and neither the pope nor Wolsey had made much of a shot at it; perhaps a godly prince would do better. Whether that was worth a unilateral declaration of independence divided clerical opinion, but it was generally assumed that when the king had settled his affairs, and got an heir, the whole situation would be renegotiated. It was hardly worth risking martyrdom for a temporary aberration, and by the time that they realized that they had misjudged Henry, it was too late to make a stand.

Whether Englishmen on the whole supported the king, or merely acquiesced in what he was doing, we shall probably never know. There is plenty of evidence on both sides. When it came to facing the Church courts, it did not make much difference; bishops, archdeacons and churchwardens carried on as before, and if you made a disturbance in church, refused to take communion at Easter, or withheld your tithe, you would still be in trouble with the law. The canon law was now trimmed to remove the pope, and was called the king's law, but he did not make it any more than he made the common law. On the other hand, it was in Henry's reign that that universal busybody, Parliament, started to decree how worship was to be conducted and what might, or might not, be believed. In a sense this was an improvement because Parliament was, at least in theory, answerable within the realm, whereas the pope was not. Better, perhaps, the devil you knew.[32]

It was legislation that made the big difference in Henry's reign, although the common law continued to develop by interpretation. This could be ingenious. For example, trespass (that is entering uninvited into someone else's property) was an unlawful act, but because the King's Bench division was quicker and more decisive than Common Pleas, it became conventional to describe such offences as having been carried out *vi et armis* (with 'force and arms'), thus making it a criminal action.[33] It was well known that the force was fictional, but since one could not trespass on one's own property, this became a convenient way of testing rights and ownership.

This fictional action was already fully developed before Henry's time, but as the king's policies began to stir up fierce controversy, and accusations flew backwards and forwards, it also became apparent that the common law provided no adequate protection against slander. So the concept was developed of trespassing on someone else's reputation, an offence that came to be known as 'trespass on the case'. This fictional pleading was used in hundreds of cases, both in Henry's reign and later.[34] Similarly, cases from the country could be brought into King's Bench by a fictitious 'bill of Middlesex', alleging a trespass in that county.

Statute was used rather differently, and much more frequently after 1529. Several new felonies were created, and penalties for existing crimes increased. Treason, in particular, was redefined several times in accordance with Henry's shifting policies.[35] Because conviction for treason involved the forfeiture of all property to the crown, it was normal to repeat such forfeitures, known as 'attainders', by act of Parliament, which confirmed the king's title to the property. An act might, however, be used instead of a trial. This was not altogether unprecedented: when Edward IV had accused his brother the Duke of Clarence of treason in Parliament, no trial had followed, the king's word being deemed sufficient. It was, however, very unusual. During Henry's reign, acts of attainder, as they were called, were used against Elizabeth Barton in 1533, against Thomas Cromwell in 1540 and against Catherine Howard in 1541,[36] but most accused traitors were tried either by the Court of the High Steward (in the case of peers) or by commissions of *oyer et terminer*.

Treason legislation did not, in any case, affect very many people. Far more were involved in the various administrative regulations that Parliament laid down; acts for the making of ropes at Bridport, for example, or for hats and caps at Leicester. These regulations overrode the existing local customs, and were often enacted at the suit of interested parties, sometimes to be repealed in the next session when other interest groups had gained the ear of members.

Two types of statute, however, affected everyone in Henry's reign. The first comprised those acts concerning vagabonds and the poor, and the second comprised the regulations concerning the teaching and ministry of the Church. Pre-Tudor legislation on beggars had been punitive. In 1349 the giving of alms to the able-bodied was forbidden, and by an act of 1383 'sturdy rogues' could be committed to the assizes.[37] At first the Tudors had done no more, and a statute of 1495 had merely provided that such people should be forcibly returned to their places of origin. In 1531, however, an entirely new principle appeared for the first time. The statute of that year distinguished between the 'whole and mighty in body, and able to labour', who were to be treated as before— that is whipped and sent home—and the 'aged, poor and impotent persons', who were allowed to solicit alms.

This was the very minimal beginning upon which the later Poor Law was to be based. It was minimal because it did no more than recognize the distinction. JPs were empowered to inflict punishments and to licence those entitled to beg, but no one was expected to accept responsibility for the latter.[38] The giving of alms to such people, like the similar giving to pious causes, was entirely a matter of Christian conscience. In 1536 a further critical advance was made. The statute of 27 Henry VIII, c.25, dealing with 'sturdy vagabonds', placed the legal responsibility for the relief of the sick and disabled upon their parishes of origin, or, if they were unable to travel, upon their parishes of residence. In the wake of this act, overseers of the poor appear for the first time, and poor-relief funds were established. By later standards the provision was inadequate. No distinction was made between 'able bodied vagabonds' and those who were willing to work but unable to find employment—a distinction crucial to the later law —and the whole system depended upon voluntary contributions. It was now required by law that parishes make provision for poor relief, but not that such coffers should be replenished.[39]

AN ACT FOR THE PUNISHMENT OF STURDY VAGABONDS

1535 (extracts)

ITEM, *it is ordained and enacted by the authority aforesaid [Lords spiritual and temporal and Commons in Parliament] that all and every Mayors, Governors and Head Officers of every city, borough and town corporate, and the Churchwardens or two others of every parish of this realm shall in good and charitable wise take such discreet and convenient order, by gathering and procuring of such charitable and voluntary alms of the good Christian people within the same with boxes every Sunday, holy day, and other festival days or otherwise among themselves, in such good and discreet wise as the poor, impotent, lame, feeble, sick and diseased people, being not able to work, may be provided, holpen and relieved, so that in no wise they nor none of them be suffered to go openly in begging. And that such as be lusty, or having their limbs strong enough to labour may be clearly kept in continual labour, whereby every one of them may get their own [substance]*

*and living with their own hands; upon pain that all and every the
said Mayors, Governors, Aldermen, Head Officers and other the
king's officers and ministers of every of the said cities, boroughs,
towns corporate, hundreds, parishes and hamlets shall [lose] and
forfeit for every month that is omitted and undone the sum of
twenty shillings …*

*Item, be it also enacted by the authority aforesaid that the said
Governors … [etc.] shall have authority by virtue of this present
Act to take up all and singular children in every parish within
their limits that be not grieved with any notable disease or
sickness, and being under the age of xiiii and above the age of five
years in begging or idleness, and to appoint them to masters of
husbandry or other crafts or labours to be taught, by the which
they may get their livings when they shall come to age, giving to
them of the said charitable collection, as it may be conveniently
sustained and borne, a raiment to enter into such service. And if
any above the age of twelve years and under the age of sixteen
years refuse such work or depart from the same without some
reasonable cause [then] they to be arrested and apprehended by
any of the said officers and to be brought before the Mayor,
Aldermen, Justices of the Peace, Bailiffs, Governors, Constables
or other officers and ministers of that limit and circuit where they
be taken. And if it shall appear by his or their confession or other
sufficient testimony before the same officers and ministers, that he
or they have refused to serve or have departed from their service
without cause reasonable, he shall then in the parish where he was
apprehended be openly whipped with rods by discretion of the said
Governor or Bailiffs. And thereupon to be set again to his service,
and so to be served as often as he shall be apprehended and
convicted in form aforesaid …*

[Statute 27 Henry VIII, c.25. From *Statutes of the Realm*, III, pp. 558-9.]

It should perhaps be noted that both these statutes preceded the
dissolution of even the smaller monasteries, and that there was no
connection between these two acts of policy. There was some

anxiety in the 1530s about rising levels of rural unemployment, or more accurately underemployment, but this was unconnected with any release of ex-monks and ex-monastic servants onto the labour market. Indeed it is very uncertain that the latter happened at all. The lands of the dissolved abbeys did not disappear. The new owners still required men to work that land, and more often than not the houses themselves were converted into gentry homes that similarly required service. There was disruption—worse in some places than others—but it is unlikely that this had much impact on the employment situation. The displaced monks themselves were given the option of joining larger houses, or becoming secular clergy, and those who chose the latter option were soon absorbed by the parochial system.

Rural unemployment, which may have been dimly perceived in these early poor laws, was the result of an unacknowledged, and probably unnoticed, growth in the population. It is impossible to quantify accurately, but probably the population of England rose by about half a million in the 38 years of Henry's reign. This was enough to put a strain on the land market; to mean that tenements, the land held on tenancies, became divided on inheritance to an uneconomic extent, and that younger sons were often displaced altogether.[40] An increasing paranoia about rogues and vagabonds, which can be more clearly seen in the half century following Henry's death, had its origin in this phenomenon.

Whether there was any real increase in criminal behaviour may be doubted, but there were certainly more poor people travelling the roads and looking for work, and that was unsettling. A man (or an unmarried woman) was largely identified by his (or her) occupation and employer, and a person without regular employment was 'masterless'. Traditionally 'masterless man' was almost synonymous with outlaw, a person living outside the recognized social structures and constraints, and therefore potentially dangerous. The statutes of 1531 and 1536 began to tackle this problem of perception by taking the sick and impotent out of the equation, and by labelling them as 'unfortunates' to give them again a recognized

[1] HENRY VIII, THE
RENAISSANCE PRINCE,
aged around 35, as painted
in miniature by Lucas
Horenbout (*c.*1490–1544),
appointed royal painter
in 1534.

[2] HENRY as depicted
with his symbols of royal
authority on the third Great
Seal, this example from
letters patent granting land
to the Earl of Hertford
(1544).

[3] A PORTRAIT presumed to be that of the young Catherine of Aragon, wife of both Henry and his older brother Arthur. It was painted by Michel Sittow (1485–1536).

[4] THOMAS WOLSEY (*below*), lord chancellor, cardinal and Henry's chief minister 1514–29, in a contemporary Flemish drawing.

[5] A CONTROVERSIAL RECORD (*lower right*). This is Henry's registration of his 'scruple of conscience' (1 July 1529) before the legatine court, convened to consider the case for terminating his first marriage. One of two originals at the National Archives, which recently came to light during conservation work, it is most likely the source of stories by Cavendish (*see* Chapter 4) and others, in which John Fisher, Bishop of Rochester, who opposed the divorce, claimed his signature and seal (third from left) had been forged.

[6] SEXUALITY AND WIT COMBINED. This portrait of Anne Boleyn, probably 17th-century, suggests the combination of those qualities which attracted Henry. Despite her own fall from grace, she gave birth to England's future queen, Elizabeth.

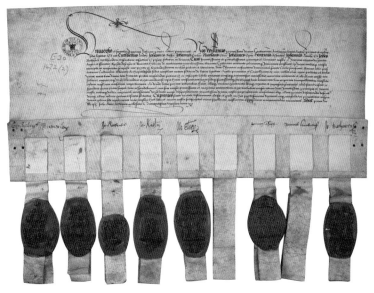

Tho: Moor L. Chancelour

[7] A SERIOUS OPPONENT (*left*). Thomas More was chancellor after Wolsey, but his opposition to the Royal Supremacy cost him his life. He was drawn by Holbein the Younger in *c*.1527.

[8] A MARRIAGE ANNULLED (*below*). This is the sentence of Cranmer's court at Dunstable in the proceedings of Henry and Catherine, 1533.

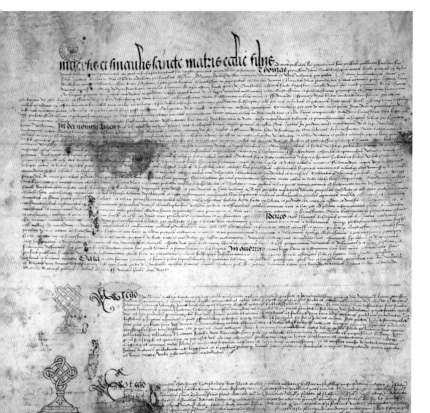

[9] THE KING IN HIS GLORY (*above*). This is one of the classic views of Henry, produced by Holbein the Younger in 1536, in which the monarch exudes majesty and sheer presence.

[10] THE SUPREMACY IN ACTION. Detail of a page from a 1533 volume of the *Valor ecclesiasticus*—the survey undertaken to assess church wealth, now held at the National Archives. The illuminated capital for Staffordshire shows Henry backed by, but still dominating, his secular and clerical notables.

[11] A WILY ADVISER (*below*). Thomas Cromwell was Henry's chief minister in 1532–40.

[12] A MUCH EASIER ANNULMENT (*opposite, top*). In this notarially attested document (11 July 1540), Anne of Cleves agrees to the end of her royal marriage.

[13] FALL OF THE HOUSE OF HOWARD (*opposite*). Charges drafted by the lord chancellor Thomas, Lord Wriothesley, against the Duke of Norfolk in 1546. Henry's own death saved Norfolk from execution.

[14] POLITICAL IMAGERY (*below*). In a *c*.1545 painting, Queen Jane and Edward anachronistically inhabit the centre of power; princesses Mary and Elizabeth lurk on the margins.

In dei noie Amen ...

[Top membrane: a lengthy legal instrument in 16th-century secretary hand, largely illegible, bearing four pendant seals on vellum tags. Signatures and a date "1588" appear at the foot.]

173

... the colaterall lyne to the heyre of ...
... to have thermof of Emp and ...
the seconde quarter wth the difference of ...
... Doo stampe his right place
and leave then in the first quarter leavinge
out the same difference of ... and
... the Lion thereof ...
... the heire male apparant ...
... any manner goie or flaunder the
... of the Prince or ...
and howe it wayeth in one ...

presume to
If a man take into his owne ... of the
Crowne and ... it wthout ...
... maye be to the goie or flaunder of
... the very heire of the Crowne, or be takes
to tende to his disturbaunce in the same
... in what goie ... he that ... that ...

himselfe to governe the realme doe actually
... to rule the Empere and ...
If a man ...
for that purpose undisch ...
... a baron his pardon ...

[15, 16] IMAGES OF A KING.
The engraving of Henry
in decay (*right*) by Antwerp's
Cornelis Matsys (*c.*1510–57)
contrasts strikingly with
this respectful chalk drawing
(*above*) of *c.*1540, probably
copied from Holbein. Per-
haps the truth of the mature
Henry lay somewhere
between the two.

position, albeit a dependent one. A disabled man could not be expected to have a master.

Statutes arising from the exercise of the royal supremacy might also have an impact on ordinary people. They were not much concerned with acts that made provision for the appointment of bishops, but when it came to 'abolishing diversity of opinions', they were much more likely to become engaged. Heresy had been an offence under the common law since at least the 14th century, when it had been established in the case of one Sawtrey that *de heretico cumburendo* ('for the burning of heretics') was a writ under the common law, although the conviction had been reached under the canon law in an ecclesiastical court.[41] This provision had been reinforced by the Heresy Acts of 1401 and 1414, aimed against the Lollards, the first of which had decreed death by burning as the punishment for the impenitent or relapsed, while the second had empowered justices in quarter sessions to receive indictments for heresy, although not to try such cases.[42]

An act of 1533, before the enactment of the royal supremacy, had modified this situation in a number of ways. By repealing the statute of 1401 it deprived bishops of the power to arrest on mere suspicion, and by confirming that of 1414 made it virtually essential for heresy cases to proceed by way of indictment in a court of common law. It also declared that speaking against the papal authority, or against the canon law, was no longer to be deemed heretical, and that no indictment on those grounds would be received.[43] The common law and the canon law were therefore no strangers to each other, although as we have seen relations between the lawyers tended to be strained.

In 1539 the small precedent set in 1531 was followed up in a much more sweeping fashion. Apart from de-criminalizing abuse of the pope, no statute hitherto had attempted to define what constituted heresy. The Act for the Abolishing Diversity of Opinion, better known as the Act of Six Articles, did precisely that. Denial of transubstantiation, advocacy of marriage for priests, rejection of the efficacy of private masses, or the denial of auricular confession were declared to be heresies for which the holders of such opinions, 'their aiders, comforters, counsellors and abettors', being duly convicted by an ecclesiastical court and refusing to abjure, 'shall therefore have and suffer, judgement, execution and pains of death by way of burning …'[44] At the same time the refusal of confession or communion, while not heretical, was an offence to be punished in the first instance with fine and imprisonment, and on the second offence a felony punishable by death—although not by burning.

Because this statute for the most part confirmed the definitions of the existing canon law, its significance has not always been recognized. For the first time the Church in England had a confessional statement that had force under, and was defined by, a secular law. Between 1533 and 1539 prosecutions for heresy had fallen away, partly because the presence of Thomas Cromwell as 'vice regent in spirituals' had tended to discourage them, and partly because of the need to proceed by way of indictment under the common law. Within a year after the passing of the Act of Six Articles, Cromwell had fallen from power, and the new statute acted as a spur. With the common law now firmly behind them, the bishops were emboldened to bring many more cases, and there was an upsurge of prosecutions for which the act was largely, and rightly, blamed.

At a time when notions of orthodoxy had been destabilized by the royal supremacy, the advent of the English Bible and the dissolution of the monasteries, many ordinary men and women had begun to question traditional definitions of the faith. That did not mean that they were Protestants, but it did mean that they were asking questions that would not have occurred to their parents or grandparents.[45] How important this was depended upon the nature, and location, of the community to which the persons concerned belonged. Anyone within reach of Bishop Longland of Lincoln, whose diocese covered the county and university of Oxford, or Bishop Gardiner of Winchester, whose diocese included Southwark, was very likely to be on the sharp end of an inquisition. However if your diocesan bishop was Thomas Goodrich of Ely (which covered Cambridge), the risk was much less.

In most environments the educated were more at risk than the uneducated, but in communities with strong Lollard traditions the unlettered were equally vulnerable. Places such as Cranbrook in Kent or Burford in Oxfordshire, which had had large numbers of retractions of heresy in earlier visitations, were especially endangered. The old fashioned Lollard was much more likely to be illiterate than the newer evangelical, and also much more likely to abjure if caught. This made relapse extremely dangerous, and most of those who suffered at this time did so for that reason. Neighbouring towns, or even parishes, might have quite different traditions, often depending on the predilections of the incumbent or his predecessor. London, where Lutheran tendencies were stronger than elsewhere, had some very conservative parishes, which in circumstances such as those of 1540, after the Act of Six Articles, tended to prey on their neighbours.[46]

Another factor of importance was the attitude of the local justices. Zealous 'old believers' would cooperate enthusiastically with the ecclesiastical authorities, and be active in securing indictments. Others might be so uncooperative as to provoke complaints from the bishop. Although most people no doubt tried to carry on as though nothing had happened, the royal supremacy and the Act of Six Articles genuinely divided opinion in the country, and although the intervention of statute clarified the legal position, it did nothing to resolve the arguments.

Literacy, as we have seen, was important, and is not easy to assess, because reading and writing were separate skills and not everyone who could read could also write.[47] The nobility and gentry, male and female, were literate in English, and that accounted for about 10 per cent of the population. Urban merchants and craftsmen were similar, and that was about another 10 per cent. Among the remaining 80 per cent the skills were spread erratically. A yeoman was more likely to be literate than a husbandman, and a man than a woman, but individual examples of literacy can be found at all social levels. The clergy, who numbered about 10,000 in 1540, were theoretically literate in both Latin and English, and many were, but they comprised an insignificant proportion of the population. It is probable that between 25 and 30 per cent were literate to some degree, and nearly every community would contain someone who could read. This became important when the English Bible was introduced, and when radical pamphlets began to circulate. Reading the first was urged by injunction, and the latter forbidden by proclamation, but most people would have been unable to do either unaided.[48] However, virtually everyone could listen to such books being read, either in the church or in the alehouse.

It was unlawful to dissent from either the doctrine of the Church or the ecclesiastical order after 1539, and the full weight of the king's authority was being used to keep the lid on what was increasingly a boiling pot. The ambitiously entitled Act for the Abolishing of Diversity of Opinion committed the common law to an uphill battle that was to far outlast Henry's reign, or even the century. It was not until the end of the 17th century that the Church *established* by law ceased to be the Church *enforced* by law.

§6 The King's Government

THE FOCUS of Henry's government, both executive and administrative, was the king's council. The king made all the important decisions, but the council carried them out, and exercised a general supervisory control, which also involved making many routine decisions for the implementation of policy.[1] The council was as old as the monarchy itself, since there had never been a time when kings ruled without advisers, or when those advisers had not needed to meet as some kind of a group. In theory the composition of the council was entirely at the king's discretion, but in practice that had never been the case. Certain great officers sat *ex officio*—the lord chancellor, the lord treasurer, the Archbishop of Canterbury—and although the king also made such appointments, he was often constrained by political circumstances, and elevations to Canterbury always had to be agreed with the pope.

There were also great magnates to be considered, men who by virtue of their lineage and resources the king could not ignore. When Henry VI had tried to ignore the Duke of York (whom the queen could not stand), the duke had responded (unsuccessfully) that he was a 'councillor born', and that his proximity to the throne entitled him to a seat.[2] A councillor proper took a special oath of fealty and service, but there were many others who styled themselves 'councillors' who did not take the oath, and who appeared only when specifically summoned. Nowadays such men would be termed 'special advisers', and such was normally their function. They might be lawyers or merchants or soldiers, but they were not parties to the state secrets with which their sworn colleagues dealt. Even among those who were sworn there were differences of degree. In every reign there was an 'inner circle' of those whom the king particularly trusted, and whom he consulted, both individually and collectively, upon a regular basis. Outside of that, there were those—sometimes including some senior office holders—who did not attend regularly, and who might well be absent, taking care of various other duties.[3]

In the 15th century and before, the council had had, up to a point, a representative function as well. Wise monarchs tried to ensure that different regions, and different power groups, were given access to the court by this means. Excluded interests, particularly if they were also excluded from patronage, could be dangerous. It was from such an exclusion that the Wars of the Roses had arisen.[4] Henry VII had used his council in an entirely traditional way. It had been a large and somewhat amorphous body, probably numbering between 60 and 70 members at any given time, the majority of whom would have taken the council oath. For the whole 24-year reign, 227 known councillors are recorded.[5] Henry VII had his favourites—John Morton, Richard Fox, Reginald Bray—and these with a few others constituted the inner ring. A number of senior peers were also councillors, but only Henry's uncle, Jasper Tudor, Duke of Bedford, was close to the king. Although some of his policies (and some of his councillors) were unpopular, nobody took issue with the way in which Henry VII handled his council.

At first the new reign saw little change, either in membership or function, but that altered with the rise of Wolsey between 1512 and 1515. Wolsey was accused of being a 'one-man council', and of monopolizing access to the king. It was alleged that he developed the Court of Star Chamber to keep his fellow councillors busy as judges, and distract them from the regular practice of politics.[6] For about ten years his influence with Henry was so great that the charge was plausible, but it was never true. Henry listened to whom he chose, and for a while the queen's influence was as great as the cardinal's, although she was never (of course) a councillor.

What Wolsey did do was to manage the council on the king's behalf. Henry intervened from time to time as he felt inclined— and sometimes showed surprising knowledge of the issues—but by and large he let the cardinal get on with it. It was Wolsey who decided who did what, reserving for his own attention key issues such as foreign policy, and the need to raise additional funds. He frequently used his own servants for this, when he should have used the king's, and this was a breach of etiquette that left him vulnerable to criticism.

WOLSEY THE OVERREACHER

*A*FTER THIS [*the creation of Henry FitzRoy as Earl of Richmond, 1525*] *the Cardinal took upon him as the king's chief councillor, to see a reformation in the order of the King's Household, wherein he made certain ordinances. He also made all new officers in the house of the Duke of Richmond, which was then newly begun. Also at that time he ordained a council and established another household for the Lady Mary, then being Princess of the Realm, so that all thing that was done was done by him, and without his assent nothing was done: he took so much upon him, and made the king believe that all things should be to his honour, and that he needed not to take any pain, so that to him was the charge of all things committed, at the which wise men becked [cavilled] and light men laughed, thinking great folly to his high presumption. And at this time the said Cardinal gave to the King the lease of the manor of Hampton Court, which he had of the lease of the Lord of St Johns, and on which he had done great cost. Therefore the king of his gentle nature, licensed him to lie in his manor of Richmond at his pleasure, and so he lay there at certain times: but when the common people, and in especial such as had been King Henry the seventh's servants, saw the Cardinal keep house in the manor Royal of Richmond, which King Henry the seventh so highly esteemed, it was marvel to hear how they grudged and said, see a Butcher's Dog lie in the manor of Richmond: these with many opprobrious words were spoken*

against the Cardinal, whose pride was so high that he nothing
regarded, and yet he was hated of most men.

[Taken from Richard Grafton, *A Chronicle and mere history* …, 1809
edition, pp. 382–3.]

Wolsey is even alleged on one occasion to have used the revealing
phrase 'I and my king', but he was never as all powerful as his
detractors chose to believe, and after 1525 the king's confidence in
him became increasingly uncertain.[7] What he also did for Henry,
and with the latter's full approval, was to increase the authority of
central government. He was not directly responsible for the downfall of the overweening Duke of Buckingham (see Chapter 7), but
he did manipulate the case, realizing that although the duke may
not have been much of a threat, he was a symbol of the old order
of aristocratic power.

It was probably Wolsey's desire to increase royal authority in
the north and in the marches of Wales that led to the promotion
of Mary and Henry FitzRoy, Duke of Richmond, in 1525, and the
re-establishment of the councils that were associated with their
households.[8] It was also Wolsey's desire to raise the profile of royal
justice that led to the major development of the Star Chamber,
and the less obvious but equally significant growth of the Court
of Requests. Wolsey fell from power, not because of any aristocratic reaction, or because he was deemed to have mishandled the
government of the country, but because of his failure to secure an
annulment of Henry's first marriage, and the fiasco over the Amicable Grant, which had initially weakened the king's trust in him
and left him exposed to his numerous enemies.

THE FALL OF WOLSEY

H ERE FOLLOWETH *a brief remembrance of how the affairs*
of this realm have been conducted since it pleased our
Sovereign to make my Lord Cardinal's grace his chiefest and only
councillor …

We [*Wolsey is referred to as 'we' throughout*] *triumphed*

*also when we brought the king his title of Defensor Fidei, and
departed early from our lodging in Greenwich to the Friars, that
we might be received into the court as ambassador from the Pope,
when the Pope was dead.*

*Now followeth how violent we were and hasty to come into this
high authority, and how rigorously we have handled the king's
subjects, especially the nobles if they fell in the danger of the law,
and what sore exactions have been levied since he was in his said
authority:—*

*We took away from my Lord of Canterbury [William
Warham] the chancellorship, and to take therefore the fee,
notwithstanding our great livelihood.*

*We took away from my Lord of Winchester [Richard Fox] the
Privy Seal.*

We found the means to order the signet at our pleasure ...

*We have wearied and put away, both out of the king's council
and of his house, all such officers and councillors as would do or
say anything freely, and retained such as would never contrary us.*

*We have put so importable [unsupportable] charges to the
noblemen in the king's name, what in his wars and what in his
triumphings, that some have been constrained to mortgage their
lands to the king, some to sell it outright, some to obtain the
king's letters and go a begging in the realm.*

*We have in a manner undone all the young gentlemen of
England that served us, and sent some beyond the seas on embassies, and devised means to linger them there still, and to promote
some into Ireland because we would have them out of the way ...*

*We have promoted none in manner of the church to no manner
wealth but such as served about the king, to bring to pass our
purposes, and to establish us in our authority, or were of our
council, or in such things as honest men would not vouchsafe or
be acquainted with ...*

*We have besides the yearly revenue of a hundred thousand
pounds, dispent in our first wars with France £1,300,000, in our
last £40,000 we have gathered of our commons; six fifteenths of*

*the spirituality; ten dismes, besides head money; and now the
tenth part of all the moveables temporal in the realm ... — and yet
this sorry Cardinal findeth flatterers enough to tell the king and
him that all is well ...*

[Paraphrase, taken from *Letters and Papers*, IV, iii, no. 5750. The original
is in the National Archives, TNA SP1/54 pp. 244–52.]

Wolsey's fall in 1529 was followed by a period of about three years
during which the king dealt directly with his council, in the traditional manner. This way of proceeding did not last because it
did not suit Henry's style. He preferred, at this stage of his reign, to
deal with a chief minister who would mediate his wishes, and was
soon regretting the loss of his cardinal. By 1533 he had found a
replacement in the person of one of Wolsey's former servants, the
self-taught lawyer and ex-soldier of fortune, Thomas Cromwell.

The secret of Cromwell's success lay partly in a phenomenal
capacity for hard work, and partly in astute political judgement.[9]
It was he who found ways to convert the king's rather vague ideas
about ecclesiastical jurisdiction into parliamentary legislation,
which both annulled the troublesome marriage and created the
royal supremacy. Cromwell was first secretary and then lord privy
seal. It was he who brought about the fall of Henry's troublesome
second wife, manipulated Princess Mary into surrender, and
drafted the legislation that dissolved the monasteries.

Cromwell's method was one of ubiquitous personal control.
He had spies and agents everywhere, and his police work in enforcing Henry's controversial policies was exemplary.[10] He managed the council no less effectively than Wolsey, but he did this by
persuading the king to make amenable appointments rather than
by monopolizing business — a tactic that he also used on the privy
chamber. Like Wolsey, he was a great believer in centralized control, which he aimed to achieve partly by legislation, and partly
by keeping key matters, such as finance, in his own hands. It was
Cromwell who abolished the franchises that had disrupted the
universal running of the king's writs (see Chapter 5), and who

created the financial courts (such as Augmentations and First Fruits and Tenths) into the offices of which he was able to place his own friends and sympathizers. Cromwell was a bureaucrat rather than a courtier, but he recognized the importance of the king's privy chamber, and was careful to persuade Henry to appoint some sympathetic gentlemen, the importance of which emerged in the years after his fall.

Like Wolsey, Cromwell could be accused of being a one-man council. Perhaps he would like to have been, but he was not. Great as his influence was between 1533 and 1540, the direction of policy was always decided by the king. Cromwell was *par excellence* a finder of ways and means, and Henry always had other sources of advice, although he did not usually heed them. What brought Cromwell down was religion. Appointed the first (and only) 'vice regent in spirituals' at a time when he was high in favour, he used his authority more enthusiastically in the reforming interest than Henry came to approve.[11] Cromwell's enemies drove a wedge between him and the king, as they had done with Wolsey, and destroyed him in the summer of 1540. For several years Cromwell seems to have been planning to reform the council, to make it more focused and professional, but his own desire to exercise a personal control over all important business had militated against that.

Cromwell's removal consequently forced the pace of change, and later in 1540 the council was reorganized. In place of the loosely organized traditional body, with an informal inner ring, there now appeared a privy council of about twenty members, each of whom was an office holder or a major nobleman.[12] The rest of the old body were relegated to the status of 'councillors at large', who were expected to appear, like the old fringe members, only when specially summoned. Only the new privy councillors were now expected to take the oath, and appointments to the council at large virtually ceased. The work of the privy council did not fundamentally change, but it now met regularly, and frequently on its own initiative, and its clerk kept minutes of all routine business. This council waited on the king when summoned to do so, and when sensitive issues of policy were under discussion, the clerk was excluded. It was both more visible and more disciplined than its predecessor, and it also dealt directly with the king, because after Cromwell's fall there was no further chief minister.[13] Politics now found a focus in the council as never before, and several of the conflicts of the later part of the reign were carried out in that forum. But its members were left in no doubt as to who was the master, a fact that had become more starkly evident when the mediating position of the lord privy seal was removed.

It was the council that oversaw the work of the justices of the peace, and consequently the implementation of most legislation. Councillors sat both in the House of Commons and the House of Lords, and were expected to speak in the king's interest, and to steer debates.[14] After 1540, however, the council made no attempt to be representative. That function was now taken over by Parliament, and the regular engagement of councillors, both in debates and in the drafting of bills, reflects a subtle but significant change in the function of both, but particularly of the high court.

Parliament consisted of three units, the consent of each of which was necessary for the creation of an act—the monarch, the Lords and the Commons. The Lords were in theory assembled at the discretion of the king, but in practice that had long since applied only to the mitred abbots and the eldest sons of major peers, such as dukes and marquises.[15] Bishops and all recognized peers of full age received writs of summons as a matter of course. Henry occasionally warned individuals that he did not want them to attend, but the warning was always accompanied by a normal writ. The 'great council', the Lords meeting without the Commons, had once been a significant assembly, and had been used as late as Henry VII's reign, but it did not meet under Henry VIII.[16]

The Commons, as Sir Thomas Smith pointed out, was deemed to carry the proxies of all the non-noble inhabitants of the kingdom, although its actual representation was much more narrowly based. By 1485 there were 74 county members, representing the gentry of 37 shires, and about 225 borough members, representing 110 towns. All these members were in theory elected, but the franchise was very limited, and in many boroughs patrons or other powerful men of the neighbourhood placed their own men.[17] Major towns, such as London or Norwich, which were not amenable to such control, nevertheless had citizen franchises that embraced no more than 10 per cent of the population. In the counties the vote was held only by those with freehold land worth 40 shillings a year. This was not a high ceiling and a few quite humble men qualified, but by and large the county courts, which conducted the elections, were gentry preserves, and it was quite normal for the powerful families of the shire to agree in advance about who should sit. Contested elections were very rare, and happened only when the various interests could not agree.

In the course of Henry's reign about forty members were added to the House of Commons, representing the newly created Welsh counties, a few Welsh boroughs, Calais, and some other towns that were enfranchised by the granting of charters. The House of Lords was proportionately diminished when the disappearance of the mitred abbots after 1540 was only partly compensated by the creation of six new sees. Very unusually among the similar assemblies that existed in most European countries, the English Parliament had no House of Clergy. Without the abbots, the bishops formed only a minority of the House of Lords, and the lower clergy were represented only in the convocations of the two provinces, Canterbury and York, which were not a part of Parliament, and which had only limited functions.[18] In the Reformation Parliament in particular, which passed the statutes of 1529–36, this secular bias was to be extremely important.

Far more important than any change in composition, however, was the development that took place in the functions of Parliament during the reign. Originally Parliament had existed mainly for the granting of direct taxation, which was why the Commons had become important at an early date, and for the receiving and promotion of petitions. In other words it had had no role in policy decisions, either foreign or domestic. Henry's need for support over his Great Matter changed all that. Between 1533 and 1536 Parliament legislated, on the king's initiative, in several vital issues over which it had previously claimed no competence — the succession, ecclesiastical jurisdiction, and the abolition of traditional vested interests. The last of these operations followed naturally from the second. The Church had been the greatest franchise in the realm, with its own code of law, its allegiance to an outside authority, and its vast landed endowment. The Act of Appeals and the Act of Supremacy changed that status completely. The Church was now wholly subject to the king, its jurisdiction redirected, and its whole function accessible to scrutiny.[19]

THE ACT OF SUPREMACY

'An Act concerning the King's Highness to be Supreme Head of the Church of England, and to have authority to reform and redress all errors, heresies and abuses in the same', 1534.

A LBEIT *the King's Majesty justly and rightfully is and ought to be the Supreme Head of the Church of England, and so is recognized by the clergy of this realm in their Convocations; yet nevertheless for the corroboration and confirmation thereof, and for increase of virtue in Christ's religion within this realm of England, and to repress and extirpate all errors, heresies and other enormities and abuses heretofore used in the same. Be it enacted by authority of this present parliament that the King our Sovereign Lord, his heirs and successors kings of this realm, shall be taken, accepted and reputed the only supreme head in earth of the Church of England called* Anglicana Ecclesia, *and shall have and enjoy annexed and united to the imperial crown of this realm as well the title and style thereof, as all honours, dignities, pre-eminences, jurisdictions, privileges, authorities, immunities, profits and commodities to the said dignity of supreme head of the same Church belonging and appertaining. And that our said Sovereign Lord, his heirs and successors kings of this realm, shall have full power and authority from time to time to visit, repress, redress, reform, order, correct, restrain and amend all such errors, heresies, abuses, offences, contempts and enormities, whatsoever they be, which by any manner spiritual authority or jurisdiction ought or may lawfully be reformed, repressed, ordered, redressed, corrected, restrained or amended, most to the pleasure of Almighty God, the increase of virtue in Christ's religion, and for the con-servation of the peace, unity and tranquillity of this realm: any usage, custom, foreign laws, foreign authority, prescription or any other thing or things to the contrary hereof nothwithstanding.*

[Statute 26 Henry VIII, c.1. Taken from *Statutes of the Realm*, III, p. 492.]

The precedent that was thus set was immediately employed in other directions. In two acts of 1536 and 1543 all franchises, whether secular or religious, were abolished, so that the king's writ ran uniformly through the realm. In a sense such franchises had always been vulnerable, because they had all been created by the crown in the past. However, with the very limited exception of Tynedale and Redesdale in the reign of Henry VII, no attempt had been made to reduce them, except by the somewhat lateral process of 'escheat', by which a franchise could revert to the crown either by normal laws of inheritance or in the absence of legal heirs. At the same time the abolition of the Welsh marcher lordships was accompanied by the creation of 12 new shires in Wales, complete with parliamentary representation and commis-sions of the peace—the first time that such jurisdictions had been created since the Norman Conquest.

THE CURTAILING OF FRANCHISES

'An Act for the recontinuing of certain Liberties and Franchises heretofore taken from the Crown', 1536.

WHERE DIVERS *of the most ancient prerogatives and authorities of justice appertaining to the imperial crown of this realm have been severed and taken from the same by sundry gifts of the King's most noble progenitors, kings of this realm, to*

*the great diminution and detriment of the royal estate of the same
and to the hindrance and great delay of justice. For reformation
whereof be it enacted by the authority of this present parliament
that no person or persons, of what estate or degree soever they be
of, from the first day of July which shall be in the year of our Lord
1536, shall have any power or authority to pardon or remit any
treasons, murders, manslaughters or any kinds of felonies ... or
any outlawries for any such offences afore rehearsed, committed,
perpetrated, done or divulged, or hereafter to be committed, done
or divulged, by or against any person or persons in any part of this
realm, Wales or the marches of the same; but that the King's
Highness, his heirs and successors kings of this realm, shall have
the whole and sole power and authority thereof united and knit to
the imperial crown of this realm, as of good right and equity it
appertaineth, any grants, usages, prescription, act or acts of
parliament, or any other thing to the contrary thereof
notwithstanding.*

*II. And be it also enacted ... that no person or persons, of what
estate, degree, or condition soever they be, from the said first day of
July, shall have any power or authority to make any justices of
eyre [an early type of assize], justices of assize, justices of peace or
justices of gaol delivery, but that all such officers and ministers
shall be made by letters patent under the king's great seal in the
name and by authority of the King's Highness, his heirs kings of
this realm, in all shires, counties, counties palatine and other
places of this realm, Wales and [the] marches of the same, or in
any other his dominions ...*

[Statute 27 Henry VIII, c.24. Taken from *Statutes of the Realm*, III,
pp.555–8.]

At the same time the king by statute also imposed injunctions and
doctrines upon the Church, abolished religious houses upon an
arbitrary definition of their usefulness, and vested the property of
all surrendered houses in the king.[20] All these extraordinary ex-
tensions of power were accepted by the country on the grounds

that Parliament spoke for the whole realm—even though that was in some respects manifestly untrue. The definition that Sir Thomas Smith was to make in 1565 was already substantially accurate by 1547:

> THE PARLIAMENT *abrogateth old laws, maketh new, giveth orders for things past, and for things hereafter to be followed, changeth rights and possessions of private men, legitimateth bastards, establisheth forms of religion, altereth weights and measures, giveth forms of succession to the Crown ... appointeth subsidies, tallies, taxes and impositions, giveth most free pardons and absolutions ... And to be short all that ever the people of Rome might do either in* centuriatis comitiis *or* tributis [*community or senate*], *the same may be done by the parliament of England.*[21]

This was little short of a revolution in government, which set a pattern for the future, not only in the 16th century, but well beyond. What had been before 1523 an occasional assembly, called by the king for certain limited purposes, now became an essential institution whose competence the lawyers struggled to define because it was in fact new, and they were not used to dealing with new situations.

One of the consequences of these changes, which was certainly not anticipated by Henry, was that certain aspects of royal power became formally subjected to the process of consent that Parliament embodied. Parliament now monopolized consent, so that a limitation on the power of the monarch that had always been acknowledged, but which had been conveniently vague in its location, now had a local habitation and a name. The time would come when this powerful assembly would attempt to prescribe policies to the monarch, and to demand the right to offer counsel. This arose directly from the increase in the powers of Parliament that occurred at this time, but did not happen in Henry's lifetime. The other price that the monarchy paid, perhaps willingly, was that the Tudors were unable to follow the course that the Valois followed in France and tax without consent.[22]

The revenues of the English crown came in two forms—ordinary and extraordinary. Ordinary revenues were the profits of the crown lands, the income from the courts of justice, and the proceeds of the royal franchises, such as the Duchy of Lancaster. Extraordinary revenue was everything else—foreign subsidies, the profits of trading, customs dues (which were voted by Parliament at the beginning of each reign), loans, benevolences and direct taxes. The original direct tax was the 'tenth and fifteenth' (a tenth of the value of goods and a fifteenth of the value of lands; the payer was assessed on one or the other), which by the 16th century yielded about £30,000.[23] By longstanding custom a tenth and fifteenth could only be asked for in times of emergency, of which war was the most common, and if the need was exceptionally great (and recognized as such) more than one might be granted.

Benevolences, which were essentially prerogative taxes (taxes raised without parliamentary consent), had been banned by statute in 1484, and thereafter tended to be disguised as loans, to which there was at least a theoretical obligation of repayment. Between 1512 and 1515 Wolsey began to experiment with a new and more flexible type of taxation, called the subsidy, which could be directly assessed at different levels according to need. In 1523 he overreached himself by pitching his demand too high, and was rebuffed by the Commons, but the subsidy became thereafter the main parliamentary tax, and in the 1530s was worth about £120,000.[24]

As first defence and then war expenditure escalated after 1534, Henry resorted several times to subsidy demands, and the traditional association with open warfare was bypassed.[25] His demands were met more or less willingly, and during the 1540s raised some £650,000. The war of 1543–6, however, cost about £2 million, and the balance was made up partly by selling monastic land (£800,000–£1,000,000), and partly by loans taken out both at home and abroad. The latter were raised mainly from the banking houses of Antwerp, and about £100,000 was outstanding when the king died. Henry was always short of money after the end of his first war in 1514, and that, combined with his indebtedness to Parliament for other reasons, kept him firmly in line as far as money was concerned.

It is sometimes argued that Thomas Cromwell saw the dissolution of the monasteries as the means to create a long-term endowment for the crown that would have made resort to Parliament unnecessary, but since he began to sell that land almost as soon as it was acquired, it seems more likely that what he was intent on—and indeed succeeded in—creating was a vested interest in the royal supremacy, for those who purchased confiscated monastic land from the crown were unlikely to argue against the crown's title to it.[26] On the whole the Parliaments of the 1530s served the king (and Cromwell) very well, and he had little incentive to try to bypass one of its main functions.

CROMWELL IN THE HOUSE OF COMMONS
Ralph Sadler to Thomas Cromwell, 1 November 1529.

A LITTLE BEFORE *the receipt of your letter, I spoke with Mr Gage [Sir John Gage, the vice chamberlain] at the court, and, as you commanded, moved him to speak to the Duke of Norfolk for the burgess room of the parliament on your behalf, which he did. The Duke said that he had spoken with the King, who was well contented that you should be a burgess, if you would follow the Duke's instructions. The Duke wishes to speak with you tomorrow, and has sent you as token, by Mr Gage, your ring with a turquoise, which I now send by the bearer. I will speak with Mr Russhe tonight and know whether you shall be burgess for Oxford [in fact, Orford] or not. If you are not elected there, I will desire Mr [Sir William] Paulet to name you as burgess for one of my Lord's [Wolsey's] towns of his bishopric of Winchester★. It would be well for you to speak with the Duke of Norfolk as soon as possible tomorrow, to know the King's pleasure how you shall order yourself in the parliament house … All Saints Day, 4 p.m.*

[*signed*]

[Taken from *Letters and Papers*, IV, iii, Appendix 238. Original BL
Cotton Ms Cleopatra E.IV, f. 178.]

★ The Parliament convened on 4 November, and Cromwell sat for
Taunton.

The elevation of Parliament is the real substance behind the 'revolution in government' that Geoffrey Elton attributed to Cromwell, but it was not, Elton argued, the only aspect.[27] As we have
seen, the reorganization of the council can be attributed to him
only very indirectly, but two other aspects of his work demand
some further consideration. He was responsible, very largely, for
the reorganization of financial administration. Before 1485, most
of the king's money had passed through the exchequer, an ancient
and distinctly hidebound institution, with total inflexibility of
procedure and obsolete accounting methods. For that reason
Henry VII had shifted most of his financial business to the treasury
of the chamber, which had originally been the king's 'privy chest'
but now became the major spending department.

Wolsey had continued with that system, but Cromwell, more
sensitive to the power and priorities of money, was determined to
change it. Over the course of about five years he reduced the treasury of the chamber to something like its original function, and
redirected most of the king's money into four new revenue courts:
Wards and Liveries, General Surveyors, First Fruits and Tenths, and
Augmentations, each with a defined constituency, double-entry
book-keeping, and the jurisdiction proper to a financial court.[28]
Previously only the exchequer had had that power. The exchequer
remained, processing some traditional revenues, but effectively
moribund and cut off from the main financial stream.

Each of these new courts had its staff, including regional
receivers, and Augmentations in particular constituted a small
empire with nationwide ramifications. Cromwell did not control
any of these courts directly, but he effectively appointed the men
who did, and that was sufficient for his purpose. His system did
not last, and therefore cannot be classed as revolutionary, because
General Surveyors and Augmentations were merged in 1547, and

the second Court of Augmentations was absorbed into the exchequer in 1554. First Fruits and Tenths was abolished in 1555, and by 1558 only Wards and Liveries and the Duchy of Lancaster stood outside the exchequer.[29] However, this did not mean a full return to the 'ancient course', that antiquated system of book-keeping. Lord Treasurer Winchester was far too acute for that, and the new augmentations office retained its receivers, and its double-entry book-keeping. As Sir William Paulet, Winchester had been a close colleague of Cromwell, so part of the lord privy seal's legacy was preserved. Of course, as treasurer Winchester controlled the exchequer, which was something Cromwell had never been able to do.

The other department that Cromwell is alleged to have revolutionized is the office of secretary. Under his control the secretary's office became the clearing house for all business, which he and his staff redirected to the appropriate department. Dispatches from diplomats, requests from petitioners, intelligence reports, protests and correspondence of every kind came across his desk. He ran his own network of spies, both at home and abroad, and their reports came directly to him. This never amounted to complete control, because Cromwell could not manipulate people such as the Duke of Suffolk or the Archbishop of Canterbury, who had their own networks, and their own independent access to the king, but it did give him very great power.

This was a completely personal creation, which was associated with the office of secretary because that was where Cromwell was. When he moved on to become lord privy seal in 1536, the whole system went with him, and the office of secretary largely reverted to its earlier status. It was not until Sir William Cecil held the office from 1558 to 1572 that the secretariat became institutionalized as a clearing house.[30] What Thomas Cromwell did do was to create a precedent for a style of organizing business. It was not followed up immediately after his fall, when administration again became fragmented, but after William Cecil, first Francis Walsingham and then Robert Cecil made sure that there was no similar

backsliding, and the office of secretary of state descends directly
from them.

Cromwell was never lord chancellor, which is one reason why
he played little part in the development of equity jurisdiction (see
Chapter 5), which continued during his time in office. Wolsey
was succeeded by Sir Thomas More, then by Sir Thomas Audley,
and finally in 1544 by Thomas Wriothesley. None of these men
had quite the cardinal's range of competence, nor his high political profile. Each of them—Audley and Wriothesley in particular
—were practising lawyers with limited skills outside their proper
sphere. The chancellor headed what had once been the king's
writing office, but had long since ceased to be part of the court. It
was a partner institution to the exchequer, but whereas the latter
had largely lost its function of handling money and become primarily an accounting and judicial office, the chancery went on
doing what it was designed for. It issued writs for every conceivable
process leading to the Great or Privy Seal, and for the authentication of any judicial process.[31] No fugitive could have his goods
confiscated without a writ of *capias*, and no heretic dispatched
without a writ of *de heretico comburendo*.

Whereas first the secretariat and then the office of the lord
privy seal drove all the informal work of government, the chancery
drove the formal work. It was a profitable business for the clerks,
because it was not only the crown that originated writs; they had
to be issued for all sorts of judicial and quasi-judicial purposes,
and since fees had to be paid for this service, the clerkships were
much sought after. The chancery remained largely immune to
the storms and upheavals of Henry VIII's reign, and the writs that
were issued retained their traditional and totally stylized nature.
No new form of action had been developed for centuries, and the
changing needs of both the judiciary and the general public continued to be forced into the mould of the existing forms. Neither
Wolsey nor Cromwell made any significant difference, and writs
continued to be essential for what might be termed the transmis-
sion of government.[32]

The essential unit of local government was the county or shire, which was divided into hundreds, or into sokes and wapentakes, according to location.[33] As we have seen, the traditional royal officer in charge of the shire was the sheriff, who presided at the county court. Anciently each hundred or wapentake had also had its court, but by the 16th century all the judicial functions of these courts had been taken over by the commission of the peace, and they retained only a ghostly existence for the election of MPs and local officers. The justices of the peace, and most particularly those core members known as the quorum, effectively administered the county in addition to judging its crimes and disputes. A justice who took his responsibilities seriously (as some did not for a variety of reasons) was a hard-working civil servant, carrying out the council's instructions. As late as the end of the 15th century much of this work had been done by the servants and retainers of territorial magnates, and although they might equally be acting in the name of the king, their authority derived largely from the status of their masters.

By Henry VIII's reign, and particularly the later part of it, such privatized jurisdiction was a thing of the past: only holders of the king's commission were authorized to act in his name. The commission of the peace was by no means the only such body. There were commissions of gaol delivery, which were judicial, and commissions of sewers, which were administrative, as well as numerous special commissions of investigation or inquiry. All these contributed to the sense among many people — growing through the reign — that the reach and extent of government was steadily increasing.[34] The 'county community' can be overemphasized as a determinant of identity, but it certainly had some reality. Gentry with court connections, for example, frequently married outside their home county, but there was a sense of corporate identity. With no standing army, and no police force, much of the real work of government was devolved by commission to the counties.

Towns, being smaller communities, and much closer knit, had even stronger identities. A few were counties in their own right, and had their own commissions, but most were governed in local matters by councils drawn from the wealthier citizens, and from the members of particular guilds or companies, which formed close oligarchies.[35] The terminology varied from place to place. In the larger and royal boroughs the head officer would be the mayor, and he would be assisted by a body of aldermen and an elected council, but in some smaller places the chief officer would be a bailiff or steward, and the aldermen also formed the council.

The structure, and the franchise, depended upon the terms of the charter. The sense of identity derived partly from physical proximity, partly from shared economic activity, and partly from the experience of limited self-government. For all major issues these towns were subject to the county commissions, although in some cases the mayor might serve as a justice *ex officio*. The identity of most Englishmen was circumscribed by their parish of residence, although economic migrants were numerous, from the unemployed weavers or husbandmen in search of work to younger sons of remote Northumberland gentlemen seeking their fortunes in London or at the universities. Nicholas Ridley, for example, who never seems to have returned to Tynedale after migrating to Cambridge, nevertheless retained a strong sense of his roots.[36]

Most cities and counties were administered directly by the privy council, or in practice by a chief minister when one existed, but in areas that had recently been subject to the overlordship of some magnate a different course was adopted. The shires of Northumberland and Cumberland abutted upon Scotland, and in addition to the normal county administration were subjected to the military rule of the wardens of the marches.[37] These positions were in theory free royal appointments, but in practice were always held by powerful local families, the Percys and the Dacres in particular.

When Richard of Gloucester had ruled the north for his brother, Edward IV, he had done so by means of a council, which carried out most of the functions elsewhere performed by the king's council. After Richard became king, that council became moribund until it was revived in 1525 by Wolsey. In theory this served the infant Henry FitzRoy as lieutenant of the north, but in practice it was answerable to the cardinal, and through him to the king. After Wolsey's fall in 1529, and Richmond's death in 1536, the council remained. It had jurisdiction over the whole area from Yorkshire northward (with the exception of Lancashire), administering equity, issuing administrative instructions, and keeping close control over the marcher wardens.[38] After the death of Henry Percy, the 6th Earl of Northumberland, in 1537, Percy control over the East March, which was the largest and most important along the Scottish Border, was in any case broken.

The other marches, those of Wales, were different in that there were no military wardens, but until 1536 the area was notoriously lawless because of the weak control of the marcher lordships, which were franchises. Henry's elder brother, Arthur, as Prince of Wales, had had a council in Wales like that of the Duke of Gloucester in the north. This had jurisdiction over the whole principality, the marcher lordships, and the neighbouring English counties as far east as Gloucestershire.[39] After Arthur's death that council had also remained in existence, but became moribund. As with the council in the north, it was revived by Wolsey in 1525, in theory to serve the 9-year-old Princess Mary, but in practice to represent the king. Mary was withdrawn in 1527, the franchises abolished in 1536 and Wales was shired by 1543, but the council remained. Like its fellow in the north, it had equity jurisdiction, a standing commission of *oyer et terminer*, and a general administrative brief.

These councils did not act independently of the privy council in London, and were ultimately subject to it, but they were able to deal with much routine business, and to do so more expeditiously than would have been the case if decisions had always had to be referred to the capital. These regional councils thus served two purposes: to improve the efficiency of government with their jurisdictions; and to make it clear that the king was not a remote figure who could be safely ignored, but had a real authority on the ground, even in Westmorland or Pembrokeshire.[40]

It was this latter consideration that also brought about a subtle

but profound change in Henry's relations with his senior peers. At
first he had taken the nobility pretty much as he found it, sharing
its chivalric culture and respecting its claims to natural authority
and ancient lineage. For that reason he created Margaret Pole
Countess of Salisbury in 1514. However, the pretensions of the
Duke of Buckingham, who claimed the hereditary high constableship and exercised widespread authority in the Welsh marches,
seem to have begun to change his mind.[41] Buckingham was executed on somewhat flimsy charges of treason in 1521, and that also
seems to have taught the king a lesson.

Henry may have been influenced by Wolsey, whose relations
with the traditional aristocracy were very bad, but perhaps not,
and he began to distrust any claims to authority that were not
derived from himself. His father had built up the royal affinity, or
personal following, to make the county gentry less dependent
upon noble patronage, and after an interval, by the 1520s Henry
VIII was doing the same. He needed to establish, in Lawrence
Stone's famous phrase, that 'the king was a better lord than the
Earl of Derby'.[42] In other words good lordship in the traditional
sense was now to be found only in the royal service. This did not
mean that Henry disliked noblemen, but they now had to engage
with the political process on his terms.

Some ancient families, such as the Talbot earls of Shrewsbury
and the Stanley earls of Derby, adapted to this new mode of service, kept a fairly low profile, and survived. Others—the Percy earls
of Northumberland, the Courtenay Marquis of Exeter, Margaret
Pole, and eventually the Howards—were destroyed, as we shall
see, the last explicitly because of the lineage claims raised by
Henry Howard, Earl of Surrey, son of the Duke of Norfolk.[43]

Henry created many peers, but after 1525 none of these cre-
ations was based on the claims of ancestry. Some, such as Charles
Brandon, Duke of Suffolk, were elevated for personal reasons.
Some were the kindred of his consorts: Thomas Boleyn became
Earl of Wiltshire; Edward Seymour, Earl of Hertford; and William
Parr, Earl of Essex. Hertford would probably have earned his

promotion as a soldier in any case, but the others were definitely through kinship. Most, however, were elevated for service, present or anticipated: Henry Clifford was made Earl of Cumberland; Thomas Cromwell, Earl of Essex before Parr gained that title; George Hastings, Earl of Huntingdon; Thomas Manners, Earl of Rutland; William FitzWilliam, Earl of Southampton; Robert Radcliffe, Earl of Sussex; John Dudley, Viscount Lisle; and William Paulet, Lord St John. By the end of Henry's reign, although some ancient families were still represented, the majority of peers were of the king's own creation, and constituted a 'service nobility'.[44]

Such service could be important. Quite apart from diplomatic missions and administrative duties, it was the loyalty of Norfolk, Shrewsbury and Derby that frustrated the Pilgrimage of Grace, when it showed some signs of sweeping in the disaffected nobility. Henry's attitude can be well summarized in a remark made to his last Parliament in 1545 in respect of the government of the north. He would not, he declared, be bound to be served by nobles as wardens of the marches, 'but by such as we shall appoint to the position'. In other words, the king's authority was a sufficient warrant in all circumstances, and needed no endorsement from the personal resources of the officer concerned.

In saying this, Henry was being over-optimistic. In spite of his ambition, it was much easier to govern with the grain of local noble influence than against it, as both his chief ministers (men of notoriously non-noble origin) discovered to their cost. Nevertheless, an important corner was turned during Henry's reign: this was the process that turned the provincial magnate of the 15th century into the court-based politician of the Elizabethan period, and eventually into the political patron and party manager of the 18th century. In 1547 the House of Lords was still more important than the House of Commons, but Thomas Cromwell's parliamentary strategy had set the latter on a course that was to have profound constitutional implications, and which would have filled Henry VIII with horror and alarm.

§7 The King's Enemies

HENRY would only have used the word 'enemy' to describe his neighbours during the periodic breakdowns in their relations. The king of France was his enemy in 1512, 1523 and 1544; at other times he was a friend. The king of Scots was his enemy in 1513 and again in 1542; at other times he was a kinsman. The Emperor was his enemy in 1529, and the pope regularly after 1533. The king's enemies within the realm, or among his subjects in exile, were 'traitors'. However, the term will here be used more widely to describe all those opposed to the king's policies who took any action against him, and the scope of this chapter will take in discontent, resistance and rebellion (but not war).

Henry's accession had been unopposed, but not entirely unthreatened. The main Yorkist claimant had been Edward, Earl of Warwick (the son of George, Duke of Clarence, younger brother of Edward IV) — but he had been executed in 1499.[1] Only one of Edward IV's other siblings had left issue, his sister Elizabeth, who had married John de la Pole, Duke of Suffolk. It had been their son, John, Earl of Lincoln, whom Richard III had designated as his successor, and who had died in 1487. He had two brothers, both of whom were alive in 1509, and who presented a possible challenge.[2] Edmund de la Pole, styled Earl of Suffolk, had taken refuge in the Low Countries, and had been handed over to Henry VII by the Emperor Maximilian as part of the terms of their treaty in 1506. In 1509 Edmund was in the Tower. His younger brother Richard, however, had gone to France, where he remained, known in some quarters as 'the White Rose'.

Edward IV's sons, of course, had been the 'Princes in the Tower', who (in spite of some rumours to the contrary) by 1509 had long since been presumed dead. Edward's eldest daughter, Elizabeth, had been Henry VIII's mother, but her two sisters had also married: Anne to Thomas Howard, who became the 3rd Duke of Norfolk in 1525, and Katherine to William Courtenay, Earl of Devon. The Earl of Warwick's sister, Margaret, had also married, in her case to Sir Richard Pole.[3]

There were thus four families with possible claims to the throne. Henry had no brothers, and at the beginning of his reign only his elder sister, Margaret, was married, her husband being James IV of Scotland. His younger sister, Mary, was unmarried at the time of his accession.

In due course, as the succession issue became more tangled, their royal connections were to prove fatal to most of these families, but at first it was only the de la Poles who were taken seriously. The reason for this is not immediately clear, but it was probably the result of Richard III's recognition of the Earl of Lincoln. Although it is hard to believe that anyone was taking Richard's dispositions seriously by 1512, the earl had died without issue, and so Edmund de la Pole was his heir. As Henry prepared for war with France, he was looking anxiously over his shoulder, and in 1513, without Edmund having said or done anything to justify execution, he was brought out of the Tower and beheaded.[4]

The pretext for this appears to have been the fact that his brother, Richard de la Pole, who was in the service of Louis XII, was technically in arms against his natural lord. Richard gained a sort of revenge later in the same year when Louis recognized him as king of England, but the French made no attempt to press this claim when peace was signed in 1514. When England and France were again at war in 1523, Francis I toyed with the idea of sending Richard at the head of an invading army to claim his realm, but the scheme never came anywhere near fruition, and Richard was killed at the Battle of Pavia in 1525. Meanwhile Henry's sister Mary, briefly married to the elderly Louis as part of the peace settlement, had subsequently espoused Henry's friend Charles Brandon, Duke of Suffolk, and borne two daughters to add to the army of women who were beginning to besiege the throne.[5]

The Courtenays and the Poles both to some extent fell victims to dynastic anxiety, but as we shall see, they did give some grounds for suspicion, and the charges of treason against them were not entirely fabricated. Rather surprisingly, the only family to fall almost exclusively because of their own hubris was the Howards. The Duke of Norfolk had given a lifetime of service to the crown, and was over 70 years old, but his son, Henry Howard, Earl of Surrey, had proved less satisfactory. Apart from being a splendid poet, he was a rather rash and adventurous soldier, and an over-bearing personality. Unlike his father (who knew better) he was proud of his royal ancestry, and took the technically treasonable step of adding the arms of Edward the Confessor to his own. There was a little more to this than symbolic exhibitionism, because what Surrey was also implying was that his royal ancestry entitled him to wealth and power, irrespective of what the incumbent monarch might think of him.[6]

In 1547 he paid for this mistake with his head, because not only was the king in his last days extremely sensitive to any possible challenge to his son, he was also deeply suspicious of any claims to status that he could not control. Surrey's father, the duke, was condemned for aiding and abetting (see plate 13) rather than for any overt action of his own, and it was perhaps a kind of justice that saw him reprieved by the king's own death. For the time being the fall of the Howards was complete, and most of their estates and affinity was shortly after handed over to the Princess Mary. She in due course restored the duke as an act of filial contrition, and when he died in 1554 at the age of 81, his grandson duly succeeded. The 4th duke, however, had been too young to learn from his father's fate, and went to the block in his turn in 1572 for aspiring to the hand of the Scottish queen.[7]

The first major peer to die for treasonable aspirations was Edward Stafford, Duke of Buckingham, in 1521. Stafford did indeed have a remote claim to the throne, going back to Anne, the daughter of Thomas of Woodstock (the sixth son of Edward III) who had married Edmond, Earl of Stafford. However, that was not really the point in 1521. As recently as 1519 Sebastian Guistianini, the Venetian ambassador, had believed that Buckingham would secure the throne if the king died without heirs, but since Henry already had a daughter and an illegitimate son, that was a fairly remote speculation.[8]

Buckingham was a member of the king's council, and although his voice did not carry much weight, that was as much the result of his perceived lack of competence as of any mistrust. He was, however, a proud man, and obtusely persistent in his attempts to secure the high constableship of England, an office to which he claimed hereditary entitlement. The position had been withheld by Henry VI from his great grandfather Humphrey Stafford when the latter had achieved his majority. He had been allowed to sue for it, but it had not been granted.[9] One of the reasons for this reluctance may have been that there was a legendary (and untested) prerogative attached to the office, which empowered the constable to arrest the king if he was accused of misgovernment.

Some such thought may have been in Henry VIII's mind, but it is more likely that he saw the office as redundant (possibly prompted by Wolsey) and had no great confidence in the claimant. Buckingham, however, persisted, and this caused the king great annoyance. Henry may, or may not, have had a confrontation with the duke on account of alleged attentions paid by the king to the latter's sister, but for whatever reason, Buckingham was out of favour by 1520. He was also a wealthy regional magnate, with castles and *manred* (i.e. the ability to command service) in Wales and the marches, an area that Wolsey was eying askance as being under very imperfect control and the source of much lawlessness. Buckingham had also married a Percy, whose power in the north was still formidable, and his sister had married another well-endowed magnate, George Hastings, Earl of Huntingdon.[10]

For all these reasons, he should have trodden delicately, but being Edward Stafford he did no such thing. He grumbled, loudly and audibly, about the king's foreign policy, about Wolsey's ascendancy, and about what parvenus the Tudors were. Buckingham was not the only peer suspected of harbouring such thoughts, and Wolsey's spies were active, but the duke was the only one to be clumsy enough to antagonize several key men by dismissing them from his service. It was remembered that he had retained Sir William Bulmer, who was a knight of the king's body, against the law, and a case against him began to build up. Buckingham should, of course, have stayed in attendance and outfaced his critics, but instead in October 1520 he withdrew to his castle at Thornbury, and the following month began to raise an armed guard.[11] He probably had no more sinister intention than that of making a progress through his properties in the marches, but in the circumstances it was an incredibly foolish thing to do. In April 1521 he was summoned to court, and incarcerated in the Tower. Within a few weeks his servants and ex-servants were queuing up to testify against him. Robert Gilbert, his chancellor, and Edmund Dellacourt, his confessor, provided the most damning testimony. On 13 May Buckingham was tried by his peers and found guilty. On the 17th he was executed.[12]

Buckingham had actually done nothing, but he had spoken out of turn, and left himself wide open to misrepresentation. His fall proved two things. In the first place not even the most powerful man could afford to ride roughshod over the sensibilities of his subordinates. If he did, he gave them occasion against him, and destroyed the bonds of loyalty and mutual trust that should have held his affinity together. In the second place, not even the greatest magnate could defy or insult the king with impunity. When it came to the crisis point, neither his kindred nor anyone else rallied to Buckingham's defence, and he was destroyed with little more effort than would have been required to bring down a much humbler man. If Henry played his cards circumspectly, and did not inspire the English nobility to combine against him, he had nothing to fear from them. This was a lesson that was learned to lasting effect upon both sides.

THE ATTAINDER OF BUCKINGHAM
1523

FORASMUCH *as Edward, late Duke of Buckingham, late of Thornbury in the county of Gloucester, the xxiiith day of April in the fourth year of the reign of our Sovereign Lord the King that now is* [1512], *and divers times after, imagined and compassed Traitorously and unnaturally the destruction of the most royal person of our said Sovereign Lord and subversion of his realm, and then traitorously committed and did diverse and many treasons against our said Sovereign Lord the King, contrary to his allegiance in the counties of Gloucester and Somerset, the City of London,* [and] *the counties of Kent and Surrey. Of the which treasons and offences the said late Duke in the said counties was severally indicted. And afterward for and upon the same treasons, the xiii day of May* [in] *the xiiith year of the reign of our said Sovereign Lord the King, at Westminster in the county of Middlesex, before Thomas Duke of Norfolk for the time only being Great Steward of England by the king's letters patent, by verdict of his peers and by judgement of the said Steward against the said late Duke then and there given after the due order of the law and custom of England, was attainted of high treason as by the records thereof more plainly appeareth. WHEREFORE be it ordained, enacted and established by the King our Sovereign Lord, with the assent of the Lords spiritual and temporal and the commons in this present parliament assembled and by authority of the same, that the said late Duke, for the offences above rehearsed, stand and be convicted, adjudged and attainted of high treason, and forfeit to the King our Sovereign Lord and his heirs for ever, all honours, castles, manors, lordships, hundreds, franchises, liberties, privileges, advowsons, notatives, knights fees, lands, tenements, rents, services, reversions, remainders, portions, annuities, pensions, rights, possessions, and other hereditaments whatsoever* …

[Statute 14 & 15 Henry VIII, c.20. Taken from *Statutes of the Realm*, III, p. 246.]

So much for Buckingham. Other developments in the 1520s exercised the patience and loyalties of the king's subjects. When Wolsey tried to extract a subsidy from Parliament in 1523, he met with strenuous resistance and was forced to reduce his demand, but this was a proper function of the House of Commons, and cannot be construed as opposition to the king's policies, let alone disaffection. The demand for an extra-parliamentary tax, hopefully known as the 'Amicable Grant', two years later produced a similar reaction in the community at large. This opposition, which we would now call a 'tax payers' strike', was not covered by parliamentary immunity simply because the demand had not been made there.[13] The idea for such a grant had probably been the king's, but as the resistance built up and became more effective, it suddenly became Wolsey's responsibility. The opposition was not linked to any demand for policy changes, and certainly to no ambition for regime change, so that although the refusers were resentful of Wolsey, and made more so by the king's 'escape clause', they were not in any sense Henry's enemies. But they were totally successful, and the king backed down—something that he always hated doing. The cardinal dutifully accepted the blame for this fiasco, and thereby weakened his long-term credit.[14]

The king's 'Great Matter', of course, stirred up powerful emotions on both sides, but it was treated, at least at first, as a matter for discussion and debate rather than as a test of allegiance. Catherine had many supporters, both among those who believed that her case in canon law was sound, and among those who believed that the king was acting unreasonably and uncharitably. Among the latter was Henry's own sister, Mary, Duchess of Suffolk. The most outspoken of the former was John Fisher, Bishop of Rochester. Anne Boleyn was a spanner in the works, because her appearance on the scene raised the political stakes and introduced a new faction into the court. By 1529 it was clear that the king intended to marry her, and a major issue was thereby created. The ambitious, or even just the politically alert, now had to gamble on the outcome of the king's bid. If he won, Anne would be in the ascendant and her friends and supporters would be rewarded. If he lost, or was forced to give up, then there would be a reconciliation with Catherine and (knowing Henry) Anne and all her family would be dispatched to the wilderness.[15] This was a gamble on the strength of the king's willpower, and both sides professed their warmest allegiance, although with just a suggestion that that allegiance might be conditional upon the outcome of the king's suit.

The events of 1533 changed the rules of engagement. Henry rejected both Catherine and the pope, and staked his authority upon the outcome. Open support for the former queen was now no longer an option. As long as she confined her resistance to words, covert support might be tolerated, but the pope showed every sign of fighting back, and by 1534 support for him was high treason.[16] All those who continued to accept the traditional order of the Western Church thus became the king's enemies.

For most of those caught in the crossfire, this was a tragic dilemma, because they had no desire to be seen as disloyal, nor had they any other alternative to offer in Henry's place. There was also the thought in many men's minds that Henry's actions were a temporary aberration, and that sooner or later he would come to his senses—in which case it would be quixotic to make the supreme sacrifice that open treason would entail. Consequently, although many were suspect, and quite a few investigated, the number eventually convicted for this type of treason was comparatively small. In all, about 345 people were executed or died in prison after conviction for treason during Henry's reign, an average of nine a year. Nearly 900 appear to have been investigated.[17]

The man who was in many ways Henry's most persistent enemy during these years could not be touched by any legal process, because he was Eustace Chapuys, the Emperor's ambassador. Chapuys spent about ten years trying to persuade his master to invade England, at first to rescue Catherine and Mary from the terrible indignities that they were suffering at the king's hands, and later in defence of the 'true faith'. His letters were often intercepted, and Thomas Cromwell knew perfectly well what he was about, but his presence was tolerated. This was partly because neither Henry nor Cromwell wanted to precipitate a complete breakdown of diplomatic relations with so powerful a ruler; partly because Cromwell knew that Chapuys's campaign did not reflect the Emperor's real intentions, and that his influence in Brussels was limited; and partly because intercepted dispatches warned the government which Englishmen they should be keeping an eye on.[18]

Chapuys was in touch with malcontents of every hue, particularly the ex-queen's supporters, and was constantly urging them to rebel, in order to give him the necessary 'leverage' to persuade Charles to intervene. All he succeeded in doing, apart from annoying the king beyond measure, was to put Cromwell's bloodhounds onto a number of useful scents. Chapuys lectured the king and the council regularly upon the iniquity of their ways, but his presence, irritating though it must have been, was in itself a guarantee against that complete estrangement that Henry feared, and the king knew that every nuance of his relations with Francis I would be reflected in Chapuys's despatches, and that his own ambassadors resident with the Emperor would be able to pick up the responsive vibes. The ambassador's observations that 'all good men' in England were longing for the Emperor to come and set things right may be discounted as diplomatic hyperbole, but just occasionally he was contacted by Englishmen who were genuinely prepared to set their natural allegiance aside in defence of the Roman cause, and one of those was Bishop John Fisher.[19]

Fisher had never made any secret of his support for Catherine, but that in itself was not treasonable (see pages 93–5 and plate 5). He had been a thorn in the king's side since 1527, but that was not treasonable either. In 1533, however, he had crossed the divide that separated disaffection from treason by appealing to the Emperor. Cromwell's agents did not detect this move, but in 1534 a new treason act required all office holders (including bishops) to swear an oath to accept not only the legitimacy of Elizabeth as heir to the throne, but also the lawfulness of the royal supremacy.

Fisher declined both, and was sent to the Tower.[20] For this stand he was elected cardinal by the new pope, Paul III, in 1535, but as one contemporary dryly observed, 'The head was off before the hat was on, and so the twain met not.' Fisher was condemned and executed under the terms of the statute of 1534, but he was also guilty under the much older definition of treason, which went back to 1352. Neither Henry nor his judges knew that at the time. Only Chapuys and the Emperor's council were in on that secret, and they were not going to let on as they made the best propaganda that they could out of the bishop's martyrdom. The execution of a prince of the Church was sufficiently uncommon for the news to reverberate around Europe, and all sorts of rulers who had not the slightest interest in the affairs of England secured a few credit points with the papacy by jumping on the band-wagon—notably Henry's nephew James V of Scotland.

Although prompted by the highest motives, John Fisher died as the king's enemy, but whether the same can be said of his fellow victim, Sir Thomas More, is much more questionable. More had never appealed to any foreign power, and did not therefore lie under the same condemnation as Fisher. He had also supported Catherine, but much less conspicuously, and when Henry had persuaded him to take the chancellorship after Wolsey's fall, it was on the understanding that his conscience on that sensitive issue would not be offended.[21] More, however, who is most affection-ately remembered in his earlier incarnation as a humanist, a friend of Erasmus and a gentle wit, had by 1530 become a bigoted defender of the Catholic faith, and a fierce persecutor of dissent.

His views on the royal supremacy were much the same as Fisher's, and when the clergy had made their first surrender to the king in 1532, he resigned the Great Seal. This he was permitted to do on the condition that he retired from public life, a condition that he ostensibly observed, while remaining active in encourag-ing opposition to the king's policies behind the scenes.[22] He in his turn was arrested, convicted (allegedly on the perjured evidence of Sir Richard Rich), and executed in 1535. The legality of More's conviction has always been doubtful, because it was based upon a statute that had not been enacted until after the alleged offences had been committed.[23] There can be no doubt, however, concerning More's determination to challenge the king's policies, and in the circumstances that made him a dangerous man. More would have classed himself not as the king's enemy, but as the enemy of evil counsel, and the same would have applied to many other less high-profile victims of Henry's obsession. Altogether about 45 men, mostly clergy and many of them monks and friars, were executed for this particular kind of treason—all of them professing loyalty to the king.

A PETITION FROM THE WIFE AND CHILDREN OF SIR THOMAS MORE

IN LAMENTABLE WISE *beseech your most noble grace your most humble subjects and accustomed bedefolk [supplicants] the poor miserable wife and children of your true, poor heavy subject and bedeman Sir Thomas More Knight, that whereas the same Sir Thomas, being your grace's prisoner in your Tower of London by the space of eight months and above, in great continual sickness of body, and heaviness of heart, during all which space, notwithstanding that the same Sir Thomas More had, by refusing of the oath forfeited unto your most noble grace all his good and chattels, and the profits of all his lands, annuities and fees, that as well himself as your said bedeswoman his wife should live by, yet your most gracious highness, of your most blessed disposition, suffered your said bedeswoman, his poor wife, to retain and keep still his moveable goods, and the revenues of his lands, to keep her said husband and her poor household with. So it is now, most gracious sovereign, that now late, by means of a new Act or twain made in this last past prorogation of your parliament [18 December 1534], not only the said former forfeiture is confirmed, but also the inheritance of all such lands and tenements as the same Sir Thomas had of your most bountiful gift, amounting to*

the yearly value [of] lx li is forfeit also, And thus (except your
merciful favour be shewed), your said poor bedeswoman his wife,
which brought fair substance to him, which is all spent in your
grace's service, is likely to be utterly undone and his poor son, one
of your said humble suppliants, standing charged and bounden for
the payment of great sums of money due by the said Sir Thomas
unto your grace, standeth in danger to be cast away and undone in
this world also. But over all this the said Sir Thomas himself, after
his long service to his power, diligently done to your grace, is likely
in his age and continual sickness, for lack of comfort and good
keeping to be shortly destroyed, to the woeful heaviness and deadly
discomfort of all your said sorrowful suppliants. In consideration of
the premises, that his offence is grown not of any malice or obstin-
ate mind, but of such a long continued and deep rooted scruple as
passeth his power to avoid and put away, it may like your most
noble majesty, of your most abundant grace, to remit and pardon
your most grievous displeasure to the said Sir Thomas, and to
have tender pity and compassion upon his long distress and great
heaviness, and for the tender mercy of God deliver him out of
prison, and suffer him to live quietly the remnant of his life
with your said poor bedeswoman his wife, and other your poor
suppliants his children, with only such entertainment of living as
it shall like your most noble majesty, of your gracious alms and
pity to appoint him. And this in the way of mercy and pity, and
all your said bedesfolk shall daily during their lives, pray to God
for the preservation of your most royal estate.

[Taken from 'Inedited Documents relating to the Imprisonment and
Condemnation of Sir Thomas More', edited by John Bruce, *Archaeolo-*
gia, XXVII, 1838, pp. 361–74. Original BL Arundel MS 152, f. 320.]

Reginald Pole, probably because he was out of reach, felt constrained to make no such profession. He was the youngest son of
the Countess of Salisbury, and hence the king's second cousin.
Because of this he had been carefully educated at Henry's
expense, and it had seemed at one stage that he was destined for

an archbishopric.[24] In 1529 he had been used by the king to canvass opinions from the European universities in respect of his marriage, but as it became clear that Henry's mind was made up, and that he was looking only for endorsement, Pole became increasingly alienated.

Perhaps he was more percipient than Thomas More, or perhaps he just had better opportunities, but in 1530, when it was clear to him that he could no longer accommodate his conscience to the king's requirements, he sought (and obtained) licence to study abroad, and went back to Italy.[25] There he quickly became *persona grata,* partly because of his learning, but more on account of his royal blood and his potential usefulness as a weapon against his difficult kinsman. As was most of Catholic Europe, Pole was horrified by the executions of More and Fisher (especially the latter), and at some time between September 1535 and March 1536 he wrote an extended letter to the king. Pole insisted that this was for the king's eyes only, but it is difficult to take that assertion seriously. It was published shortly after in Rome, entitled *Reginaldi Poli ad henricum Octavum, Britanniae regem, pro ecclesiasticae unitate defensione* ('Reginald Pole to Henry VIII, king of Britain, for the defence of the unity of the Church')—usually known as *De unitate*—and was quickly recognized as a piece of committed polemic.[26] Pole pulled no punches: the king was a schismatic and a tyrant; a lecher who put his own gratification before the interests of his kingdom or the laws of the Church. There was no pretence of friendly counsel; this was outright denunciation.

Unsurprisingly, the king was furious. That such a tirade should have come out of Italy was not surprising, but that the author should not only be his subject, but a kinsman who had enjoyed his bounty on a lavish scale, made the whole situation intolerable. Shortly after he delivered this broadside, Pole was created cardinal and sent to northern Europe for the specific purpose of inciting Charles and Francis to attack England in the cause of Rome.[27]

It was a forlorn venture, but that is not the point. By acting as he did, Pole declared himself to be the king's enemy in the most obvious and traditional sense. He was attainted of treason by act of Parliament, and Cromwell's agents did their best to secure his abduction or assassination, should orthodox extradition be unsuccessful. He was expelled from France, and hovered insecurely in the Low Countries until he was recalled to Rome in June 1537.[28] Although hardly anyone in England can have read *De unitate*, its repercussions were severe. The king became not only deeply distrustful of anyone with connections to Reginald Pole, but also experienced a revival of his old fears about Yorkist conspiracies. In the late summer of 1538 Henry struck at the Poles and the Courtenays, using Cromwell and his inevitable spies and agents. Sir Geoffrey Pole, the cardinal's brother, was arrested and interrogated. Geoffrey was a weak man, and the mere threat of torture seems to have been enough to persuade him to sing lustily. Of course he had been in touch with Reginald—so had his brother Henry, Lord Montague, and his mother Margaret, the Countess of Salisbury. Servants and messengers were questioned, and a damning case was built up.

The historian Hazel Pierce, who has conducted the most recent examination of these proceedings, has concluded that whereas specific treason was never proved, the alienation of the whole Pole clan from Henry and his policies was radical and profound.[29] Whether that makes them the king's enemies in the same sense as Reginald was an enemy is difficult to say. They would have denied it vigorously, and did, but the charges were not as petty and irrational as is sometimes suggested. Margaret, Henry, Lord Montague and Geoffrey were all tried and convicted. Henry was executed in 1539, and the countess (eventually) in 1541. Geoffrey, who had 'turned king's evidence', was pardoned, but discredited.

The Poles were not of course isolated; they had their own networks and connections. The wind blew close to Sir William Paulet, their Hampshire neighbour, but he was Cromwell's trusted friend and he escaped unscathed.[30] Henry Courtenay, Marquis of Exeter, and Sir Edward Neville were less fortunate. Both were implicated by servants' gossip and evidence of messages sent and responded to. Courtenay was in additional danger because his mother had been Katherine, Edward IV's daughter, and he therefore stood in relation to the crown rather as the de la Pole brothers had done earlier. In his younger days he had been a close companion of the king, but that now counted for nothing. Henry had only one infant son, and the people of Devon were (apparently) saying what an excellent king the marquis would make.[31] Such a combination of circumstances sealed Courtenay's fate, and he and Neville were both executed on 9 December 1538. This so-called 'Exeter conspiracy' does not prove that there was any purposeful group in England working to achieve Reginald's objective of overthrowing the tyrant, but it does prove that there was a lot of disaffection, both in high places and low, and Henry felt it incumbent upon him to act ruthlessly in order to prevent such emotions from running out of control. Assisted by the threat of foreign invasion, which followed in 1539, he was successful.

In a sense Reginald Pole's aiders and abettors were an afterthought. Had Courtenay and Montague declared their hands earlier, and more unequivocally, they might have achieved rather more than their own executions. The difficulty was that by far the largest and most dangerous protest movement of the reign had not, for the most part, endorsed the cardinal's radical agenda. The Pilgrimage of Grace was not intended to overthrow Henry in the interests of the pope, or the Emperor, or anyone else. It was a protest movement, intended to change the king's mind over certain key aspects of his policy.[32] The pilgrims protested vigorously that they were no traitors, but the king's loyal subjects. This was eventually to prove their undoing. They were certainly not the king's enemies in any normal sense, but since he chose to regard them as traitors—and treated many of them as such—their movement must certainly be considered under this heading.

The rebellion, which began at Louth in Lincolnshire on 2 October 1536, was partly a grassroots reaction against what was supposed to be government policy. 'Supposed', because some of the alleged policies were never such at all. It was, for example, rumoured that parish churches would be abolished and their goods confiscated; and that the parish registers that had been introduced by the royal injunctions in the summer, were a surreptitious method of assessing a new poll tax.[33] Other grievances were more substantial. The dissolution of the smaller religious houses was unpopular, and the general drift of religious policy towards reform was much resented, particularly by the clergy. The king, it was alleged, was listening to base-born councillors, such as Cranmer and Cromwell, instead of the ancient nobility of England. Less obvious, but a very real complaint among the gentlemen of Lincolnshire, was the way in which Henry had built up his favourite, the Duke of Suffolk, in the county, to the exclusion of local interests.

The situation, it is clear, was tinder dry, and the subsidy commissioners, who had come to assess a lawfully voted tax, were set upon and scattered. News that Lincolnshire was 'up' rapidly reached London, and the fire spread rapidly from town to town, village to village. Within a few days 10,000 men (it was alleged) had entered Lincoln, and a number of gentlemen were forced (they later alleged) to take the rebels' oath, and to go with them.[34]

Gentry leadership was a mixed blessing. Once sworn to the rebels' cause, they could not be ignored, but their strategy quickly had the effect of cooling things down. Once at Lincoln, they insisted upon sending a set of articles to the king, and awaiting his response. These articles, five in number, concentrated upon such grievances as monastic dissolution, taxation, the Statute of Uses (a purely gentry concern, concerning the disposal of lands in wills), base-born councillors and general heresy. The five articles were couched in terms of a humble petition and request. Although the king observed suspiciously that the gentlemen of Lincolnshire were 'not as whole as they pretended', stalling the movement at Lincoln took a lot of the momentum out of it. Henry promised no concessions, but only a pardon, and by the time that his herald arrived at Lincoln on 11 October, a force was already mustering against the rebels at Stamford, led by the Duke of Suffolk himself.

The gentlemen were left with the option of making their peace with the duke, which most of them took, while the commons, now left leaderless by this desertion, were easily persuaded to disperse. Although the conservative clergy, who had inspired the outburst in the first place, were no doubt left gnashing their teeth, there was little more that they could do. The five articles had been distinctly short on constructive ideas, and George Wyatt's later observation that, left to themselves, the fury of the commons is soon appeased, was proved true in this instance.[35] Although Cromwell went after some of the ringleaders with a deliberate persistence that took months, the Lincolnshire rising was effectively over in about two weeks. If that had been the end of the matter, it might have counted as a minor shot across the bows, or it might have given encouragement to Cromwell and his assistants, conveying the message that opposition was unlikely to be sustained or purposeful.

It was not, however, the end of the matter. Some fugitives from the collapsing movement in Lincolnshire spread their resentments into south and east Yorkshire, where the ground was equally fertile, and the response was swift and widespread. The Pilgrimage of Grace, as it is called, was a very large and very complex movement, embracing every kind of grievance from neo-feudal resentments against the centralization of government to the use of gressoms (fines relating to tenures of land) and the abolition of saints' days. The regional emphasis varied, and in accordance with the priorities of local leadership, but its driving force came, as it had in Lincolnshire, from the disgruntled commons.

This was to some extent concealed by the connivance, indeed the active involvement, of some traditionally minded peers such as Lord Darcy and Lord Hussey, who had been talking to Eustace Chapuys for two or three years. Lord Darcy had declared that the king's proceedings dishonoured not only himself, but all those who were parties to them, and seems to have felt that his allegiance was dissolved by such faithlessness; while Lord Hussey had been a servant and leading supporter of Catherine of Aragon.[36]

These men would probably not have stirred if it had not been for the dynamism supplied by the general disaffection. They acted willingly enough, but they were figureheads.

The real leadership on the ground was provided by Robert Aske, a gentleman-lawyer and dependent of the Earl of Northumberland. Aske was an ideologue, who objected to the whole drift of the king's proceedings. The dissolution of the small monasteries was a grievance, but a comparatively minor one in his eyes. The kingdom was in schism and drifting into heresy thanks to Henry's mistakes. It was too late to urge Henry to take back his first wife, but he should recognize his daughter Mary as legitimate, restore the primacy to the see of Rome, and punish all those wicked heretics who had been leading him astray.[37]

It is highly unlikely that most of those who were 'up' with the pilgrims shared Aske's political priorities, although they would surely not have objected to them. They wanted the friars back, their abrogated holidays restored, and matters of customary tenure resolved in their favour. By late October the harvest was in, and they were sufficiently indignant to use the time that they now had available to make a show of force. Aided by a number of sympathetic gentlemen, Aske had the formidable task of turning this cataract of humanity into some kind of purposeful-looking demonstration. An oath was devised, emphasizing their public spirit, devotion to the Church and the commonwealth, and their desire to preserve the 'king's person and his issue'.[38] The blame for everything that had gone wrong was laid, in the most traditional manner, on 'evil councillors', of whom Thomas Cromwell was the worst.

By 4 December an estimated 30,000 men had assembled at Pontefract, and no one in the north had either the will or the ability to stand against them. Henry, responding as best he could, appointed the Duke of Norfolk as his lieutenant, and began to assemble a force in the south to go against the northern men. It was slow work, because sympathy with the rebels' purposes was widespread, and by early December Norfolk had nothing like enough for a confrontation.

In spite of appearances, however, things were not going all the pilgrims' way. The northern gentlemen generally, and lords Darcy and Hussey in particular, were looking for one of the great magnates to lead them, but no such leader appeared. They could hardly have expected the Duke of Norfolk to turn his coat, but neither the Earl of Derby nor the Earl of Shrewsbury, both powerful in the north, showed any inclination to become involved. Instead these nobles declared for the king and proceeded to exercise their great influence to restrain their tenants and dependents.[39] The earls of Cumberland and Westmorland similarly remained aloof, and even the Earl of Northumberland, the greatest man in the northeast, showed no sympathy. Northumberland was a sick man, and his family did not share his reluctance, but that produced a rift in the clan rather than any great accession of support for the Pilgrimage.

Meanwhile the assembly at Doncaster had sent Sir Thomas Hilton with a list of 24 articles to the Duke of Norfolk.[40] These show unmistakable signs of Aske's influence, but were also very much concerned to seek the restoration of all clerical and ecclesiastical privileges, including the re-establishment of the temporal power of the palatinate of Durham and its 'prince-bishops', and with the demand for a Parliament to be held in the north. Regional priorities were strong. No one was to be subpoenaed out of the north, but only to York. Common-law grievances also featured in a number of articles, and the general impression given is that the pilgrims objected to everything that the king had done, whether in respect of the Church, the faith, the succession, government or administration over the previous twenty years. They formed as sweeping a statement of sheer conservatism as could well be imagined. This was their strength in terms of popular support, but a weakness when it came to dealing with the king. He could not reasonably have been expected to accept such an indictment of his entire regime, especially as many of the changes had been introduced for good and sufficient reasons—and, of course, with the consent of Parliament.

THE PILGRIMAGE OF GRACE

Instructions for Sir Thomas Hilton and others sent as representatives of the northern pilgrims to the Duke of Norfolk, the king's lieutenant, November 1536.

1. First to declare to the Duke of Norfolk and other the lords that the intent of our meeting surely is met and thought of assured truth without any manner of deceit or malignancy.

2. The second is to receive the king's safe conduct under the broad seal of England and to deliver our safe conduct and promise under our hands for the assurance of the lords there.

3. The third is to entreat of our general pardon for all causes and that all persons the which is within this realm which in heart, word, and deed assisted, joined, aided, or procured the furtherance in this our quarrel may be pardoned life, lands and goods [fees and offices*] and that in the said pardon nor other the king's records nor writings, we be not reputed, written nor taken as rebels and traitors, nor so rehearsed in the same [but the king's true subjects*].

4. The fourth that Thomas Cromwell nor none of his band nor sort be not at our meeting at Doncaster, but absent the same council.

5. The fifth to receive the king's answer by the declaration of the lords and to certify the very intent thereof to us here ...

[Taken from the transcript in R.W. Hoyle, *The Pilgrimage of Grace and the Politics of the 1530s*, 2001, p.460. The original is in the National Archives, TNA SP1/112, f.118r.]

* These words appear only in a variant version of the text at the National Archives (SP1/112 ff.122–4).

Because he did not have the force to respond in the way that he would no doubt have preferred, Henry instructed Norfolk to negotiate. Some concessions were offered. There would be a Parliament in the north, the Statute of Uses would be looked at again, the enclosure acts caps would be more rigorously enforced, and so on. A free pardon would be granted to all those who had protested. However, no ground was given on the ecclesiastical supremacy, or on the composition of the council.

Inadequate as it was, this response seized the initiative. It was now up to the pilgrims' leaders to decide what to do. If they rejected compromise and marched south, how long would their numerical superiority last? Some of the rank and file were already wanting to go home. Moreover, the pilgrims did not know how strong the king's party in the south might turn out to be. Above all, they had professed their loyalty to the king; would they now trust him—or not? Just as the Pilgrimage had been assembled from a miscellaneous collection of local movements, so its counsels were now divided. Some were all for forcing the king's hand, but the majority, mindful of their own propaganda, urged acceptance and dispersal, and that was what happened.[41]

THE IMPERIAL VIEW OF ENGLAND AND THE PILGRIMAGE

A transcribed summary of letters from England to the Emperor Charles V, 22 November 1536.

ALL THE NOBILITY *of the Duchy of [York] is risen. They muster 40,000 combatants, and among them 10,000 horse. They are in good order and have a crucifix for their principal banner. The Archbishop of York* and Lord Darcy are in the army. The king blames the latter more than any man. Norfolk and his colleagues do not wish for a battle. They are all good Christians, showing tacitly that the petitions of the insurgents are lawful, and giving them hopes that the king will yield.*

The determination of the King cannot yet be known. It is feared that his arrogance and the persuasions of those who govern him, will prevent him from granting the demands, and also that he congratulates himself that the French king has offered to come and help him with 4,000 or 5,000 men. The men of the north are able to defend themselves, and their number will probably grow every day, but they have little money, in which the Pope ought to help them. If the Pope has determined to send Master Pole, it can

*easily be done because he is at present in Rome (this Pole has
recently been made a Cardinal, and is one of the principal men of
England) ...*

*The other parts of the Kingdom wish the men of the north to
come on and join them, or at least to stand firm and not listen
to the good words and practices which the king employs to make
a division among them. It is to be feared that they will allow
themselves to be deceived, as their leaders have no means of
providing money. If the Pope would send Reginald Pole with
funds, matters would be remedied in a moment, especially if
some musketeers were sent over as there is a great need of them.*

*Answer has been given to the ambassadors that the King will
not change anything that has been settled by parliament, and
therefore [will] do nothing that they ask, much less reform his
Privy Council to please them, as it is a thing in which they have
no right to meddle.*

*That the Emperor may know the dissimulation and
inconstancy of the King of England, it is not a month ago that he
allowed himself to say publicly that he was much obliged to the
French King who wished for his daughter [Mary] as a wife for the
Duke of Orleans, although she was a bastard ...*

[Paraphrases taken from *Letters and Papers*, XI, 1143. The original MS,
in Spanish, is BL Add. MS 28589, f. 101.]

* Edward Lee, who appears to have seen himself as mediator, and who
  escaped the blame attached to Darcy.

Whether Henry would have kept his word in other circumstances, we do not know. Probably not, as he would have felt that
he had acted under constraint. As it was, a minor, and really rather
irrelevant, attempt to restart the rising in Yorkshire in February
1537 gave him the perfect pretext to renege.[42] No Parliament met
in the north, and within a few months all the leaders of the original Pilgrimage, including Aske, Darcy and Hussey, had been
rounded up, tried and executed. The north was not to rise again
for another thirty years. In spite of the pilgrims' professions,

Henry had little choice but to treat them as his enemies, because what they were demanding amounted to a complete retraction of twenty years of policy and an unthinkable surrender to democratic dictatorship. In due course some of their demands were quietly accepted: Cromwell fell; Mary was restored to the succession; and the Act of Wills followed the Statute of Uses. But none of these things were the direct result of the rebellion. Had the pilgrims attempted to declare Henry deposed, or summoned the aid of the Emperor, or even dealt directly with Reginald Pole, they would have been much more clearly the king's enemies in the traditional sense. They did none of those things, and yet paid as high a price as if they had.

Henry executed many traitors—including two wives for treasonable adultery—who were not in any sense his enemies. But those clergy who died in defence of the papal authority (the majority) should perhaps be so classified. Henry was excommunicated and declared deposed by popes who were perfectly happy to call upon his neighbouring rulers to carry out their sentence. Anyone supporting that position was not only a traitor by statute, but also by the ancient definition: they were adherents to a hostile foreign power. The fact that this was also an issue of conscience muddied the moral waters, and has since led to many of those executed for treason being described as martyrs. In the event, not many of those who disliked the king's proceedings were prepared to stand up and be counted—except inadvertently, when their grumblings were detected—and that makes it very hard to decide how many enemies Henry had within his own realm. This is important, because it marks the distinction between a tyrant who imposed his will by force, and a ruler who (however ruthless) had for the most part majority consent. It is probably fairest to conclude that Henry's subjects by and large acquiesced in what he was doing, and that turned to more positive support after 1540. The Pilgrimage is a test case. However strongly most of the participants disagreed with the king, they were not prepared to push their discontentment into an open confrontation. They did not want another king, they wanted the king to behave in a different way, and they were in their own eyes demonstrators and not rebels.

Henry, however, also had another realm over which he claimed authority, but where his writ had never run uniformly, and many of whose inhabitants rejected his lordship entirely. That realm was Ireland, and as we shall see, the rules of engagement there were completely different ones.

§8 The King's Other Island

TUDOR POLICY in Ireland, the king's other island, was not a success. Although, when the Nine Years' War eventually came to an end in 1603, the Irish were subdued, that in itself was a failure in terms of the aspirations that had prevailed earlier in the previous century. The English, or rather Anglo-Norman, presence in Ireland went back a long way, to the days when Hugh de Lacy had been appointed 'Justice and Custos' (vice-regent), in 1172.[1] By the late 15th century the island was divided roughly into three zones. The first was the Pale—Dublin and its environs—which was under effective English rule, where the common law was applied, and where the king's writ ran without question. The second was the so-called 'obedient land', of Leinster and Munster, which was ruled by Anglo-Irish peers such as the earls of Kildare and Desmond. These peers acknowledged the overlordship of the kings of England, and used common law and Gaelic custom as appropriate. The third zone was the 'wild Irishry' of Connacht and Ulster, which was ruled by Gaelic chieftains, without reference to the king, whose overlordship was not acknowledged; here Gaelic custom was the only law.

Gaelic Ireland was in no sense united, and in the perpetual small wars that prevailed there, alliance with the Anglo-Irish peers, or with the English governor himself, was not out of the question.[2] In theory the whole of Ireland was a lordship under the English crown, but in practice the king's effective rule extended to less than a third of the island, and tended to fluctuate with the strength of the English crown at home. Both Lambert Simnel and

Perkin Warbeck, those pretenders to Henry VII's throne, found support in Ireland for their ambitions. For his part, Henry VII was, by and large, happy to settle for the submission of the Anglo-Irish peers, while allowing them to continue governing the country in the king's name.[3]

At first Henry VIII was equally happy to continue with this situation, and reappointed Gerald, the 8th Earl of Kildare, as chief governor immediately after his accession. An understanding of what followed is dependent upon an appreciation of the nature of Kildare's position. On the one hand he was *Gearoid Mor*, 'the Great FitzGerald', a chieftain of power and resources, respected and feared by the Irish clans.[4] On the other hand he was the king's representative, whose authority to govern the Pale depended entirely upon a royal commission. At the same time, on his own great estates he had a following that was both English and Irish, and whose first loyalty was to him as their overlord. His position could thus be compared to that of the great English magnates of the 15th century, such as the earls of Warwick or Northumberland, whose capacity to make trouble for the king was so great that he was virtually forced to govern through them.

Kildare was proud of his connections with the English crown and court, and contemptuous of Irish manners. But he was also an amphibian who could operate in both elements. Gaelic political consciousness was highly particularist and dynastic, and the FitzGerald family could be fitted into that context with little adaptation. Kildare's children were married into both communities.[5] The Celtic praise-singers might laud his position as the royal governor rather than as the successor to the ancient High Kings of All Ireland, but the substance of what they were saying was much the same. It is hardly surprising that the earl therefore saw any strengthening of his position amongst the tribes as an enhancement of the authority of the crown. Nor is it surprising that his activities, when viewed from London, took on a rather different perspective. A man who was as at home in the Gaelic language and culture as he was in English naturally exposed himself to misunderstanding, yet such expertise was essential to his position.

The distinction between the Irish and English communities, in terms of language, law and lifestyle, was clear enough, and there was plenty of mutual antagonism, but there were also big areas of overlap. Land titles in the marcher areas were fearsomely complicated, a complexity increased by the fact that the area of English settlement had shrunk during the troubled times of the mid-15th century. This had left some places in Gaelic occupation, and presently subject to Celtic law, but to which English title remained. This could be exploited as settler fortunes revived, but only at the cost of confused legal process, and often violence. Some English settlers also preferred the ancient Celtic brehon law for certain purposes. It was less draconian than the common law, and allowed (for example) 'composition' (a compensatory fine) for homicide.[6] In the lordships of the marches that option was available.

Similarly some Irish tenants in the same lordships preferred English law for property disputes, because of the greater clarity and firmness of the remedies it offered. To the Irish tribes the king of England was not so much an ethnic or ideological enemy as an alien presence who had to be accommodated, and who could be a useful ally when the circumstances were right. If the English of the Pale had a complaint against government from London in the first decade of the 16th century, it was that they saw too little of it. The FitzGerald ascendancy was not unacceptable, but it could be oppressive, particularly when the earl was juggling his priorities with the 'wild' Irish.

There was a Parliament in Ireland, modelled on that in England, but until 1494 it was not entirely clear who had the right to summon it. In that year the lord deputy, Sir Edward Poynings, secured the passage of an act that rested the initiative firmly with the English crown, and prescribed that only matters initiated by the council in London should be considered for legislation. This so-called 'Poynings' Law' governed the operations of the Irish Parliament thereafter.[7] Partly for that reason it was never as independent or as important as its English counterpart, and of course it represented only the Pale, the obedient land, and the English towns of the southwest, such as Galway and Limerick. The native Irish were unrepresented, and did not recognize its jurisdiction.

The 8th Earl of Kildare died in 1513, having made no noticeable adjustments to his style of government, and not having been called upon to do so. He was succeeded in office by his son, the 9th Earl, and everything seemed set to continue as before. However, Henry VIII was more inquisitive about what happened in the 'other island' than his father had been, and more inclined to bestow Irish offices upon his English courtiers. He appointed Sir William Compton, the chief gentleman of his privy chamber, as chancellor. Compton never went to Ireland, and discharged his office through a competent deputy.[8] He similarly appointed John Kite to the archbishopric of Armagh in 1513, before transferring him to Carlisle in 1521. Unlike Compton, Kite did reside in Ireland—which he regarded as a kind of exile—and his recall to the remotest, and one of the poorest, English sees says a lot about the priority with which Ireland was regarded.

Kildare lacked his father's sureness of touch, and the feeling began to grow among the gentry of the Pale that the FitzGerald ascendancy might not be the unmitigated blessing that they had supposed. In 1514 the earl made the mistake of dismissing two of his baronial council, William Darcy and Robert Crowley, who promptly made their way to London and began to bend the ears of the king's council about the chief governor's mismanagement.[9] He had, it was alleged, made war and peace without the consent of his council, and introduced both Irish men and Irish customs into his government to an unacceptable degree. Apart from a small area around Dublin, the 'Englishry' was losing its identity, and if nothing was done the whole colony stood in danger of disappearing. Kildare was summoned to London in 1515, and he confronted his accusers. Their charges, it soon transpired, were personally motivated and wildly exaggerated. The earl was exonerated and confirmed in office. However, the whole episode had served as a timely reminder of the chief governor's ultimate dependence upon the king. This time he had not only been endorsed, but significantly rewarded; next time he might not be so successful, and almost immediately after his return an obstacle was thrown into his path by the death of Thomas Butler, Earl of Ormond.

Thomas died without a direct male heir, and the inheritance was disputed between his cousin, Sir Piers Butler, and his two daughters. Piers looked to his friend Kildare for support, but Henry had unequivocally instructed his chief governor to recognize the claims of Ormond's daughters, Anne St Leger and Margaret Boleyn, both well connected at the English court.[10] Margaret indeed was the mother of Sir Thomas Boleyn and thus grandmother to Mary and Anne, the former of whom was just beginning to attract the king's favourable notice. In December 1515 Henry recognized the daughters' entitlement to all the Ormond lands in England, Wales and Ireland, but Kildare and the Irish council accepted the claims of Sir Piers, and the Irish lands went in practice to him. He began to style himself Earl of Ormond, but the king did not for some time recognize him as such, and, feeling that the chief governor had let him down, Butler quarrelled bitterly with FitzGerald in 1520.

Henry, on the other hand, considered that his instructions had not been obeyed, and when further complaints arose against the chief governor's regime, he was less inclined to look on him with favour. By 1520 the Kildare ascendancy was beginning to unravel, and Henry, prompted no doubt by Wolsey, was thinking that the devolved government of Ireland, which had worked for nearly thirty years, was no longer performing satisfactorily. In March 1520 he sent across a reliable English nobleman, Thomas Howard, Earl of Surrey, as lord lieutenant in Kildare's place.[11]

Howard's instructions were sweeping: 'to inform [his] highness by what means and way [his] grace might reduce this land to obedience and good order'. He was to recall the lords in the marches to their direct allegiance, and to levy the king's revenues throughout the obedient land.[12] Kildare was summoned back to

London, and kept there for the time being. Unfortunately, the resources that Howard was given (and over which there was a good deal of haggling) were not sufficient for so ambitious a programme. In spite of ostensibly proposing a sweeping programme of change, the English gentry of the Pale offered little in the way of practical support, and the backing of the nobles' personal followings was patchy and unpredictable.

By 1521 Surrey's lieutenancy was costing the king £10,000 a year above the revenues of Ireland, and had achieved virtually nothing. The earl was insistent that only a military conquest could subdue even the Anglo-Irish lords, let alone the 'wild Irish', but Henry was unconvinced, looking instead for a process of more or less peaceful pressure.[13] This soon became a fundamental disagreement, because the traditional English attitude towards the Irish was that they were a subject people, who could be expropriated at will. This was, by and large, the position that Surrey adopted, but the king and Wolsey favoured instead an attempt to win over the Irish chieftains, which, ironically, was much closer to the practice of the Anglo-Irish peers. Not for the last time, the English government became bogged down in the contradictions and illogicalities of Irish politics.

Meanwhile the FitzGeralds were seething with discontent, and Kildare himself was returning to favour at court. In September 1521 Surrey was recalled. In tangible terms he had accomplished nothing, but what his mission had done was to set out in stark terms the alternatives that confronted the king in his other realm. Either he must commit the large resources of men and money that would be required for a military conquest, and to go on doing so for a long time in support of a regime controlled directly from England, or he must fudge and compromise with the various factions and groups that constituted the Englishry, and try by gradual persuasion to improve relations with the native Irish. Meanwhile, Kildare still not being fully rehabilitated, Henry appointed no less a person than Piers Butler as lord deputy, presumably on the grounds that he controlled the second largest affinity in the obedient land, and was a reliable opponent of the Geraldines (as Kildare's followers were called).[14] Henry offered Butler favour, and a good marriage, but did not recognize him as Earl of Ormond until 1528.

Piers Butler's estates, it soon transpired, were in the wrong place, his resources inadequate and the Geraldines uncontrollable. At the same time, a third Anglo-Irish peer, the Earl of Desmond, complicated the issue further by entering into direct negotiations with Francis I during the second Anglo-French war, and by recognizing Richard de la Pole as king of England.[15] This was little more than a nuisance as far as Henry was concerned, but the deteriorating situation prompted him to receive Kildare back into favour in 1523, and to dispatch the earl back to Ireland to pacify his kindred. Butler and Kildare immediately quarrelled, and in the summer of 1524 Wolsey attempted another cheap form of direct involvement by sending a special commission over to resolve the dispute.

Ostensibly this was successful, both peers entering into bonds to keep the peace towards each other, but the equilibrium was again upset when Kildare was restored as chief governor later in 1524, whereupon his feud with Butler promptly flared up again. Complaints and counter-complaints were soon flying backwards and forwards across the Irish Sea, and it was alleged that Kildare was inciting the Irish tribes to attack his rival's estates. Although Kildare's reappointment restored order to the Pale, this continuing quarrel, plus Kildare's failure to apprehend the rogue Earl of Desmond, prompted another rethink in 1528. Both protagonists were summoned to London and detained, while the governorship was placed in the hands of Thomas FitzGerald of Leixlip, as lord justice.[16] This reduced the main faction fight to skirmishing, but weakened the government in the face of Irish incursions; pleas for more money and military resources were soon resumed. Only in one respect was the situation eased: the Earl of Desmond died in June 1529, and the desire of his successor for royal recognition led to his submission and the settlement of that particular issue.

Uncertainty seems to have prevailed during the last days of Wolsey's ascendancy. Piers Butler was restored in August 1528, now recognized as Earl of Ormond, and then in June 1529 the king's illegitimate son, Henry FitzRoy, Duke of Richmond, was appointed lord lieutenant.[17] This appears to represent a complete change of direction, because FitzRoy never visited Ireland, and for about a year the office was discharged by a 'secret council' headed by John Allin, the Archbishop of Dublin.

After Wolsey's fall, in the summer of 1530, William Skeffington was appointed deputy. Skeffington, who was backed by a modest but effective military force, succeeded in bringing an end to the feud between Desmond and Ormond, and persuaded Henry to send Kildare back to Ireland, with the specific brief of managing the borders with the Irish tribes. The improvement, however, was purely temporary. By the summer of 1531 Skeffington and Kildare had fallen out, and the Parliament of October 1531 threw out the subsidy bill, reducing the government to impotence. In the summer of 1532 Skeffingon was recalled and charged with all sorts of malpractices.[18] Apparently despairing of any better solution, the king restored Kildare to office, only this time as deputy.

However, by the summer of 1533 Thomas Cromwell was turning his omni-competent gaze towards Ireland, and not liking what he saw. He began a policy of 'subliminal intervention', securing control of Irish patronage, and promoting Ormond or Desmond supporters to lesser but significant offices. Kildare was summoned to London, but he sent his excuses, and there was talk of sending William Skeffington back to Ireland. By late 1533 English politics were impacting in Ireland, and resentment over the king's marital proceedings (and their consequences) were adding further fuel to the many fires of controversy. In 1534 Kildare rethought his position, and decided to obey the summons, once he had been given permission to appoint his son Thomas, Lord Offaly, to act in his absence.

This was the signal for a crisis. By May Kildare was facing charges of treason, and on 11 June Lord Offaly stormed into the

Irish council, resigned his office, and denounced the king's policies from every possible angle.[19] Exactly what persuaded Offaly to
ignore the subtleties and ambiguities of Irish politics in this forth-
right way, we do not know, but within a month he was in open
rebellion, murdered the Archbishop of Dublin, and laid siege to
Dublin Castle. 'Silken Thomas', as he was known, claimed to be
leading a Catholic crusade against the schismatical king of England, and sought support both among dissident peers in England
and also from the Emperor. For a variety of reasons, none was
forthcoming. Charles V was interested for a while, but eventually
was not drawn, and men like Lord Darcy, who sympathized with
his ostensible intentions, were not prepared to act.[20]

Had the Irish revolt coincided with the Pilgrimage of Grace it
might have been a different story, but it did not. In Irish terms,
however, it was a considerable conflagration, being partly religious
in its motivation, and partly provoked by the increasing signs of
central interference in the affairs of the lordship. Although Kildare
was off the scene, his affinity rallied to his heir, as did many of those
whom Kildare had appointed to office before his departure. Both
the Pale gentry and their natural enemies, the Irish tribes, were
involved. This combination had its drawbacks, because those
most opposed to the Kildare affinity, or most hostile to the native
Irish, had every incentive to remain loyal. Viewed from the outside, the rebellion looked more like a civil war. Neither the king
nor Cromwell showed the slightest inclination to compromise, and
although it took some time to mobilize a response, Henry happened to be free from other military commitments at this point.[21]

At first the rebels had the better of a very confused conflict, but
the return of Skeffington in October 1534 with over 2,000 troops
transformed the situation. This was a very large army by Irish
standards, where battles were normally fought by scores or hundreds, and it quickly restored the Pale and most of the obedient
land to its allegiance. As his English followers dropped away, or
were defeated, Offaly found himself increasingly dependent upon
his Irish allies, and this gave a new, and ultimately sinister, twist to

the conflict. After his own main fortress of Maynooth had fallen to the royal forces in March 1535, 'Silken Thomas' took refuge with the tribes, and during the summer of 1535 the war acquired an ethnic dimension of Gael against Gall (foreigner), which had not been present before. It may be that Offaly, by this time the 10th Earl of Kildare,[22] was himself perturbed by the implications of this, because in August of that year he surrendered and the rebellion came to an end.

Kildare may well have expected that this conflict would conclude, as was normal in Ireland, with submission, settlement, and eventually a return to favour. He probably expected no worse than a period in the wilderness, such as had often been inflicted on his family in the past. If so, he was to be disillusioned. He had insulted the king, and sought foreign allies. Meanwhile the Pilgrimage of Grace reminded the king that he could no more afford to be tolerant of opposition in Ireland than he could in England. After the end of the Pilgrimage, in February 1537, the earl and his five uncles were all executed in London. The Kildare ascendancy had been brought to a bloody end.

THE KILDARE REVOLT

Paraphrase of a letter from John Alen (at this time clerk of the council and master of the rolls) to Thomas Cromwell, 26 December 1534.

D OUBTS NOT *that the Treasurer [James, Lord Butler] and others will write of the late journey to Waterford. [He] is grieved to see the expense of this army, and not such service done as might be. Journeyed with 300 horsemen through Kildare and Cartlagh, and by MacMorgho and O'More. The traitor [Thomas, Lord Offaly] and O'More dared not set upon them, but meanwhile robbed and burned Trym and Dunboyne. The Deputy [William Skeffington] then made a truce with him, which [the writer] thinks not honourable. O'Nele on the other side burned part of the baron of Slane's lands, all Betaghe's lands and a great part of Uriell. This rebel cannot be destroyed if the King's army stays in Dublin. He expected to be banished a month ago, but now grows in pride and strength again. The King and Cromwell should write to the Deputy and captains to approach to the war and leave Dublin and Drogheda. The traitor has not more than 100 horse and 300 foot, among whom there is not one archer, nor 10 handguns, and he has no ordnance. He intends to have Trym, the Nawon, Athboy, the Naas, Kildare and other towns, and will break his own garrisons and burn his own lands lest Englishmen should profit by them. Understands that he expects an army from Spain, and has lately sent the Official of Meath, the dean of Kildare, parson Webbe, the Bishop of Killallo and other papists to Spain to ask for aid against the King as a heretic.*

Advises the king either to pardon him out of hand, or to send here a proclamation that he never intends to pardon him, or any who take part with him thereafter. If the army would go abroad it would not be long before he would be subdued. A marshal should be appointed who is not a Welshman, for they rob both friend and foe ...

The deputy is old, and cannot take pains by reason of sickness. Suggests the advisability of having 200 more northern horse.

Offers that he and the Chief Baron will go with the army, if they may have 24 spearmen and six archers or gunners on horseback. Objects to the appointing of Captains as Privy Councillors. It were better they should be commanded than commanders. The Deputy, the Lord Chancellor [John Barnewell, Lord Trimblestone], Lord Butler and the baron of Delven know how to subdue this traitor better than all the captains of England, except the Duke of Norfolk. Desires credence for the bearer, Edward Becke. Dublin, 26 December.

Trusts that the Commons of England will grant the King £100,000 for subduing this false traitor.

[Paraphrase from *Letters and Papers*, VII, 1573. TNA SP60/2 pp. 78–9.]

This marked an important turning point, because Ireland was now a welter of competing affinities and interests, no one of which had the edge. After Henry FitzRoy, Duke of Richmond, died in the summer of 1536, it was decided that the country should be governed more directly, by an English deputy supported by a sizeable garrison. Lord Leonard Grey was actually appointed before Richmond's death, and under his auspices the Irish Reformation Parliament met in 1537, which dutifully extended the royal supremacy to the Church in Ireland.[23] In spite of the fury that the implementation of such a policy had seemed to threaten only three years before, these measures were accepted without serious resistance. However, there was still no agreement as to general policy in Ireland. Grey, backed by the Irish administration, favoured a full conquest of the island, arguing that the collapse of Silken Thomas's insurgency presented a unique opportunity.[24] Henry, on the other hand, was acutely conscious of the cost of such a 'forward' policy, and of the risks of getting literally bogged down in the tribal lands.

Between September 1537 and April 1538 a specially appointed commission for Irish affairs examined the options, and recommended that in future the council in Dublin should confine itself to governing and defending the Englishry, and that administrative reforms should be introduced to increase control over the obedient land. Relations with the Irish chieftains should be confined to the giving and taking of pledges for the peace, and otherwise there should be no attempt to expand into tribal land.[25] Lord Grey, who was not happy with these recommendations, was replaced in 1540 by Sir Anthony St Leger, who was to remain as lord deputy for the rest of the reign—and beyond. By this time Cromwell had also gone, and the way was now open for a new initiative.

PROBLEMS OF ORDER

From the 'book' of David Sutton, a minor official who composed memoranda, 20 September 1537.

THIS BOOK *made the 20 September 29 Henry VIII by commandment of the Commissioners then being in Ireland, which had me sworn to declare the truth of how the counties of Kildare and Carlow was used by the late Earl of Kildare, and sithens [since then] and now.*

Enumerates many extortions practiced by Kildare upon the people. He used the King's laws or Brehens laws [native or Gaelic law] as suited him best, and his own proclamations were taken for law.

The Lord of Kilkullyn is now the only man who sets coyne and livery* on the king's tenants, as his own lands would not keep half his men of war. They are nominally for the defence of the country, but many of them are naughty men, and if not with him, or executed, would be doing hurt, as Piers FitzGarrett's sons do. Great exactions practised by William Brymycham, who among other things has proclaimed throughout his barony of Carbre that no man shall take anything to market, but only to his wife, and she to make the price. Two strong thieves were taken lately in 'harst' [red-handed]; one is with the Deputy, the other William Brymycham let go because he was Cayre Acconer's servant. He harbours the Connors.

Philip Morris sets coyne and livery in Allan and my Lord Bishop's lands there, and keeps the Danceys with him, who are the best spies in our country. James McGerald accompanies with the Daunceys and with strong thieves. Many of the Lord of Kilcolyn's men [and] James Gerald's men exact 'foyse' (that is meat). Piers FitzGarrett's sons are succoured by the baron of Noragh. When we are at peace with the Leysse and the Danceys, they come in companies to ask meat, and the borderers, being afraid to refuse, are so impoverished that the king's tenants have given warning to quit their holdings. James FitzGarrett of Ballysonnan succours the thieves of Leyxe, and his brother Piers leads them. They take their spoils the first night to the Black Wood, next night to Ballysonnan, next night to Leyxe, and so from place to place that they cannot be traced.

[Taken from *Letters and Papers*, XII, ii, 729. Original TNA SP1/84 p.101.]

* Coyne and livery = a general term for various exactions of Gaelic origin, arising from the free quartering of the chief's dependents on the country.

St Leger's name is always associated with the last, and the most hopeful, phase of Henry's Irish policy, which was symbolized by his erection of the traditional lordship of Ireland into a kingdom in 1541.[26] This was in part a natural consequence of the rejection of papal authority, because there was a general (and well-founded) belief that the king of England held the lordship of Ireland as a fief from the pope. Henry would have nothing to do with such a view, and chose this method to demonstrate his sovereignty.

However, it was also intended to indicate an 'equal but separate' system of government. Instead of embarking upon a vastly expensive and confrontational policy of conquest, he would attempt to incorporate the tribal lands into the new kingdom by a policy of inclusion and reconciliation. This was the policy of 'surrender and regrant', which was attempted by St Leger between 1541 and 1547. The basic idea was simple. Each tribal chieftain would surrender his lands to the king of Ireland, and receive them back as a fief to be held of the king in chief. Along with each grant would go a barony, which carried with it a place in the Irish House of Lords.[27]

STRATEGIES OF CONTROL

Renumbered extracts from the notes of John Alen (now clerk of the privy council of Ireland, and later lord chancellor), 20 September 1537.

[1] *The Irish have long looked upon the Kings of England but as governors here for the Bishop of Rome. An Act should be passed recognizing the King as King of Ireland, and the Irish captains should be sworn to him as such.*

[2] *As it is enacted that the King is Supreme Head of the Church in Ireland, every man should sworn to it, and this oath should be offered by commissions in each county, and given to the Lords at the next parliament.*

[3] *Danger of great Power of individuals …*

[4] *Every man of great power should have some grave personage joined with him, so as to divide his influence …*

[5] *It should be enacted that in case a lord marcher lack capacity*

to defend the Pale, another of his 'nation' be appointed by the Deputy and Council to do so, with a reasonable stipend out of the said lord's lands.

[6]   *There is such a lack of English blood that we are bound to take Irishmen, our natural enemies, as tenants and even as servants; but it should be enacted that none bide amongst us whose grandfather, father and self have not been born in the Pale.*

[7]   *Irishmen calling themselves Englishmen's servants go about stealing, for there is no difference between our marchers and the Irish in habit; all inhabitants of the Pale should be ordered to have no upper beard called a crommell or turffid head, but either wear a bonnet or else polled heads.*

[8]   *Such as have made marriages, given byinges or fastual [tributes] to any Irishman of late should be punished and forbidden to do so again.*

[9]   *It should be enacted that no Irishman should have the keeping of an Englishman's castle on the borders ...*

[10]   *In towns people should be compelled to teach their children English; every owner of a plough should wear a coat after the English fashion, and every merchant worth over £40 ride in a saddle.*

[11]   *Archery to be encouraged ...*

[12]   *As the nature of Irishmen is that for money one shall have the son to row against the father, and the father against the child, the King should always have treasure ready.*

[Taken from *Letters and Papers*, XII, ii, 729 (4). Original TNA SP60/5.]

It was assumed that a process of anglicization and 'civilization' would then follow. The early results were promising. After the ritual gestures of coercion that formed part of the traditional liturgy of Irish politics, chieftains such as McMurrough, O'More, O'Connor, Desmond, Burke of Clanrickard and O'Neill all sought reconciliation, and entered into indentures to recognize the king as their lord, and to apply for crown grants and the peerages that went with them.

Unfortunately nothing in Ireland was as simple as this would suggest. In the first place, by Gaelic law the land belonged to the tribe, and not to the chief, in other words it was not his to surrender; although if he managed to get away with it, the new grant would confer a valid title by English law, which would be vested in himself alone. This meant that the chiefs were very much keener than their followers and kinsmen, and when it came to the actual details, the negotiations frequently broke down.[28] So tortuous did these negotiations often become that the whole policy was effectively suspended in 1543, when only a small number of transactions had been completed. It was not abandoned, but no fresh initiative took its place in Henry's lifetime, and it was a big discouragement to St Leger, who found himself effectively marking time in his relations with the Irishry.

HENRY, KING OF IRELAND

Imperial ambassador Eustace Chapuys to the Emperor Charles V, 16 July 1541.

NOTHING IMPORTANT *has happened here since my last [2 July]. Some days ago the King ordered the estates of that portion of Ireland which is now under his rule to be convoked for the purpose of communicating to them, among other things, that he wishes and intends to set up under the name 'The Kingdom of Ireland' that part of the country where his lordship and rule are at present obeyed; and consequently to call and entitle himself King of Ireland; in expectation of which new title all business has for some days been suspended in Chancery, as well as in the Exchequer Court, in order that all of a sudden, and conjointly as it were, the king's name may appear decorated with his new title of 'King of England and Ireland' in all Letters Patent, provisions etc., emanating from these two officers, and that by that means the news may be spread and circulated in every quarter.*

[Taken from the *State Papers, Spanish*, VI, 173. The original, in French, is in the Vienna Staatsarchiv.]

The Irish Church, like the community itself, was divided into zones. Within the Pale, which roughly corresponded with the archdiocese of Dublin, the standards of discipline and education were much the same as they were in England, and similar systems of patronage applied. The provinces of Armagh and Cashel each covered part of the obedient land, and dioceses such as Cashel itself and Meath were rather similar to Kildare or Ferns; but they also included Irish lands where different practices were followed, and even the succession of the bishops is often uncertain.[29] The whole of the province of Tuam was Gaelic country, and there even the archbishops are shadowy.

By the standards applied in most parts of the Western Church, the clergy of the tribal lands were in serious need of reform. Parishes were very large and ill defined, the priests often being kinsmen of the clan chiefs. The ancient Celtic habit of relying on the regular clergy for parish ministry was still followed in many places. Sometimes this was respectable enough, and the friars were busy and very well regarded in this mode, but in other places it meant that the parish priest doubled as the abbot of the local monastery, and might well be a married man with a large family.[30] There was, consequently, a considerable racial division within the Church, and provinces, or even dioceses, might have two sets of administrators—one dealing with the clergy *inter Anglicos* and the other with the clergy *inter Hibernicos*. About a dozen sees were normally in English hands, and there the bishops were provided by the crown and confirmed by the pope, as in England.

In the first twenty years of the 16th century Anglo-papal relations were good, and there were no problems. Thirteen sees were regularly in Gaelic hands, and there the pope tended to provide without reference to English wishes, because the English had no temporal control. The other nine dioceses varied, and it was there that the main problems arose. Sometime these sees were held by absentee Englishmen, sometimes by Englishmen who were resident, and sometimes by resident Celts. There were double appointments to the same position, quarrels and uncertainties in such places, and it was there that the sharpness of racial antagonism was most marked.[31] Royal and local interests were constantly in conflict, and this required regular process of negotiation and compromise. By the 1520s double provisions, at least, had been largely eliminated.

Rather surprisingly, in view of the stand that Lord Offaly had been claiming to make, the royal supremacy was accepted in Ireland with remarkably little fuss. The Parliament enacted the necessary legislation in 1537, with the only dissent coming from the 'third chamber', the proctors of the lower clergy who (in contrast to England) formed a house of the Parliament. One result of this, of course, was to sharpen the distinction between the Englishry and the Irishry, because the latter paid no attention whatsoever to the new laws, and continued to deal directly with Rome as they had done before.[32] To what extent the curia actually understood the condition of the Irish Church may be doubted, because one of the consequences of this was the preservation (and indeed promotion) of the clerical dynasties that were one of the features of the tribal lands.

The fact was that the Gaelic Church was very far from being a jewel in the papacy's crown. Although the liturgy was in Latin, education in the normal sense was very sparse. As in Wales, the bards had a learning of their own, which they imparted to selected laymen, but this served mainly to perpetuate the distinctiveness of their culture, and did not build any bridges either to England or to mainland Europe.[33] Although some parts of the scripture had been translated into the Gaelic tongue, humanism as that was normally understood had made no impression in Ireland. Piety, even by English standards, was primitive and superstitious. 'Holy warriors' gave their services to chiefs in battle, water poured into saints' bells cured sick animals, and visions and minor local miracles were a constant ingredient of popular faith. Moreover the mores of tribal conflict were regularly reflected in the behaviour of senior clergy. In 1444 Cormac MacCoughlan, Bishop of Clonmacnoise, his son the archdeacon and the Prior of Clontuskert were all killed in battle with a rival clan. In 1466 O'Brien of Thomond was allegedly slain by the evil eye, and as late as 1525 Abbot Kavanagh, the Archdeacon of Leighlin, murdered his own bishop, Mauricius O'Deoradhain, in the king's highway, allegedly to secure his see.[34] The latter crime, being committed within the obedient lands, attracted a savage justice at the hands of Lord Deputy Kildare.

Altogether, there was much in the Gaelic Church that stood in need of reform. Discipline as that was normally understood was virtually non-existent. The great exception to this generally depressing picture was, however, the growth and strength of the mendicant orders.[35] Although for the most part of Irish birth, these friars had normally been educated abroad, and brought with them different standards of both conduct and ministry. Above all, they stood apart from tribal loyalties and affinities, in marked contrast to the secular clergy.

During the 15th century nearly fifty houses of Dominicans, Franciscans and Augustinians had been established, mostly in the tribal lands. Between 1460 and 1530 many of these houses also converted to 'strict observance', and this was greatly respected among a laity whose lives were far from strict. There was a down side to this, in that chiefs, and even bishops, jostled to be buried in a friar's habit in the belief that some of this sanctity would rub off on them; but there is no doubt that the mendicants in general provided a quality of spiritual guidance and example that was not otherwise available. They were also able and willing to preach in Gaelic, which was an invaluable asset, because otherwise most of those who had the language did not have the ability, and those with the ability did not have the language. Some houses were also established in English-speaking towns, but a sensible policy of deployment did not usually waste Gaelic speakers in places where they could do no good. In the Englishry, as in England itself, the friars were generally reckoned to be at the sharp end of theological debate, and in so far as there were reformers in Ireland, they tended to be located in the mendicant houses.

By contrast, monasticism was in full decline, and in 1538 there were no more than half a dozen communities with more than six monks.[36] The rot in that quarter went back a long way, again because monastic property tended to be regarded as a part of the tribal endowment. Abbots frequently, and individual monks not uncommonly, were married, often non-resident, and made almost no pretence of observing their rule. In 1466, for example, the abbey of Lough Key was burned to the ground by the inadvertence of a canon's wife bearing a lighted candle.[37] Pluralism, the holding of more than one ecclesiastical position at the same time, was also frequent, and monastic sites were sometimes turned into strongholds for the purposes of tribal warfare.

The Cistercians, who had been in the forefront of earlier reforms, were in a desperate condition by the end of the 15th century, and in 1496 the general chapter established a national congregation, which appointed special *reformatores* in the hope of re-establishing discipline. A surviving report from Abbot Troy of Mellifont, one of these special agents, makes the scale of the problem clear. Only two communities, his own at Mellifont and one in Dublin, still observed the rule and wore the habit; the others scarcely made a pretence of maintaining any corporate life or liturgy. They were caught up in local wars, dominated by tribal chieftains, and in the obedient land riven by racial animosities.

Troy begged to be excused from visiting any more Gaelic houses, because of the violence to which he had been subjected, and of what had been threatened.[38] His brief was to be impartial, and he may not have been, but there is no evidence to suggest that he was mistaken. The other orders appear to have been little better. Within the Pale, the standard was more acceptable, but even there the monastic orders were in decline, lay benefactions going mainly to confraternities and third-order groups (i.e. the lay brothers who did not take full vows)—and, of course, the mendicants. Ormond, in the obedient land, was visited by a royal commission in 1537, and the picture painted was almost as black as that of the tribal lands: the abbot and monks of Inishloughnaght each had a concubine and a household; the priory of Cahir did not celebrate the liturgy; at St Katherine's, Waterford, the community had split up and divided the revenues—and so on.[39]

This is all rather reminiscent of the reports of similar commissions in England, and may have been designed to justify dissolution. By the time that this visitation took place, 13 of the more decrepit houses had already been dissolved by statute, and the Irish properties of English religious houses had been seized.[40] Pressure for more sweeping measures came mainly from official circles, and was closely linked with the desire to find more resources for military deployment. As in England, there were also pressures from private interests, which hoped to benefit. In September 1538 Henry decided on total suppression, and this process was carried out by another royal commission, which was issued in April 1539. This was a direct exercise of the royal supremacy, without any specific legislation by the Irish Parliament. By November 1540 another 47 houses had been added to those suppressed earlier.[41]

The monks were pensioned in accordance with the resources of their houses, and (where possible) redeployed as secular clergy. There was remarkably little resistance, or even complaint, because monasticism was little respected—for all the reasons suggested—and the friars, who were missed, were immediately redeployed into the parishes where they greatly enhanced the quality of the ministry. The effectiveness of the king's action varied in accordance with the general effectiveness of his government. In the Pale, Wexford, Ormond and the English towns of the southwest, suppression was total; in the obedient land partial, according to circumstances; while the tribal lands were virtually untouched.

Altogether about 80 of the 140 monasteries that had existed in Ireland in 1530 were dissolved, and a similar number of the 200 mendicant houses. The mendicants survived better, not because of their higher standards, but because they were more numerous in Gaelic Ireland. The pickings were nothing like as rich as they were in England, but a similar policy was followed. The largest number of recipients were Old English, descendants of the early

Anglo-Norman settlers, from the Pale; they were followed by a group of English outsiders, some of whom took up residence in Ireland (where they became known as 'New English'), but most of whom remained absentees.[42] A proportion also went to the Anglo-Irish peers, and to Gaelic chiefs who wanted to establish town houses within the Englishry, a distribution that can be linked to the policy of surrender and regrant. Most of this property was not granted away or sold, but leased, usually for 21 years, which was different from the policy followed in England, and possibly the result of the need to be much more careful in the newly established kingdom. Where the monasteries were dissolved they were little missed, and where they remained they performed no useful function in the preservation of the faith.

Reform as Cranmer or Cromwell would have understood it had hardly touched Ireland by 1547. No part of the kingdom was under Canterbury's jurisdiction, and although the calendar was altered and the English bible used in some places, that was at the discretion of the local diocesan. Had it applied to Ireland, the Act of Six Articles would have been warmly endorsed. There was no tradition of heretical discourse in Ireland, and no institution of higher education to attract dissident intellectuals. Quasi-Protestant evangelicals like Hugh Latimer were unknown, and when they began to arrive in Ireland after 1547, the shock was profound.

During the 1530s Henry had largely destroyed the traditional system of devolved government, replacing it with one much more directly answerable to London. Resented in some quarters, the weakening of the grip of the Anglo-Irish nobles was generally welcomed. It was the failure of the surrender and regrant policy, accompanied by the introduction of Protestantism, that turned the Irish polity inside out, and led first to colonization and then to an ethnic polarity of religious ideology that bedevilled Ireland in the Elizabethan period and after. At the end of Henry's reign his second kingdom was probably more governable than it had been at the beginning, but in bringing about this improvement, he had sown the seeds of future trouble in a big way.

§9 The King's Religion

HENRY had been brought up in a strictly orthodox environment. His father enjoyed excellent relations with the papacy, and actively supported the campaigns that certain of his bishops waged from time to time against the Lollards. The young prince's first recorded public action was to witness a grant, in 1496, to the abbot and convent of Glastonbury.[1] In 1672 Lord Herbert of Cherbury was to write that as long as Prince Arthur was alive, his younger brother was destined for the archbishopric of Canterbury. Appealing as that thought is, the only evidence for it is that someone taught the young Henry some theology.[2]

We know very little about the process of his education, but by the time that he came to the throne he was better read in the Scriptures and the Fathers of the Church than many who had been through the formalities of a university. He was, moreover, a man of the humanist New Learning and an admirer of Erasmus. This was one of the reasons for the outburst of joy with which the humanists welcomed his accession. This king was not merely a patron of learning — he was learned himself. Exactly how learned we can gather only from later evidence. He did not immediately rush into print, and records of his conversations are sparse. Such evidence as we have of his piety from the early years of his reign is largely negative. He completed projects that his father had left unfinished, such as King's College, Cambridge, but he undertook no new ones, and made no generous donations to religious causes. He offered regularly at the usual feasts, but with an air of habitual duty rather than enthusiasm. He made just one pilgrimage, to

Walsingham, to celebrate and give thanks for the birth of his short-lived son in 1511, and perhaps the outcome of that experience deterred him thereafter.[3]

It would appear that, like many humanists, Henry was sceptical of the value of the *opus dei,* that perpetual fountain of prayer and praise with which the monasteries justified their existence. He had been on the throne for nearly twenty years before serious questions began to be asked about the nature of his faith, and never in that time had he made any generous benefaction to a religious order — let alone founded a new house. He offered at all the traditional shrines, not only Walsingham, but at Our Lady of Pew, Missenden and Doncaster, at St Thomas of Canterbury, and at the shrine of Edward the Confessor. However, with the one exception these offerings were always delivered by proxy. When the king went about hunting, or in pursuit of secular business, it was his queen who visited shrines, wore the habit of the third order of St Francis, and distributed alms to the poor and aged.[4] In this she was being no less humanist than her husband, but it was a different kind of piety, and one deeply rooted in the rather indiscriminate charity of the past.

When Henry spent money on pious causes, it was more likely to be on masses and on sermons. From before his accession, he was accustomed to hear two or three masses a day. These were, admittedly, low masses, that is spoken not sung, which did not take very long, and the king received communion only at major festivals such as Christmas and Easter. However, such a habit indicates a notable level of devotion, which was commented upon, and serves to remind us that his indifference to shrines and to the regular life does not necessarily indicate a secular turn of mind. Preachers, particularly learned ones like the humanist John Colet, dean of St Paul's, were much favoured, and apparently accorded a freedom of speech that normal courtiers could only dream about.[5] It must also be remembered that piety was a part of the chivalric culture that Henry had absorbed from his Burgundian forebears. Henry saw himself as a knight, but, like the Arthurian

Sir Bedevere, very much a Christian knight, which was one of the reasons why he was so keen to be on the same side as the pope in 1512. The knights of the Garter were devoted to deeds of the faith as well as heroism; indeed they probably would not have made any distinction between them. In spite of his learning and humanist mind-set, there was a superstitious streak in Henry's nature that was to become important in due course, and was to account for some of the apparent contradictions in his later behaviour.

Henry's first brush with the Church had nothing to do with his personal piety. There had for many years been concern in England about the exemptions that the clergy enjoyed from normal royal jurisdiction. This focused partly on the alleged abuse of ecclesiastical sanctuaries, where, it was claimed, criminals were inadequately supervised and allowed to continue their depredations unimpeded;[6] but more importantly, the concern focused on so-called 'benefit of clergy'. This was an ancient custom that entitled anyone in holy orders to claim trial by an ecclesiastical court. This privilege had long since been confined to first offences, but given the lenient judgements handed down by the Church courts, it was still a considerable immunity.

There was little general anticlericalism in the pre-Reformation English Church, but this was a sharp point of grievance; and only the king could do anything about it. In 1512 an act of Parliament circumscribed the privilege further, confining it to certain offences, but two years later a papal declaration laid down that all such limitations were contrary to the law of God.[7] In the early days of the reign, Edmund Dudley, writing his testament in the Tower, had declared that only the king could manage the affairs of the Church within his realm, a view that (had he known about it) Leo X would certainly have anathematized even more emphatically. The seeds of a first-class row had therefore been sown long before anyone had heard of Luther, or his protest.

The quarrel that actually arose, however, was not between the king and the pope but between the Bishop of London and the secular jurisdiction of the city. In 1511 one Richard Hunne, a rich but cantankerous merchant, had become embroiled in a legal dispute with his curate, in the course of which Hunne had brought a writ of *praemunire*, alleging clerical infringement of secular jurisdiction.[8] The curate then accused Hunne of heresy, whereupon Hunne was arrested and subsequently died in the bishop's prison. The London coroner's court indicted three of the bishop's officials for murder, and the bishop was forced to wade in to prevent the case being brought to trial. Feelings ran high, appeal was made to the king, and debates held in Parliament. Extreme positions were taken on both sides, and the anticlericals were threatened with charges of heresy.[9]

This was guaranteed to exacerbate lay fury, because heresy belonged exclusively to the ecclesiastical courts, and such an accusation was seen as a mere ploy to stalemate secular jurisdiction. Wolsey struggled to make peace between the two sides, but the king was now a party rather than a mediator. Eventually Henry contented himself with a statement to the effect that he recognized no earthly superior, and called off the parliamentary bloodhounds. The issue was not resolved, but it was allowed to die down until it was revived in different circumstances 14 years later.

Perhaps the king feared that his equivocation on the issue of privileges had damaged his standing in Rome, or perhaps he was simply moved by a pious zeal, but as soon as he heard of Martin Luther's challenge to the religious status quo in Wittenberg, he put pen to paper in defence of the practice of 'indulgences', which Luther had so vigorously denounced. What Henry wrote was never published in its own right, but appears to have formed the first two chapters of the *Assertio septem sacramentorum* ('Assertion of the Seven Sacraments'), which appeared in 1521.[10] If that is correct, Henry showed a poor grasp of what Luther was about, and failed to rise above the conventional in his defence of Catholic teaching. The *Assertio* itself had a frankly political agenda, and was a rather unexpected response to Pope Leo's plea to Catholic monarchs for support against the recently excommunicated Luther, whose teachings were currently sweeping Germany. From the pen of a trained theologian it would be classed as a mediocre, if not an inadequate, piece of work, but as the product of so exalted an amateur it is not at all bad. Although it is, as one commentator has put it, 'shot through with semi-pelagianism'[11] —pelagianism being the belief that goodness of itself ensures a safe passage to heaven—it shows a sound grasp of the Scriptures, particularly of the Old Testament. As a response to Luther's *Babylonish Captivity*, a critical study of papal authority, it would hardly have moved many hearts or minds, but that was not really the point. Henry had laid down a marker of his own convictions and, more importantly, earned from the pope the cherished title 'Defender of the Faith'. He could now hold up his head in the company of the 'Most Catholic' king of Spain and the 'Most Christian' king of France.

In the course of the *Assertio* Henry had warmly defended the papal jurisdiction, and seems to have perceived nothing in it that was incompatible with his earlier assertion about having no superior in earth. The contradiction, however, was about to come back and haunt him, because one of the results of his superstitious streak was that he was inclined to seek for signs and portents. No portent could be more ominous than his lack of a male heir, and by 1527 Henry had become convinced—or had convinced himself—that his marriage was contrary to divine law.

It is easy to mock Henry's conscience, and to point out how convenient it was that his marriage should be deemed unlawful just when he was setting himself up with another woman. That, however, is to misjudge both the king and the situation. Anne Boleyn was not a factor in the early stages of these doubts, and we do not know how they first arose. Catherine later blamed Wolsey, and French representatives negotiating a marriage for Mary were also held responsible.[12] John Longland, the king's confessor, has also had the finger pointed at him. It is entirely likely that both Wolsey and Longland talked to the king about his doubts, but the chances are that the worries arose fundamentally from the nature of his own piety, and from the fact that he knew his Bible. Perhaps Henry was honest when he aired his doubts and asked for reassurance, or perhaps not. It is probable that the conviction did not come to him overnight, and that for some time he was, as he claimed, in genuine and painful perplexity.

However, it is clear that by 1529 Henry's mind was made up, and that what he faced with Catherine was a genuine battle between two opposed and complete convictions. It was, of course, Catherine's conviction as to the validity of her marriage that corresponded with the general perception. If there had been any canonical doubts about the marriage, the pope had dispensed them—and that was that. Consequently Henry found himself forced onto unfamiliar ground, where he was compelled to argue that the law of God as laid down in the Scriptures was absolute and not subject to any canonical manipulation, not even by the pope.[13]

This was uncomfortably close to the Lutheran position of *sola scriptura*—that the word of God must take precedence over any earthly authority—and although the king himself may not have been aware of this, some of his advisers undoubtedly were. Thomas Cranmer, busy about his justification of the king's position, and those who were responsible for the advice known as the *collectanea satis copiosa*, prepared in 1530, were all convinced that Julius II had acted beyond his powers in granting the dispensation, and were moving towards a position in which the papacy had no legitimate jurisdiction outside of the see of Rome.[14]

The king himself did not come to that position overnight, and as late as 1532 was still sending envoys to Rome in the hope of changing Pope Clement's mind. Whether it was the political circumstances of 1533 that forced him to make up his mind, or whether his decision generated the circumstances, we do not really know. What we do know is that by the summer of 1533 Henry had made up his mind that the Scriptures contained no justification for the claims that the popes had traditionally made, and that the *plenitudo potestatis*, that breadth of jurisdiction claimed by the papacy, was of purely human origin, designed to promote the 'lucre' of successive popes.

That this represented a change from the position Henry had taken in 1521, he freely admitted. 'Then,' he declared, 'we were but young and [had] but little experience in the feats of the world ... Now we write not as we did.'[15] From this position, once reached, neither persuasion nor changing circumstances would shift him. He may by that time have been listening to Cranmer, or to Thomas Cromwell, but there is no doubt that the king made his own decision, and otherwise conservative prelates such as Cuthbert Tunstall and Stephen Gardiner were forced to toe his line. The statutes that embodied the royal supremacy were probably drafted by Thomas Cromwell, but only in careful consultation with Henry, whose views they expressed. By 1535, following the execution of John Fisher and Thomas More, both Henry's orthodoxy and his humanist credentials lay in tatters. Henry was excommunicated on 30 August 1535, and the realm was in schism.[16]

These developments must have tested the king's idiosyncratic self-righteousness, but it showed no sign of buckling. Instead, he took his responsibilities as the Church's supreme head with great seriousness. He grappled with the problems of the Church in a way that neither Archbishop Warham nor Wolsey had attempted. Clergy who clung to the pope's authority were deemed traitors, and over forty of them were executed; but at the same time those who allowed themselves to be persuaded by Luther or Zwingli were regarded as heretics, and a number of them were burned.

One of the great changes that came about in the 1530s was in the official attitude to the Bible. When William Tyndale had first translated the New Testament into modern English in 1526, his book was burned and Bishop Tunstall claimed to find over 2,000 errors in the translation.[17] Tyndale himself was burned as a heretic in the Low Countries in 1535, but within four years a vernacular Bible (see plate 27), which was very largely his work, was not merely approved for publication in England, but was prescribed for use in churches.[18] Glad though Cranmer and Cromwell may have been at this development, and strongly as they may have urged it, the decision was once again the king's. He was proud of his biblical knowledge, and he annotated the draft of the translation before it was published; but he was equally convinced that the Bible was the word of God, and that its saving message should be available to all his subjects. He did not accept the Protestant view that the Bible contained everything necessary for a man's salvation, but in rejecting the papacy he had blown a large hole in the argument from tradition, and what remained was his own (more or less arbitrary) choice. He similarly used his own discretion in pruning the calendar of the Church, which had become somewhat overgrown with festivals and days of obligation. A number of these were removed altogether by proclamation, particularly with a view to facilitating the harvest, and festivals of patron saints were ordered to be concentrated upon a single day.[19]

What all this tells us about the king's piety is that there were large grey areas—*adiaphora* (literally 'things indifferent'), as it was becoming fashionable to call them—and that he was following his own agenda. Conservatives disliked the English Bible; reformers were deeply suspicious of the king's continued devotion to the mass, which seems to have risen to three or even four performances a day by this time; and hardly any educated divine (or privy councillor) agreed with him every step of the way. The Bishops Book of 1537, and the royal injunctions of 1536 and 1538, although issued by Cromwell in his role as vice-regent in spirituals, nevertheless reflected accurately the balance of the king's mind at that particular moment.

THE FIRST ROYAL INJUNCTIONS OF HENRY VIII

Extract, 1536.

7. ITEM, *that every parson or proprietary of any parish church within this realm, shall on this side of the feast of St Peter ad Vincula [1 August] next coming provide a book of the whole bible, both in Latin and also in English, and lay the same in the*

choir for every man that will to look and read thereon, and shall
discourage no man from the reading of any part of the bible, either
in Latin or in English; but rather comfort, exhort and admonish
every man to read the same as the very word of God, and the
spiritual food of man's soul, whereby they may the better know
their duties to God, to their sovereign lord the king, and their
neighbour: ever gently and charitably exhorting them that using a
sober and modest behaviour in the reading and inquisition of the
true sense of the same, they do in no wise stiffly or eagerly contend
or strive one with another about the same but refer the declaration
of those places that be in controversy to the judgement of them that
be better learned.

[Taken from W.H. Frere and W.M. Kennedy, *Visitation Articles and Injunctions of the Period of the Reformation*, 1910, p. 9. Original in Corpus Christi College, Cambridge, vol. cxxi, p. 483.]

If most people at the time, and many historians since, believed that the royal supremacy was all about the king 'changing his woman', they did Henry a serious injustice. By 1536 he believed, passionately and sincerely, that God had entrusted him with the Church of England, and that he would eventually be answerable for the purity of its faith. Similarly, those who have argued that his campaign against pilgrimages and shrines in 1537 and 1538 was a cynical exercise, one designed to provide a pretext for widespread looting, have missed the point.

Henry had never been particularly keen on pilgrimages, in which, as in other things, he followed the lead of Erasmus. Nor was he enthusiastic about what he called 'popish purgatory', which he interpreted to mean a mechanistic view of the efficacy of requiem masses and prayers for the dead.[20] He was not against such prayers or masses, but believed them to be works of devotion that did not work automatically.[21] Their effect, in short, depended upon the will of God, not upon any papal decree. Nor was there any additional merit in going to a particular place to offer them. Genuine saints, and that included the Virgin Mary, were worthy of all honour and respect, but should not be worshipped as though they had a stake in the Godhead. Many saints, in any case, were bogus, and they (and their relics) were merely set up by greedy clergy to con the gullible. The most bogus saint of them all was Thomas Becket, who had merely been a traitor to his ancestor, Henry II, and had frustrated his reforming intentions for the Church.[22] Saints, it should be said, were not the king's particular type of superstition. So purgatory was sidelined (although not rejected) in Henry's Ten Articles of 1537, and the shrines were demolished. The work was carried out by royal commissioners, and cartloads of valuables were removed to the royal coffers. Some, of course, stuck to the hands of agents on the way, and this surreptitious distribution facilitated the work, because even in conservative places like Durham, where 'St Cuthbert' had been a rallying cry for centuries, and there was much resentment, there was no overt resistance.

Alongside this policy, and closely related to it, came an even more dramatic assault on traditional religion—the dissolution of the regular religious orders. The king had never been a patron of the monks, but nothing can have prepared the clergy at large, let alone the laity, for such a radical development. The traditional explanation is that Thomas Cromwell, who monopolized the king's attention at this time, spied an opportunity to create a vast new landed estate for the crown, and persuaded the king by pointing out that the regulars were the most tiresome adherents of his enemy the pope. The latter assertion was true to only a very limited extent, because most houses were in the hands of those who acquiesced to the royal supremacy well before the policy of dissolution began; and the former point misrepresents the nature of the relationship between the king and his chief minister.

It was not Cromwell's business to form policy (any more than it had been Wolsey's); Cromwell's task was to advise the king of the likely consequences of his various policy options, and when the latter had made up his mind, to devise ways and means of implementation.[23] It may well have been Cromwell's idea to go for the smaller houses first, and to proceed by statute rather than prerogative, but the policy itself reflected the king's own sense of religious responsibility.[24] At first it seems that his mind was not quite made up, and when the first teams of investigators were sent out in 1535, their reports were equivocal. It is possible that at this point his chief minister decided that the king needed a nudge, because as the later reports came in, they became increasingly negative, and it is thought that this was a consequence of some modification in the instructions, probably conveyed verbally.[25]

However it came about, by 1536 the king had become convinced that the smaller monasteries were sinks of iniquity—and useless into the bargain. Why, however, was the distinction between the 'vicious, carnal and abominable' smaller houses and the 'great and honourable' ones fixed at 'a clear yearly value of £200'?[26] The natural suspicion is that this was simply an expedient, a seizure that the king thought that he could get away with, because in fact many small houses were in a bad way. Thus the seizure of the small houses could be represented as a worthy reform, rather than an attack on the whole system.

THE DISSOLUTION OF THE MONASTERIES

Instructions to the Commissioners, November 1536.

1. *The Commissioners shall first repair to the monasteries, and take into their hands the common and convent seals, and cause them to be broken or kept to the King's use.*

2. *They shall call before them the governors and officers of the said houses, and order them to declare upon oath the state and plight of the houses, and what leases, corrodies,* fees etc have been granted by them before 4 February 27 Henry VIII [1536].*

3. *They shall make a true inventory of the lead, bells and superfluous buildings, and of all plate, jewels, ornaments, good, chattels, debts, corn stock and store of the said houses.*

4. *They survey all the possessions, spiritual and temporal of the same houses, in the form heretofore used of such other like houses*

of religion dissolved by reason of the said Act of Parliament
[Statute 27 Henry VIII, c.28].

5. They shall enquire of the debts due to the house.

6. And put in safe custody to the king's use all evidences and writings.

7. They shall appoint pensions to the governors and notify them to the Chancellor and Council of the Court of Augmentations, with the latest values of the possessions, then dispatch the governors and all other religious persons with convenient rewards.

8. They shall make letters for the capacities of the governors and other religious persons, to be obtained gratis, in the manner used in other houses heretofore suppressed.†

9. They shall sell all the corn, grain, household stuff etc. except the lead, bells, plate, jewels and principle ornaments in the form heretofore accustomed under the act.

10. They shall pay all the servants wages and debts due for corn, cattle, victuals etc, and all other debts not exceeding £6 13s 4d.

11. They shall deliver possession to such persons as the king shall appoint.

12. They shall certify their proceedings under their seals and signs manual at the day limited.

[Taken from *Letters and Papers*, XI, Appendix, 15. Original TNA SP1.]

* corrodies = monastic places available to lay persons on payment of a sum.

† Item 8 is deleted in the manuscript.

It may indeed be that the king was feeling his way, because the preamble to the statute is distinctly contradictory as a religious statement. Had Henry been as tentative as this suggests, however, it might have been expected that the Pilgrimage of Grace against the king's religious policies (see Chapter 7) would have served as a deterrent. In fact no such withdrawal took place. Instead pressure began to be applied to the larger houses, and they surrendered one by one, finishing with Waltham Abbey on 23 March 1540.[27] Henry's profession of respect for the large houses, expressed in 1536, was either fraudulent or overtaken by events. As we have seen over the papal authority, the king's conscience was not immune from evolution, and it may well be that at some point between the summer of 1536 and the summer of 1539 Henry finally became convinced that the whole system was rotten beyond redemption.

If that is what happened, a number of pragmatic events may have assisted in the process. In the first place the reports of his commissioners made no distinction between great and small; according to them it was simply not true that small houses were corrupt and great ones not. All were tarred with the same brush. Secondly, the part that the regulars had played in the Pilgrimage of Grace was sufficient to infect them all with the scent of treason. Finally, the reaction of the majority of the nobility and gentry of the realm was not one of shock or resentment, but rather a clamour for a share of the spoils.[28]

It does not look as though this vast operation was carefully planned, by Cromwell or anyone else. The pressure applied to abbots and priors was *ad hoc* and opportunist, not via any general statement or threat, and lands began to be sold piecemeal as the surrenders took place. The only development that argues a degree of planning was the erection of the Court of Augmentations in April 1536, but that was before even the smaller monasteries had gone, and apparently before any decision had been taken against the greater ones.

Great as the financial gains were to be over the next few years, the dissolution of the monasteries should not be seen primarily as a huge manipulation of the land market, but as an aspect of Henry's perception of his duty of stewardship. This can be well illustrated by what happened at Boxley Priory in Kent. Boxley was a minor house except in one respect: it had an ostensibly miraculous rood, which interacted in various ways with the devotees who came to see its marvels in great numbers. Such pilgrims kept the canons in considerable comfort as a result. When the house was dissolved in February 1538 however, the rood came under scrutiny. It was revealed to be hollow, fitted inside with various ingenious wires that had enabled the attendant canon to manipulate the image's reactions in whatever way seemed appropriate. The fraud was exposed in a stinging sermon, and the rood consigned to the flames.[29]

Boxley was not the only example; similar frauds were detected at Bury St Edmunds and Bermondsey and (most scandalous of all) the celebrated blood of Hailes, venerated for generation, was exposed as a kind of gum—or, according to some accounts, the blood of a duck.[30] Henry was genuinely outraged by these deceptions; the simple faith of his people was being mocked by wicked and fraudulent monks. It is not surprising that papal authority, superstition, monasticism and treason should have coalesced in his mind into one malign conspiracy.

The king's stewardship was shown to the friars of his realm in rather a different way. In contrast to the situation in Ireland, the fortunes of the English friars were at a low ebb. By the late 1530s only about 10 per cent of benefactions for pious purposes was going to the mendicant orders, and nothing was being received in London.[31] The reason for this is not very clear, but fashions in piety change unaccountably, and by 1538 the English friars were seriously unfashionable. In February of that year Richard Ingworth, Cranmer's suffragan, was commissioned to make a visitation, and he found, or purported to find, that the great majority of friaries were economically unviable. By presenting his findings as he did, he was able to persuade most of them into voluntary surrender.[32] Those friaries that could not be persuaded were gently coerced by threats of draconian reforms, and while most eyes were on the downfall of the great monasteries, the friars were quietly extinguished.

In theory the same condition applied as applied to the monks, who were pensioned in proportion to the resources of their houses, but the friaries were too poor to provide anyone with a living, and the Franciscans, Dominicans and Augustinians were swiftly absorbed into the parochial ministry—a process made easier by the fact that they had never been cloistered in the first place.

Nobody ever accused Henry of dissolving the friaries for their resources, nor were they conspicuously 'papist', so the reason for their demise must be that the king had decided that they no longer discharged any useful function—the same consideration, ultimately, that led to the dispersal of the monks. There were better ways, Henry believed, for the charitable donations of the godly to be used in the service of Christ than by supporting professional beggars, or idle and dissolute cloisterers.

When it came to the redeployment of monastic resources, however, the king did not set a conspicuously good example. In spite of Archbishop Cranmer's urgent pleas for a re-endowment of the parochial ministry, most of the former monastic lands, with a capital value of about £1,250,000, a truly massive sum in today's terms, were either sold or remained in the hands of the Court of Augmentations. Nevertheless, something positive was achieved. Six new bishoprics were erected, at Westminster, Peterborough, Gloucester, Chester, Oxford and Bristol; two new university colleges were founded on a grand scale, one at Trinity, Cambridge, and one at Christ Church, Oxford; and several Regius teaching positions in theology, Greek and Hebrew were endowed in both universities.[33]

The proportion of the available resources so allocated was fairly small, but it was sufficient to indicate that Henry's mindset had not changed. Both education and the effective administration of the Church remained priorities. Nor had the king's mind changed in other respects. There were those who saw his assault on monastic superstitions as an indication that his alliance of convenience with the reformers over papal jurisdiction was turning into something more positive. But such people were in for a big disappointment. This was indicated when Henry chose to display his convictions and his Bible learning in the show trial of the unfortunate John Lambert in 1538. Lambert was a sacramentarian, a follower of Ulrich Zwingli, who denied any corporeal presence of Christ in the communion bread and wine. Lambert was humble, but defiant, yielding himself only to the king's mercy. A generation

later, in *Acts and Monuments*, the Protestant martyrologist John
Foxe gave an outraged account of the trial:

A T THE LAST, *the king himself did come as judge of that great
controversy, with a great guard, clothed all in white, as covering
by that colour and dissimuling severity of all bloody judgement ...
   But the king being hasty, with anger and vehemency said: why
standest thou still? Answer as touching the Sacrament of the altar,
whether doest thou say that it is the body of Christ, or wilt deny
it? And with that word the king lifted up his cap.*

LAMBERT: *I answer with S. Augustine, that it is the body of
   Christ, after a certain manner.*
THE KING: *Answer me neither out of St Augustine, neither by
   the authority of any other, but tell me plainly whether thou saiest
   it is the body of Christ, or no? These words the king spake again
   in Latin.*
LAMBERT: *Then I deny it to be the body of Christ.*
THE KING: *Mark well; for now thou shalt be condemned even
   by Christ's own Words: hoc est corpus meum ...*

Lambert had, however, touched the very centre of the king's
faith, and in conclusion Henry (in Foxe's version) said:

*... yield not to me, I am a mortal man, and therewith rising up
and turning to the sacrament, and pulling off his bonnet, said,
yonder is the master of us all, author of truth, yield in truth to
him, that truth I will defend ...*[34]

Lambert was burned, and Foxe professed himself to be bewil-
dered by what he saw as this reactionary twist in the king's policy,
and his explanation has always received far more credit than it
deserved:

*... while [good] council was about him and could be heard, he
did much good, so again when sinister and wicked councillors
under subtle and crafty pretences had gotten ever the foot in,*

> *thrusting truth and verity out of the prince's ears, how much*
> *religion and all good things went prosperously forward before, so*
> *much on the contrary side all revolted backwards again ...*[35]

In other words the godly advice of Cranmer and Cromwell was now being undermined by the malign influence of Foxe's *bête noire*, Stephen Gardiner, Bishop of Winchester.

Such an explanation is neither plausible nor necessary. Whatever doubts Henry may have had about purgatory and other 'popish superstitions', he had never wavered in his devotion to the seven sacraments. However, by 1538 he may well have felt that he had left himself open to interested misrepresentation in that respect, and that the time had come to lay down a few guidelines. This he did—comprehensively—in the so-called Act of Six Articles of 1539, properly (and optimistically) entitled 'An Act for Abolishing Diversity in Opinions'.[36]

This statute was drafted by the king personally, and reflects his own priorities. Three of the articles dealt with the mass, one with marriage, one with vows, and one with auricular confession. Each was directed specifically against reformed teaching. Transubstantiation was reaffirmed, likewise the validity of private masses and the need for communion under one kind only (i.e. with just the bread). The marriage of clergy was denounced, auricular confession described as 'expedient and necessary', and, rather incongruously, the validity of vows of chastity upheld. This last is a sure sign of the king's own hand, because it made no logical sense to dissolve vows of poverty and obedience by abolishing monasteries, and yet insist upon the remaining vow of chastity—especially in the case of those who were not ordained.

Cranmer, as Henry well understood, was deeply distressed by these conservative affirmations, which were contrary to the tenor of his advice.[37] The fact that he retained his position, and his place in the king's confidence, is sufficient indication that both understood their respective roles. Henry was quite willing to listen, whether he accepted the advice that he was given or not—and on the one doctrine that really mattered to him, there was no rift between them. In that respect, Thomas Cromwell was to prove less sure footed. He had, admittedly, the more difficult task in that he was trying to exploit the firm antipapalism of the reformed preachers without allowing them to beat other Protestant drums. In 1538–9 there was a scandal in Calais, where his zeal to expose a popish conspiracy led to his turning a blind eye to the obvious radicalism of the preacher Adam Damplip.[38] By exploiting this error to the full, and making maximum use of other more ambiguous evidence, Cromwell's enemies, particularly Stephen Gardiner and the Duke of Norfolk, succeeded in turning the king's mind against his minister. With the same kind of mental gymnastics that had undone Anne Boleyn, Henry became convinced that Cromwell was that unforgivable sinner, a sacramentarian. It was no more likely that Cromwell was a Protestant than that Anne Boleyn had been an adultress and a witch, but once the king was convinced — his fate was sealed.

THE ACT OF SIX ARTICLES
Extract from 'An Act abolishing diversity in opinions', 1539.

W HEREUPON *after great and long deliberation and advised disputation and consultation had and made concerning the said articles, as well by the consent of the king's Highness as by the assent of the lords spiritual and temporal and other learned men of his clergy in their Convocation, and by the consent of the Commons in this present parliament assembled, it was and is finally resolved accorded and agreed in manner and form following; that is to say.*

First, that in the most blessed Sacrament of the Altar, by the strength and efficacy of Christ's mighty word, it being spoken by the priest, is present really and under the form of bread and wine, the natural body and blood of our Saviour Jesus Christ, conceived of the Virgin Mary, and that after the consecration there remaineth no substance of bread or wine, nor any other substance but the substance of Christ, God and Man;

Secondly that communion in both kinds is not necessary ad salutem *by the law of God to all persons; And that it is to be believed and not doubted, but that in the flesh under the form of bread is the very body, and with the blood under the form of wine is the very flesh, as well apart as though they were both together;*

Thirdly that Priests after the Order of Priesthood received as afore may not marry by the law of God;

Fourthly that vows of Chastity or widowhood by Man or Woman, made to God advisedly ought to be observed by the law of God, and that it exempteth from other liberties of Christian people which without that they might enjoy;

Fifthly, that it is meet and necessary that private masses be continued and admitted in the King's English Church and Congregation, as whereby good Christian people ordering them-selves accordingly do receive both godly and goodly consolations and benefits; and it is agreeable also to God's law;

Sixthly that auricular confession is expedient and necessary to be retained and continued, used and frequented in the church of God …

[Statute 31 Henry VIII, c.14. Taken from *Statutes of the Realm*, III, pp. 739–40.]

It is alleged that Cromwell's execution and the Act of Six Articles forced the reformers onto the defensive, but the evidence for committed persecution is slight. The radical Protestant John Hooper, whom Queen Mary later burnt, felt it advisable to leave the country, and a few days after Cromwell's execution the Lutheran Robert Barnes and two other Protestants went to the stake.[39] However, Hugh Latimer was permitted (most unusually) to resign his see of Worcester, and in a gruesome demonstration of even-handedness, three papists were executed for treason at Tyburn.

Only in one respect did Henry draw back from a reforming position that he had publicly endorsed, and that was over the availability of the English Bible. Perhaps the king was naive, or perhaps he had been convinced by an equally naive Cranmer, but he seems to have believed that the availability of the 'plain sense'

of God's word in English would put an end to disruptive controversy. It soon became apparent that the very opposite was true,
and he was to see the Scriptures 'jangled and disputed' in every
bar and alehouse. This deeply offended Henry, whose sense of the
sacredness of Holy Writ was as profound in its own way as his
conviction over transubstantiation. (As previously mentioned, he
continued to regard William Tyndale as a heretic, and seems to
have been unaware of the extent to which the Great Bible was, in
fact, Tyndale's work.) Cranmer and his allies began to fear a major
reversal of policy, and in March 1542 they bought some time by
persuading the king to refer the legitimacy of the vernacular
Bible to the universities for an opinion. In the event that opinion
was never delivered because a compromise was reached. In the
spring of 1543 a bill was introduced into Parliament condemning
'crafty, false and untrue' translations, and confining access to the
licensed Great Bible.[40]

This was a victory for the reformers, because it endorsed their
main position, and because it is by no means clear which alternative translations were being targeted. The compromise lay in the
fact that access was now supposed to be restricted to noblemen,
gentlemen, merchants and their families. This created a nonsense
because the 1538 injunctions, requiring a bible to be kept in every
church, were not withdrawn. Presumably whether this new law
was actually enforced depended upon the religious climate of every
particular parish, and the convictions of the incumbent. No sys-
tematic attempt at enforcement seems to have been made, and the
1543 act has to be seen as a gesture of unease on Henry's part, rather
than as anything more purposeful.

It is sometimes supposed that the fall of Catherine Howard at
the end of 1541, and the consequent disgrace of the Howards,
marked another turning point in the roller coaster of Henry's religious policy. The reformers were back! In truth they had never
been away, because not only did Cranmer remain in the council,
but as we have seen several of Cromwell's men continued in the
privy chamber.

HENRY'S RELATIONS WITH CRANMER

O N THE MORROW, *about nine of the clock before noon, the council sent a gentleman usher for the archbishop, who when he came to the council chamber door, could not be let in, but of a purpose, as it seemed, was compelled there to wait among the pages, lackeys and serving men, all alone. Doctor Butts, the King's physician, resorting that way, and espying how my lord of Canterbury was handled, went to the King's highness and said; 'My Lord of Canterbury, if it please your grace, is well promoted, for now he is become a lackey or serving man, for yonder he standeth this half hour without the council chamber door amongst them.' 'It is not so,' quoth the King, 'I trow, nor the council hath so little discretion as to use the metropolitan of the realm in that sort, specially being one of their own number; but let them alone,' said the king, 'and we shall hear more soon.'*

Anon the archbishop was called into the council chamber, to whom was alleged as before I'd rehearsed [referring to the previously discussed preaching and teaching of heresy]. *The archbishop answered in like sort as the king had advised him; and in the end, when he perceived that no manner of persuasion or entreaty could serve, he delivered to them the king's ring, revoking his cause into the king's hands. The whole council being somewhat amazed, the Earl of Bedford with a loud voice, confirming his words with a solemn oath, said, 'When you first began this matter, my Lords, I told you what would come of it. Do you think that the king will suffer this man's finger to ache? Much more, I warrant you, will he defend his life against brabbling* [brawling] *varlets. You do but cumber yourselves to hear tales and fables against him.' And so, incontinently, upon receipt of the King's token, they all rose and carried to the King his ring, surrendering that matter … into his own hands.*

When they were all come into the King's presence, his highness with a severe countenance said unto them, 'Ah, my lords, I thought I had wiser men of my council than now I find you. What discretion was this in you thus to make the primate of the realm,

and one of you in office, to wait at the council chamber door
among serving men? You might have considered that he was a
councillor as well as you, and you had no such commission of me
so to handle him. I was content that you should try him as a
councillor, and not as a mean subject. But now I well perceive that
things be done against him maliciously; and if some of you might
have had your minds, you would have tried him to the uttermost.
But I do you all to wit, and protest, that if a prince may be
beholden unto his subject' (and so solemnly laying his hand upon
his breast, said) 'By the faith I owe to God, I take this man here,
my lord of Canterbury, to be of all other a most faithful subject
unto us, and one to whom we are much beholden,' giving him
great commendation otherwise … And with that every man
caught him by the hand and made fair weather of altogethers
[*made up their dispute*] …

[Taken from the introduction to *The Writings and Disputations of
Thomas Cranmer, Archbishop of Canterbury,* ed. J.E. Cox, 1844. Based
upon a narrative from John Foxe's *Acts and Monuments.*]

Moreover, such an interpretation, of returning reformers, would
not fit with the timing of the Act for the Advancement of True
Religion, which we have just noticed. The king's return to more
or less godly ways after 1543 has to be seen in the context of his
growing anxiety over the succession. As his health (and his temper)
deteriorated, he became increasingly concerned by the fact that
Edward was likely to succeed as a minor. It was therefore imperative that those who had the care of his son, both now and after his
own death, should be men of his way of thinking. The tutors
whom he appointed, particularly Cox and Cheke, were first and
foremost men of the New Learning, who would give the boy a
sound classical and biblical training.[41] They were also known anti-
papalists, and that was important in the context of preserving the
royal supremacy. That they may have been crypto-Protestants,
Henry probably neither knew nor cared.

A similar consideration dictated the rise of the Seymours and of John Dudley to influence in the council, and the eventual eclipse of both Gardiner and the Howards. Henry had to be satisfied in his own mind that the men who would run the country during Edward's minority would be as committed to the supremacy as he was himself, and in that his judgement was sound. That Henry never budged in his aversion to sacramentarian heresy or in his commitment to the mass can be seen both from his will and from the continued incineration of offenders such as the out-and-out heretic Anne Askew.

Henry did listen to his advisers on religious matters, and did occasionally change his mind, but the core of his faith remained inflexible and untouched, and the direction of policy was always at his own choice and discretion. His so-called inconsistencies and reversals lay rather in the perception of those who recorded them than they did in any changes in himself. Nevertheless it should be remembered that there were undefined areas in the king's faith, particularly over how the Scriptures should be interpreted and presented, and over such matters as purgatory, where even the King's Book of 1543, a revision of the Bishops Book of doctrinal statements, remained ambiguous and uncertain.[42] However, the most telling image of the king's religion comes in the story of his alleged brush with his last queen, Catherine Parr, whom the conservatives believed they had ensnared in heresy.

THE PLOT AGAINST CATHERINE PARR

T̲HE QUEEN *all this while compassed about with enemies and persecutors, perceived nothing of all this, nor what was working against her, and what trappes were laid for her by [Stephen Gardiner, Bishop of] Winchester and his fellows: so closely the matter was conveyed. But see what the Lord God (who from his eternal throne of wisdom seeth and despatcheth all the inventions of Achitophel, and comprehendeth the wiley beguily themselves) did for his poor handmaiden in rescuing her from the pit of ruin, whereunto she was ready to fall unaware.*

For as the Lord would, so came it to pass, that the bill of articles drawn against the Queen, and subscribed with the king's own hand (although dissemblingly ye must understand) falling from the bosom of one of the foresaid councillors, was found and taken up of some Godly person, and brought immediately unto the Queen, who reading there the articles comprised against her, and perceiving the king's hand unto the same, for the sudden fear thereof fell incontinent into a great melancholy and agony, bewailing and taking on in such sort as was lamentable to see, as certain of her ladies and gentlewomen being yet alive, which were then present about her can testify ...

After this the Queen remembering with her self the word that M. Wendy had said unto her, devised how by some good opportunity she might repair to the king's presence. And so first commanding her ladies to convey away their books, which were against the law, the next night following after supper, she (waited upon only by the Lady Herbert her sister and the Lady Jane who carried the candle before her) went unto the king's chamber, whom she found sitting and talking with certain gentlemen of his Chamber, whom when the king did behold, he very courteously welcomed her, and breaking off the talk which before her coming he had with the gentlemen aforesaid, began of himself, contrary to his manner before accustomed, to enter into talk of religion, seeming as it were desirous to be resolved by the Queen of certain doubts which he propounded.

The Queen, perceiving to what purpose this talk did tend, not being unprovided in what sort to behave herself towards the king, with such answers resolved his questions as the time and opportunity present did require, mildly and with a reverent countenance answering again after this manner:

Your Majesty (quoth she) doth right well know, neither I myself am ignorant, what great imperfection and weakness, by our first creation is allotted unto us women, to be ordained and appointed as inferior and subject unto man as our head, from which head all our direction ought to proceed, and that as God

made man to his own shape and likeness, whereby he being
endued with more special gifts of perfection, might rather be
stirred to the contemplation of heavenly things, and to the earnest
endeavour to obey his commandments; even so also made he
woman of man, of whom and by whom she is to be governed,
commanded and directed. Whose womanly weakness & natural
imperfection, ought to be tolerated, aided and borne withal, so
that by his wisdom such things as be lacking in her ought to
be supplied.

Sithens [since then] therefore that God hath appointed such
a natural difference between man and woman, and your Majesty
being so excellent in gifts and ornaments of wisdom, and I a silly
poor woman so much inferior in all respects of nature unto you,
how then cometh it now to pass that your Majesty in such diffuse
causes of religion, will seem to require my judgement? Which
when I have uttered and said what I can, yet must I and will I,
refer my judgement in this and all other cases to your majesty's
wisdom, as my only anchor, supreme head and governor here in
earth next under God to lean unto.

Not so by St Mary quoth the King, you are become a Doctor,
Kate, to instruct us (as we take it) and not to be instructed or
directed by us.

If your Majesty take it so (quoth the Queen) then hath
your Majesty very much mistaken me, who have ever been of the
opinion, to think very unseemly and preposterous for the woman
to take upon her the office of an instructor or teacher to her lord
and husband, but rather to learn of her husband, & to be taught
by him. And where I have with your Majesty's leave heretofore
been bold to hold talk with your Majesty, wherein sometimes in
opinion there hath seemed some difference, I have not done it
so much to maintain opinion, as I did it rather to minister talk,
not only to the end that your Majesty might with less grief pass
over this painful time of your infirmity ... and hoping that your
Majesty should reap some ease thereby; but also that I hearing
your Majesty's learned discourse, might receive to myself some

*profit therefrom. Whereunto I assure your Majesty I have not
missed any part of my desire in that behalf, always referring myself
in all such matters unto your Majesty, as by ordinance of nature it
is convenient for me to do.*

*And is it even so, sweetheart, quoth the King? And tended
your arguments to no worse end? Then perfect friends are we as
ever at any time heretofore ...*

[John Foxe, *Actes and Monuments of the English Martyrs*, 1583, pp. 1242–3.]

Whether the story is true or not, it is authentic in one respect.
Henry would listen to religious discussion, take part in it, and
even tolerate different points of view, but he would not be lectured or dictated to. Catherine's fault, in his eyes, was not that she
held unorthodox views, but that she believed that she had a mission to convert her husband. When he became convinced that
this was not so, sweetness and light were restored, to the con-
founding of the conspirators.

Of all the king's qualities, that of his religion has been the most
controversial. Incensed by what he takes to be Foxe's misrepresentation, and by the extent to which that lead has been followed,
George Bernard has recently devoted a book of great weight and
erudition, *The King's Reformation*, to proving Henry's total consis-
tency and sense of purpose. As against Foxe's view of a vacillating
king dominated by his council (a view necessitated by the martyrologist's agenda) this is totally convincing, but as a portrait of a
king who never changed his mind, and always knew exactly what
he was doing, it is less so.

The two keys to the king's faith were the mass and the Scriptures. The fact that these were uneasy bedfellows, and that transubstantiation was a medieval invention, he would never for one
moment admit. The pope he could reject, and even the other sacraments could be debated, but on the mass he was totally inflexible.
Some superstitions, such as the 'Holy Blood' of Hailes, he rejected
with genuine horror; others, such as the portents of childlessness
or of witchcraft, he embraced with momentous consequences. In

other words, he was a man like any other, by turns obstinate and conciliatory, rigid and flexible. The one area in which he was absolutely consistent, at least after 1533, was in the conviction that it was the will of God that he should act as steward of the English Church, and that it was his responsibility not only to administer it, but also to determine in what ways the truth was to be presented to his subjects, for whose eternal welfare he bore such an onerous responsibility.

§10 The King's Last Years

HENRY HAD ALWAYS dominated those about him. His gigantic physique had towered over courtiers and companions alike, and in decay his bulk was awe inspiring, like a beached and disintegrating dreadnought. His dominating personality, unpredictable humours and powerful intellect had formed the centre of the political world for as long as any but his oldest servants could remember. Apart from the three years from 1529 to 1532 this had been partly screened from the public view by the existence of his two great ministers, Thomas Wolsey and Thomas Cromwell. Between them they had served him for 25 years, advising, manipulating, facilitating, and obligingly taking the blame for unpopular actions and policies. They had preserved the myth of royal infallibility, which had enabled opponents of the king's policies, from Catherine of Aragon to Robert Aske, to convince themselves that they were serving Henry's 'true' interests, or preserving his honour from the machinations of evil councillors.

Of course, such service had not been altogether altruistic. Both men had made vast personal fortunes out of controlling royal patronage, but after 1540 they were gone. Cromwell was never replaced, and although later councillors such as Stephen Gardiner, Thomas Wriothesley and Edward Seymour were powerful figures, they never screened the king in the way that Cromwell had done. After 1540 there was no doubt that the king's pleasure should be gratified, but, as his health and temper deteriorated, second guessing what that might be became increasingly tricky.

In a sense Henry had always lived in a fantasy world, where the human reality was so cloaked in symbolism as to become almost invisible. His honour, for example, which to the modern observer is so intangible and subjective, was to him as real as a piece of jewellery.[1] This sense of honour was partly military, and consisted mainly in the winning of battles. In spite of his jousting prowess Henry never (as far as we know) fought any personal combat; nor did he often command armies in person. Nevertheless it was the king's honour that was slighted by any lack of success in the field. The king's honour was also partly intellectual. The king must never be 'put down' in disputation or argument, which is one of the reasons why the evidence of his thoughts, in so many of the glosses and annotations that he made to texts, remained private.[2] When he did pronounce upon a doctrine or principle (as he did against the pope), then it immediately became heresy or high treason to disagree. So the king's honour lay in enforcing his will, and he was dishonoured by principled opposition, which was why he was so fierce against Robert Aske and Lord Darcy.

Finally, the king's honour was also partly sexual, and that was always a problematic area. Ideally a great king should have a clutch of legitimate children (as Edward III had had)—and a string of bastards, although frowned on by the Church, would do his image no harm at all. By 1520 Henry had two children by two different women, but for 14 years afterwards no child was born to the king, and his second known mistress, Mary Boleyn, never conceived. Anne Boleyn, when they eventually slept together, conceived promptly, but certain rather snide comments, attributed to his second queen and her friends at the time of her downfall, suggest that Henry was not only a very erratic performer by then, but was known to be so in the confines of the boudoir.[3] It was this 'touching' of his honour that made the king so willing to believe the charges against Anne. In mocking Henry's prowess, Anne had committed the sin against the Holy Ghost.

Jane Seymour conceived only once, but then her marriage lasted only 15 months, during which time the king is not known to have consoled himself with any other woman. By 1538 Henry was nothing like the stud that his honour demanded, and he was well aware of the fact. His problems with Anne of Cleves were, of course, all her fault, but his shattering experience with Catherine Howard left his manhood in tatters, and it had to be salvaged with vengeful fury. While any husband might have been entitled to feel betrayed by Catherine's behaviour, for the king it was an unspeakable humiliation.

When Henry eventually recovered, in 1542, nothing (naturally) was said, but the symbolic language subtly changed. He married again, but the air of expectation was restrained, and in effect war and policy took on the burden of sustaining his honour during the last six years of his life. In this respect, his relationship with God became increasingly important. Christian princes had always represented themselves as servants of God, usually in the context of defending the liberties of the Church, and at first Henry had been no different. As we have seen, however, his quarrel with the pope brought about a change in this relationship. Henry made himself responsible for the Church in a way that his predecessors had not been—at least not since Anglo-Saxon times —and his obedience to God now sailed into uncharted waters.

Not only did Henry's eternal salvation depend upon getting his decisions right, his honour also was at stake. It had been easy to do the right thing as long as someone else was making the rules, but now Henry had to make the rules himself, and his sense of conviction had to be expressed by great firmness against dissenters of all kinds.[4] He trod this narrow tightrope of his own creation with great determination during these later years, and one of his absorbing concerns became the preservation of this precarious balance beyond his own lifetime; in other words to ensure that his successor served God with the same fervour, and in the same sense, that he had done himself. There was no vice-regent in spirituals after Thomas Cromwell's fall—no one else to take the blame—and the king was left face to face with his Creator.

In March 1541 Henry had almost died. Many years of hard knocks in the lists had left him with bruised and ulcerated legs that had never completely healed, and at that point the ulcers closed, leaving him speechless and with a raging fever.[5] The crisis passed, but it served to alert everyone to just how fragile the king's health had now become. He was barely 50, but had already passed the average life expectancy of the time and was becoming, in 16th-century terms, an old man. What exactly ailed him has been the subject of much controversy. It was not venereal disease, specifically syphilis—a theory that was not suggested until 1888.[6] The symptoms are not consistent, and none of his children showed the signs of a syphilitic parent. Both his sons died in their teens, but his elder daughter lived an average span (43 years) and his younger an exceptionally long one (70). Moreover there is abundant evidence that Henry's mind remained extremely clear until the very last hours of his life, which would not be consistent with syphilitic deterioration.

It is possible that he never fully recovered from the disastrous fall that terminated his jousting career in 1536, a fall that had left him unconscious for several hours. It has been alleged that the severe headaches from which he suffered in later life, together with the extreme irascibility that afflicted him from time to time, are evidence of some residual brain damage from that accident, but he had always been of uncertain temper, and the severe pain from which he suffered in his legs was enough to make anyone bad tempered.[7] In all probability his condition was due to nothing more dramatic than the cumulative effects of years of overindulgence in a rich, ill-balanced diet, and the consequences of too much exercise of the wrong kind in youth, followed by insufficient exercise in middle age, all of which would have placed an undue strain upon his heart and ruined his general constitution. His ulcerated legs were a separate problem, but one that might in itself have proved fatal, given the primitive state of contemporary medical knowledge.

The difficulty in attempting to assess Henry's attitude towards illness and his own mortality is that there is too much evidence. Every courtier and ambassador was fascinated by the spectacle, and commented at length—each from his own point of view.[8] The king's military and diplomatic activity, particularly the latter, suggest a man who not only had no intention of dying, but would recognize no diminution in his faculties either. On the other hand he suffered from well-attested bouts of melancholia, when his old tendency to self-pity was given full and exuberant rein. As the 1540s wore on he became increasingly immobile, having to be hoisted by crane onto his war horse during the Boulogne campaign, a procedure not dictated by the weight of his armour, which in his vigorous youth he had made light of.

The armour itself tells the same story: several suits survive that were made for him at different stages of his life, and their increasing girth is dramatic.[9] Intermittently he was in severe pain, and in those circumstances needed to be approached with extreme caution, having little control over himself at such times. It would seem that intellectually Henry knew that his time was short, and every bout of illness confirmed that, but emotionally he would admit no such thing, and every time he recovered (more or less) he was buoyed up by a fresh sense of optimism.

The two sides of this contradictory attitude can be seen on the one hand in the paranoid suspicion with which he seems to have regarded everyone about him, and on the other hand in the purposeful steps that he took to ensure the appropriate education and management of his son.[10] As Professor Baldwin Smith pointed out a number of years ago, it is very easy to read the history of these last seven years backwards, knowing that Henry would die in January 1547, and seeing everything as geared to that date.[11] Of course no one knew that at the time, and the provisional state of the will that Henry eventually left as his final testament is proof of the fact that his thought was still evolving at the very last moment. Nevertheless it is difficult not to see the fall of the most prominent conservatives on the council in terms of the succession. Indeed it was precisely because he pretended a claim to the throne that the Earl of Surrey was executed in the last days of the king's life.

The dismissal of Stephen Gardiner, Bishop of Winchester, is

more problematic. Ostensibly he was 'rusticated' because of a rather crass misunderstanding over an exchange of lands.[12] However, if that had been the whole story, then it is reasonable to suppose that the king's spat of anger would have passed, and that a man with so good a record of service would have been reinstated. Sir Anthony Browne, believing that to be the case, and assuming the bishop's omission from the king's will to have been inadvertent, drew Henry's attention to the fact. He was rewarded with a very revealing tirade, in the course of which the king pointed out that Gardiner was such a 'wilful' character that he could be ruled by no one except Henry himself. Left with any access to authority after the king's death, he would have been an ungovernable nuisance.[13] This does not, of course, mean that Henry was contemplating an early departure, but it does mean that the politics of 1546 were dominated by the likely succession of a minor. After all, Henry could have lived several more years and that would still have been the case.

Suspicious as Henry seems to have been of the motives of everyone around him, the fact remains that he chose eventually to trust men such as the Earl of Hertford, Lord Lisle and Sir William Paget, rather than the Duke of Norfolk, the Bishop of Winchester or Sir Thomas Wriothesley, and the reason for this seems to have lain in his vision of his own authority. There had not been a royal minority for over a hundred years, not since Henry VI had reached the age of 18 in 1437, and there was, of course, no precedent at all for the royal supremacy in such a situation. It was perfectly possible to argue, as both Gardiner (from the sidelines) and Princess Mary were later to do, that the supremacy was personal to the monarch and would remain in abeyance until Edward came of age.[14]

That, it seems clear, was not Henry's intention. The supremacy, like every other aspect of the power of the crown, would be vested in the council. It was therefore imperative not only that his son should be brought up to inherit his own sense of responsibility, but that the councillors of Edward's youth should share the same vision. The reason why Henry was not more explicit about this, and refrained from naming a single regent, seems to have lain in his deeply suspicious nature, and in his unwillingness to let go of the reins of power. It was not so much that he distrusted any one individual as that he believed that the nomination of a specific person would automatically set up a new power structure in the court, and that expectant eyes would begin to look beyond the incumbent prince to the successor regime. That Henry was determined to prevent, and by the time that he was convinced that the end was upon him, he lacked the capacity to express any further intention. This mixture of clear purpose and procrastinating practice explains much of the apparently contradictory politics of the last two years of the reign, and similarly his earlier choice of tutors for his son.

It also helps to account for another strange phenomenon, the distribution of honours and rewards that occurred in February 1547.[15] This has often been described as the incoming regime helping itself at the unguarded fount of royal munificence, and much doubt has been cast upon the testimony of Sir William Paget upon which most of the decisions rested. However there is plenty of corroborative evidence that something of the kind was in Henry's mind in the last weeks of his life, and if Sir William's memory was imprecise that probably owed more to the fluctuating nature of the discussions than to any dishonesty on his part.

After the fall of the Howards, that is after 13 December 1546, the king expressed an intention that the forfeited estates (which were very large) should be 'liberally dispersed and given to divers noblemen and others his Majesty's good servants'.[16] No secret was made of this intention, and extensive consultations followed. Hertford was to be made a duke, Lisle and Wriothesley earls, Thomas Seymour and Richard Rich barons. Lands were also to be distributed in support of these dignities, amounting to about £1,500 a year. Paget, according to his own testimony, protested that the grants were too small, and that several worthy men, such as Sir Anthony Denny, had been omitted. Henry told him to go

and talk to his colleagues and to come back with better suggestions, and particularly to assess the value of the lands available.

The resulting discussions exposed the court as a bunch of greedy
cormorants. Several of those earmarked thought their rewards
inadequate or the grants derisory. Others were outraged at having
been passed over. This may well have been the king's intention.
He had played similar games with his councillors before, tempting them into exposing their true minds to his derisive scrutiny.[17]
Cranmer had been twice rescued from their clutches in such a
fashion, and it may be that Henry never had any intention of carrying out his declared policy. When Secretary Paget went back to
the king, he discovered that the latter had changed his mind and
decided to keep all the forfeited lands for himself. The secretary
had remonstrated: expectations had been created, there was much
good service to reward, and so on. Henry stalled. Perhaps he was
not acting like the munificent prince he had always claimed to be.
He would think about it again.

Further consultations had then followed, 'divers devices' were
drawn up, and eventually a whole new list compiled. This, Paget
was quite clear, had been agreed by Henry, and permission given
for the information to be disclosed. However, the paper itself had
remained in the king's custody and had never been recovered.[18]
Whether Henry's last conscious intention was to implement these
new decisions, or to add another layer to the onion of expectation
and deceit, we do not know. Paget's memory was almost certainly
authentic, because if he had been making it up he would have
been both clearer and more emphatic, and we know from other
sources that such plans were discussed. However, the suspicion
lingers that Henry was primarily concerned to remain the centre
of a dance of expectation, greed and disappointment, which
eventually did nothing but flatter his own ego with a demonstration of power.

The document that Henry did leave behind, and which
remains for public scrutiny, was his will. How many redactions
this may have been through before December 1546 we do not

know, but the chances are that it went back at least to 1543, when the last succession act had authorized the king to confirm or amend its provisions by his last will and testament 'signed with his most gracious hand'.[19] Indeed a version dated 1544 was originally produced for discussion on 26 December 1546, only to be rejected in favour of a later version. The version that remains in the National Archives is the one that was revised on or shortly after that date, and dated 30 December.[20] Nothing, however, is quite what it seems. Although this version clearly states 'we have signed it with our own hand in our Palace of Westminster', and was witnessed by 11 members of the privy chamber, forensic examination reveals that it was not in fact signed, but rather dry-stamped.[21]

There was nothing improper in such a procedure, because a commission for the application of the dry stamp had been in existence since early in the year, for the specific purpose of authenticating documents that the king was unwilling or unable to sign personally. Legally it made not the slightest difference whether it was signed or stamped. Only years later, in 1566, was Maitland of Lethington to argue (in favour of Mary Queen of Scots) that the succession laid down in Henry's will was invalid because it was not signed as the statute had specified.[22] No one attempted to argue in such a fashion in 1547, although many might have had cause to do so. There is a long and explicit entry in the list of documents authenticated with the stamp during January 1547, which, because it is not precisely dated, creates the possibility that this was not done until after Henry's death. However, the language of the entry does not suggest that; it runs:

YOUR MAJESTY's *last will and testament bearing the date at Westminster the thirty day of December last past, written in a book of paper, signed above in the beginning and beneath at the end, and sealed with the signet in the presence of the earl of Hertford, Mr Secretary Paget, Mr Denny and Mr Herbert, and also in the presence of certain other persons whose names are subscribed with their own hands as witnesses to the same. Which*

> *testament Your Majesty delivered then, in our sights with your*
> *own hand to the said earl of Hertford as your own deed, last will*
> *and testament, revoking and annulling all others …*[23]

This is listed as having been stamped by William Clerk, the commissioner of the dry stamp, in the presence of Anthony Denny and John Gates, and Clerk also signed the entry, to make doubly sure.

We do not know exactly what the previous version had actually said, or when it was dated, although presumably it had been drawn up in late 1544 or 1545. When it was read out, the king professed himself surprised by some of its contents. Since his excellent memory had been in no way impaired by age, this would suggest either that he had not himself drafted it, or that he was being disingenuous—probably the latter. Henry apparently claimed that his list of executors had been tampered with, which was a coded way of saying that he had changed his mind.[24] It was at this point that Sir Anthony Browne made his point about Gardiner, and was rebuffed. The Bishop of Westminster, Thomas Thirlby, we are told, was also struck out at this point as having been 'schooled by the bishop of Winchester'. The animus against Gardiner is unmistakable, and Paget's story that all those present besought the king to change his mind does not ring true.

Subsequent commentators have complicated the story of this will by pointing out that if it was really handed over to Hertford on 30 December, then it is odd that it was not stamped until January, and late in January according to its position in the dry stamp list. Were there actually two wills, and was the one that survives 'forged' right at the end of January, perhaps even after Henry's death, and made to appear as though it had been passed a month earlier?[25] Such speculation is based upon Henry's known love of keeping his servants guessing, and the fact that he was perfectly *compos mentis* in mid-January when he received the French and Imperial ambassadors. However, such speculation is not necessary to explain what we actually know of the document and its composition, and the simpler explanation is to be preferred. The sur-

viving will expresses Henry's last conscious intentions, and if he
later changed his mind, he did not do anything about it.

HENRY'S WILL
Extracts, 1546.

REMEMBERING *the great benefits given him by Almighty
God and trusting that every Christian who dies in steadfast
faith and endeavours if he have leisure to do such good deeds and
charitable works as Scripture commands, is ordained by Christ's
passion to eternal life, Henry VIII makes such a will as he trusts
shall be acceptable to God, Christ and the whole company of
heaven, and satisfactory to all Godly brethren upon earth.
Repenting his old life, and resolved never to return to the like, he
humbly bequeaths his soul to God, who in the person of his son
redeemed it, and for our better remembrance thereof left here with
us in his church militant the consecration and administration of
his precious body and blood, and he desires the Blessed Virgin and
holy company of heaven to pray for and with him while he lives,
and in the time of his passing hence, that he may after this the
sooner attain everlasting life. For himself he would be content that
his body should be buried in any place accustomed for Christian
folks, but for the reputation of the dignity to which he has been
called, he directs that it shall be laid in the choir of his college of
Windsor, midway between the stalls and the high altar in a tomb
now almost finished in which he will also have the bones of his
wife Queen Jane [Seymour], and there an altar shall be furnished
for the saying of daily masses while the world shall endure. The
tombs of Henry VI and Edward IV are to be embellished. Upon
his death his executors shall, as soon as possible, cause the service
for dead folk to be celebrated at the nearest suitable place, convey
his body to Windsor to be buried with ceremonies [listed], and
distribute 1000 marks in alms to the poor, common beggars as
much as may be avoided, with injunctions to pray for his soul. St
George's college in Windsor castle shall be endowed (if he shall
not already have done it) with land to the yearly value of £600,*

and the dean and Canons shall by indenture undertake: 1. To find two priests to say mass at the foresaid altar. 2. To keep yearly four solemn obits at which £10 shall be distributed in alms. 3. To give thirteen poor men, to be called Poor Knights each 12d a day and yearly a long gown of white cloth, etc., one of the thirteen being their governor and having in addition £3 6s 8d yearly. 4. To cause a sermon to be made every Sunday at Windsor.

As to the succession of the Crown, it shall go to Prince Edward and the heirs of his body. In default to Henry's children by his present wife, Queen Catherine, or any future wife. In default to his daughter Mary, and the heirs of her body, upon condition that she shall not marry without the written and sealed consent of a majority of the surviving members of the Privy Council appointed by him to his son Prince Edward. In default to his daughter Elizabeth, upon like condition. In default to the heirs of the body of the Lady Frances, eldest daughter of his late sister the French Queen. In default to those of the Lady Eleanor, second daughter of the said French Queen. And in default to his right heirs. Either Mary or Elizabeth failing to observe the conditions aforesaid, shall forfeit all right to the succession …

Westminster palace, 30th December 1546.

[*Signed with the king's stamp*]

[Taken from *Letters and Papers*, XXI, ii, no 634. Original at the National Archives, TNA SP1/227.]

We can be reasonably sure that this surviving will expresses the king's firm intention in respect of the disposal of his own body and soul, and in respect of the succession. On the latter issue he confirmed the provisions of the Act of Succession of 1544. So Edward was his heir, and in the event of his death without issue of his own, the crown was to pass first to Mary, then to Elizabeth, and then to the offspring of his sister Mary. The Scottish line was effectively ignored.

It was in fact the statute rather than the will that was the determining factor, and was to remain so down to 1587. It was never repealed, because to have done so would have been to undermine Elizabeth's position, but when the time came in 1603, it was quietly ignored. Henry left the government of Edward and his realm in the hands of a body of 16 executors, who, together with their assistants, were carefully scrutinized in December 1546. He appears to have envisaged a collegiate style of government, but again the appearance is probably deceptive. No one was more aware than Henry of the need to have an identifiable person at the head of a government, and in any case a boy of nine would need a governor. However, Henry had no desire to give hostages to fortune, and in any case he might live long enough to make such a provision unnecessary. So instead of naming an individual or individuals he inserted a clause stating that his executors should be empowered to take whatever steps they thought necessary for the safeguard of the realm.[26]

In spite of its air of assurance, the whole legal status of the will in respect of the successor government was suspect. The executors had a legally defined responsibility in respect of the king's bequests and his burial, but no one could govern with powers derived from a dead king. When the time came, they made no delay in proclaiming themselves the council of King Edward VI, and in obtaining his personal ratification.[27] The Earl of Hertford was immediately constituted 'Protector of the Realm and Governor of the King's Person'. These moves were not at all controversial. It was only when it came to defining the powers of the lord protector that disputes arose, and there is no reason at all to suppose that they contravened what Henry had intended.

By the beginning of January 1547 no one was in any doubt that Henry was seriously ill, but he had passed through so many crises during the previous twelve months that no one would venture to say that this would be the last. His courtiers certainly, and his physicians probably, were keenly aware that imagining the king's death was high treason, so no one was willing to be honest with the invalid. This was probably just as well, because in the middle of the month he rallied yet again, and on the 16th was discussing a new defensive league with Odet de Selve, the French ambassador, who reported him to be well, gracious, and in full command of himself and everyone around.[28] This may have been a shade optimistic, because ten days later Henry had collapsed again, and when the royal assent was given to the Duke of Norfolk's attainder on the 27th it was done by commission, the king being too ill to attend.

The following day, Anthony Denny, keeper of the Palace of Westminster, finally gathered his courage and warned Henry to prepare for the end. Rather unexpectedly, the king took this admonition calmly enough, and after a little while, sent for Thomas Cranmer, thereby acknowledging his plight. Cranmer was at Croydon, and although he responded immediately to what must have been an expected summons, by the time that he arrived Henry was already speechless. Unable to hear any confession, or even to administer the viaticum—the holy communion for the dying—the archbishop asked the king to give him some token that he trusted in God, whereupon Henry, 'holding him with his hand, did wring his hand as hard as he could'.[29] A few hours later Henry died, having characteristically put off receiving the last rites until it was too late.

There is no reason to suppose that the mode of the king's passing indicated any last-minute lurch in the direction of reformed practice. He died, as far as he was concerned, in the odour of sanctity, having earlier expressed the view that the mercy of Christ was sufficient to pardon all his sins 'though they were greater than they be'. He seems to have died without pain, and with an easy conscience. He had, according to his own perception, done his duty to God, and taken great trouble to ensure that it would go on being done. Both Elizabeth and Edward were children, and their presence at a deathbed would not have been expected, but neither Catherine Parr nor Mary were there either. Mary seems to have been unaware that her father was *in extremis*, and later complained that she had been kept in the dark, but the queen's absence is somewhat remarkable. There seems to have been no breakdown in relations between them, and Catherine certainly knew the seriousness of the situation, but she could not come without a summons, and that never came. Perhaps Henry wanted to spare her feelings, but it seems more likely that once again he left it too late, and even Anthony Denny did not dare to suggest that the time had come to send for his wife.

For over a fortnight Henry's body lay in state at Westminster, while his son was proclaimed and the minority government resolved. Then on 14 February, in accordance with his wishes, he set out on his last journey to Windsor. There, on the 16th, he was solemnly interred with a full traditional requiem mass, and a panegyric was delivered by—of all people—Stephen Gardiner.[30]

With a symbolism full of irony, Henry had intended to be buried in the great tomb in St George's Chapel, Windsor Castle, which Wolsey had begun to create for himself, but it was not finished in spite of the time that had elapsed. Henry had also expressed the desire to be buried beside his third wife, Jane Seymour, his intention no doubt being that she would be re-interred with him in the splendour of the great tomb. Instead, her grave in St George's Chapel was opened and he was buried beside her.

What happened to the unfinished tomb is not entirely clear. A decade later the Dean of Windsor is alleged to have told Queen Mary, not long before her death, that it had been dismantled by order of the Marquis of Winchester, then lord treasurer. Mary, so the report claims, was much annoyed, but did not have time to do anything about it.[31] It was Elizabeth who immediately ordered its restoration. However, another decade later Winchester was himself in correspondence with William Cecil about work that needed to be done, and it is not certain that it was ever either pulled down or set up again. Eventually its screen was taken down and the ornaments sold by order of the Long Parliament in 1646,[32] but it is not certain that even Elizabeth's sense of filial piety had ever run to completing it.

The bequests made in Henry's will were (eventually) honoured, or at least most of them were, but his grand vision of perpetual masses for his soul lasted barely two years. In 1549 the mass became illegal, and when it was restored by Mary in 1553, no one seems to have remembered to reinstate the king's chantry. When Mary came to make her own will, she endowed prayers specifically for her mother and all her progenitors, without mentioning her father by name. It hardly mattered, because Elizabeth ignored the entire provision.[33]

The fate of Henry's body is likewise uncertain. Years later the Jesuit Robert Parsons reported that Sir Francis Englefield—Mary's onetime privy councillor who had ended his life in Spain as King Philip's pensioner—had told him that Queen Mary had ordered that Henry should be exhumed and burned, a deed allegedly carried out at Windsor by Cardinal Reginald Pole. Professor Scarisbrick has argued that Parsons had no incentive to misrepresent Englefield, and that Englefield had no reason to lie.[34] However, since part of Parsons's purpose was to laud Mary's orthodoxy, and another part was to discredit Henry VIII, that is not entirely true.

The story remains a story, without any corroborating evidence beyond the fact that Henry's body has never been certainly identified among existing remains. If it had actually happened, it is astonishing that nobody at the time thought fit to mention the fact. When the bones of the notorious heretics Bucer and Fagius were exhumed and burned at Cambridge, it was done with full ecclesiastical and academic ceremonial, the whole point being to cleanse St Mary's Church of their contaminating presence.[35]

Moreover, although Pole would no doubt happily have consigned Henry to temporal as well as eternal fire, Mary's attitude to her father was much more ambiguous. Although she eventually repudiated everything that her father had done, the man she chose to blame for Henry's eccentricities was Thomas Cranmer, whom she burned publicly and with relish. Englefield, who was devoted to Mary's memory, and was also a very old man at the time of the alleged disclosure, had in fact every reason to misremember the events of his (comparative) youth—even something as important as the incineration of a royal corpse. It is possible that Mary regarded such retribution as a secret debt that she owed to her mother, but the absence of any contemporary corroboration, even by that universal busybody John Foxe, and what we know of Mary's character, make it extremely unlikely.

Henry's legacy was in a sense destroyed in the 1550s by his elder daughter, who repealed so many of his statutes and restored to favour the families he had rusticated. But it was Mary rather than Henry who was damned by subsequent generations, largely because Elizabeth 'gloried' in her father and rebuilt most of his achievement. She was, as the Count of Feria, the Spanish ambassador, shrewdly observed a few days before her accession, well schooled in the way in which her father had conducted himself.[36] She had the same need to demonstrate that she was in control, the same erratic temper, and above all the same sense of an especial duty to God. Because it had to be cast in a feminine rather than a masculine mode, this similarity is often overlooked. Elizabeth could not joust or seduce the ladies of the court, but she could play the Faerie Queene, and flirt with her councillors.

Because of Elizabeth, the Church of England was Henry's great legacy to his country. It did not emerge as he would have planned it, but without his egotistical gesture it would never have been possible at all—or at least not without civil war. His other great legacy was what we would now call 'the sovereignty of Parliament'. Because of his need for institutional support, he converted the essentially limited medieval estates of Lords and Commons into a virtually omni-competent legislature, an achievement that his son's councillors built on, and his daughter Mary did nothing to undermine. By the Elizabethan period, Parliament had come to monopolize the process of consent, which had always been recognized, but never so firmly located.

ELIZABETH, HER FATHER'S DAUGHTER

The Count of Feria to King Philip of Spain, 14 November 1558.

SHE [ELIZABETH] *was very open with me on many points, much more than I would have expected, although it is difficult to judge a person one has known for as short a time as I have*

known this woman. I shall tell your Majesty what I have been
able to gather. She is a very vain and clever woman. She must
have been thoroughly schooled in the manner in which her father
conducted his affairs, and I am very much afraid that she will not
be well disposed in matters of religion, for I see her inclined to
govern through men who are believed to be heretics, and I am told
that all the women around her are definitely so. Apart from this it
is evident that she is highly indignant about what has been done
to her during the Queen's [Mary's] lifetime. She puts great store
by the people and is very confident that they are all on her side—
which is certainly true. She declares that it was the people who put
her in her present position, and she will not acknowledge that your
majesty or the nobility of this realm had any part in it ... She is
determined to be governed by no one ...

[Taken from the edition and translation by M.-J. Rodriguez Salgado
and Simon Adams, *Camden Miscellany*, XXVIII, 1984, pp. 330–31. The
original, in Spanish, is in the Archivo General de Simancas, Estado
8340, f. 92.]

There were two other things that Henry bequeathed to his successors, less obvious but of almost equal significance. The first of
these was the Royal Navy. When he came to the throne, a 'Navy
Royal' was an event rather than an organization, and had been so
for centuries. When the king went to war, he called upon his subjects to supply him with ships, and when hostilities were over,
they were returned, or compensation paid in the event of loss.
Henry inherited some half dozen ships of his own, and although
these included the magnificent and aging carracks, the *Regent* and
the *Sovereign,* this small fleet had neither the back-up nor the
facilities to constitute a standing navy. That navy Henry created
in stages over the length of his reign: the standing fleet between
1514 and 1520; the dockyards between 1515 and 1530; and the
admiralty board in 1545 and 1546. At the same time the peacetime
budget increased from about £7,000 a year to nearly £30,000.[37]
Without the foundations that Henry had laid, the achievements

of the later 16th century (including the defeat of the Armada) would have been impossible.

The second thing that Henry did was less tangible, but equally important in its own way. To put it simply he converted the nobility from a lineage mode to a service mode, from independently powerful holders of age-old inherited power towards being agents of the crown. His father had begun this process, and it was not to be completed until well into the 17th century, but Henry's destruction of the Staffords, the Percys and the Howards, together with his promotion of the Seymours, Cliffords and Paulets, symbolized a shift in the whole conception of nobility that was to be fundamental in the long-term survival of the English aristocracy.[38]

Henry did other things that were of less permanent significance, like establishing financial courts and promoting his own equity jurisdiction. It is also arguable that he invented a new taxation system—and even that he saddled his successors with an unviable financial structure, which was eventually to bring the monarchy down in ruins. However, we should be guarded about attributing too much, either for good or ill, to one man, or one reign. Without Elizabeth, much of what Henry achieved would have been stillborn, or would have run into the sand. However, without him, not only would there have been no Elizabeth, but many of the distinctive features we associate with Tudor England would never have existed either. Without his humanist priorities, the education of the aristocracy would have evolved differently, and the universities would have been different places. Without the enormous client system developed by Thomas Cromwell and the uses to which he put it, neither the Marquis of Winchester nor William Cecil would have been qualified for the roles that they performed as statesmen under Elizabeth.

In addition to Henry's actual achievements in politics and administration, there is a wider cultural legacy. In some quarters his name became equated with national independence and national self-consciousness, in others with egocentric tyranny and wilful self-deception. Even Shakespeare represented him as a dissembler.

HENRY, THE PLAYER KING

Extract from Shakespeare's *Henry VIII*.

KATHERINE [OF ARAGON]:

> *I am solicited not by a few,*
> *And those of true condition, that of your subjects*
> *Are in great grievance; there have been commissions*
> *Sent down among 'em; which hath flawed the heart*
> *Of all these together; whereas although*
> *My good lord Cardinal [Wolsey], they vent reproaches*
> *Most bitterly on you as putter-on*
> *Of these exactions, yet the King our master—*
> *Whose honour heaven shield from soil—even he escapes not*
> *Language unmannerly, yea such which breaks*
> *The sides of loyalty, and almost appears*
> *In loud rebellion.*

NORFOLK: *Not almost appears*

> *It doth appear; for upon this taxation,*
> *The clothiers all not able to maintain*
> *The many to them longing have put off*
> *The spinsters, carders, fullers, weavers who*
> *Unfit for other life, compelled by hunger*
> *And lack of other means, in desperate manner*
> *Daring th'event to th'teeth, are all in uproar*
> *And danger serves among them.*

KING: *Taxation?*

> *Wherein? And what taxation?*
> *My Lord Cardinal, You that are blamed for it*
> *While with us. Know you of this taxation?*★

[Shakespeare, *King Henry VIII*, Act 1, scene 2. Taken from the edition by John Margeson, 1990.]

★ the unsuccessful 'tax', the Amicable Grant (1525).

Henry was indeed a complex, contradictory man: a committed humanist who was prone to superstitious fears; a man of immense self confidence who was a constant prey to depression and self-pity; a profound conservative who brought about radical innovations. With all his ambiguities, however, he was a great king, one who not only punched above his weight in the complex politics of Renaissance Europe, but who also changed his country for generations to come. Moreover, by patronising Hans Holbein the Younger he left his own image, and those of his court, as glittering testimonials to the magnificence of his turbulent and creative reign. And he was the first English king for whom the evidence survives to enable a convincing reconstruction of the interactions of power and personality to be made. For that reason alone he deserves to remain a subject of enduring fascination.

Notes on the Text

Full author names and publication dates are given for the first citation of a book or article; thereafter, short references are used.

ABBREVIATIONS USED IN THE NOTES

BL	British Library
Cal. Span.	Calendar of State Papers, Spanish
Cal. Ven.	Calendar of State Papers, Venetian
L&P	Letters and Papers ... of the Reign of Henry VIII
SP	State Papers
TNA	The National Archives

§1 The Renaissance Prince

1 Before the days of censuses, or even of parish registers, all demographic figures are extremely imprecise, and these estimates are based on guesses by a number of scholars. Similarly, the population recovery was not due to improved medicine or hygiene, but instead there seems to have been a fall in the average age of marriage, leading to greater fertility and larger families.

2 London was not, of course, a 'free city' in the same sense as Strasbourg or Augsburg. Its privileges were mainly commercial; but the mayor and aldermen were *ex officio* commissioners for a number of purposes, and kings were in the habit of treating the City with kid gloves.

3 Most notably his brother, Richard of Gloucester, the future Richard III.

4 Notably Perkin Warbeck, whose bid for the throne was just beginning at this time.

5 For a full consideration of all aspects of traditional worship at this time, see Eamon DUFFY, *The Stripping of the Altars* (1992), pp.91–126.

6 Charlotte A. SNEYD (ed.) *A Relation ... of the Island of England ... about the year 1500* (Camden Society, 1847), pp.53–4.

7 *Cal. Span*, IV, ii, 596.

8 ERASMUS, *Opus epistolarum*, ed. P.S. and H.M. Allen (1906), I, p.450.

9 Baga de Secretis, TNA KB8/4 ff. 54–5. David LOADES, *John Dudley*, p.9.

10 Garrett MATTINGLY, *Catherine of Aragon* (1963), pp.20–2.

11 Marriage created a bond of kinship in the first degree, which meant marriage between former brothers- and sisters-in-law was forbidden in the same way as marriage between siblings. However, this prohibition applied only if the union had been consummated, which was the assumption of this dispensation. An unconsummated marriage created only what was called a 'bar of public honesty'. That also required a dispensation, which was not included in this bull.

12 The Treaty of Windsor. T. RYMER, *Foedera, conventions* (1704–35), XIII, pp.123–6.

13 Fourteen (for the man) and twelve (for the girl) were the minimum ages prescribed by the canon law for the cohabitation of married couples. An espousal *per verba de praesenti* ('in words of the present tense', i.e. 'now' as opposed to in the future) was therefore possible.

14 MATTINGLY, *Catherine of Aragon*, pp.75–6.

15 The genuineness of this reason has been much debated. I am inclined to think it was a pious fraud, given the way in which relations between Henry VII and Ferdinand had deteriorated.

16 MATTINGLY, *Catherine of Aragon*, p.98.

17 F.C. DIETZ, *English Government Finance, 1485–1558* (1964), pp.86–7. Francis Bacon, in his *History of the Reign of King Henry VII* (1622), attributed to tradition an estimate of £1,800,000. Much closer to the time (1531) a Venetian estimate had been £1,300,000,

but all these traditions were wildly exaggerated.

18 MATTINGLY, p.108.

19 David LOADES, *Henry VIII and His Queens* (1994), p.21.

20 *Cal. Span,* ii, p.44. J. SCARISBRICK, *Henry VIII* (1968), p.26.

21 Edward HALL, *The Union of the Two Noble and Illustrious Houses ...* (1806 edition), p.520.

22 *L&P,* I, 1182.

23 The Pragmatic Sanction was a unilateral declaration by the French Church, affirming the primacy of royal authority, which the papacy had had no option but to accept. In that respect it resembled the English statutes of Provisors and Praemunire. Successive popes had tried in vain to obtain its withdrawal. R.J. KNECHT, *Francis I* (1982), p.52.

24 SCARISBRICK, *Henry VIII,* p.26.

25 Alessandro FERRAJOLI, 'Un breve inedito di Giulio II per la Investitura del Regno di Francia ad Enrico VIII d'Inghilterra', *Archivo della R. Societa Romana di Storia Patria,* xix (1896), pp.425 onwards. Julius was cautious enough to make investiture conditional upon actual acquisition.

26 HALL, *Union,* p.532.

27 *Cal. Span. Supplement,* pp.36–41.

28 Statute 4 Henry VIII, c.2. Peter Gwyn, *The King's Cardinal* (1990), p.46.

29 Alfred SPONT, *The French War of 1512–13* (1897), p.22.

30 Ibid., pp.103, 130, 141, 145, 159, 163.

§2 The King's Court

1 For a fuller structural analysis of the court, see David LOADES, *The Tudor Court* (1992), pp.25–54.

2 There was an established definition of the verge for the palaces of Westminster and Whitehall, which took in some of the surrounding streets. In the cases of the Tower of London and Windsor, the verge was defined by the castles themselves. When the court was on the move, the verge was defined *ad hoc* at each resting place. Jurisdictional disputes were consequently frequent.

3 Henry was not necessarily ignorant of what went on 'below stairs'. For example, Richard Hill, the sergeant of the cellar, was a frequent gambling companion of the king between 1527 and 1539. LOADES, *The Tudor Court,* p.39.

4 David STARKEY, 'The Age of the Household' in S. Medcalf (ed.), *The Later Middle Ages* (1981).

5 Entitlement to bouge depended on rank as well as residence. Councillors, for example, were entitled although not resident. Part-timers, such as gentlemen ushers and 'quarter waiters', were only entitled when on duty. In practice the rules were not very strictly enforced.

6 David STARKEY, 'Intimacy and Innovation', in his (ed.) *The English Court* (1987).

7 So called because his original function had been to empty the royal close stool, or privy. By this time, that particular task was performed by a menial servant.

8 Greg WALKER, 'The Expulsion of the Minions of 1519 Reconsidered', *Historical Journal,* 32 (1989).

9 George CAVENDISH, *The Life and Death of Cardinal Wolsey,* ed. R.S. SYLVESTER and Davis P. HARDING (1962), p.122.

10 For a detailed account of these purges, see E.W. IVES, *The Life and Death of Anne Boleyn* (2004), pp.148–62 and 319–38.

11 Anne Boleyn was unique in that her endowment went with her creation as Marquis of Pembroke. The others were endowed as queens, with lands worth between £3,000 and £4,000 per annum.

12 LOADES, *The Tudor Court,* p.32.

13 H.M. COLVIN, *The History of the Kings Works,* vol. IV (1982), pt. ii, pp.1–367.

14 For an early example of the use of the treasury of the chamber (1512), see *L&P*, II, pp. 1441–80.

15 This is an average. In the course of the reign ordinary revenue rose (roughly in line with inflation) from about £100,000 to about £150,000. A single 'fifteenth and tenth' tax levy was worth about £15,000, and a subsidy (parliamentary tax) around £50,000. These are approximate figures; the actual yield depended upon circumstances.

16 D.E. HOAK, 'The Secret History of the Tudor Court', *Journal of British Studies,* 26 (1987).

17 Ibid.

18 There is a vivid and unflattering account of a skirmish at the court gate during that rebellion in the narrative of Edward Underhill, who was a gentleman at arms. This is in BL Harleian MS 425, and is printed in A.F. POLLARD, *Tudor Tracts* (1903), pp. 170–98.

19 W.J. TIGHE, 'Gentlemen Pensioners in the Reign of Elizabeth' (Cambridge Ph.D. thesis, 1984); this has a good historical introduction.

20 LOADES, *Tudor Court*, pp. 54–5. For a fuller account, albeit of a later period, see Lawrence STONE, *The Crisis of the Aristocracy, 1558–1641* (1965), pp. 223–34.

21 Catherine of Aragon's most famous intercession was for the rioters of the Evil May Day in 1517. *Cal. Ven.*, ii, p. 887. The ladies of later queens tended to concentrate on smaller and more specific requests.

22 Sometimes these were in the form of public proclamations, as was done in 1533. *Tudor Royal Proclamations,* I, 141: 'The King's royal majesty straightly chargeth and commandeth that all vagabonds, masterless folk, rascals and other idle persons which have used to hang on, haunt, and follow the court, do depart from thence within 24 hours of this proclamation made, upon such pains as in his laws therefore is appointed.'

23 LOADES, *Tudor Court*, p. 56.

24 B.A. MURPHY, *Bastard Prince* (2001), p. 16.

25 Cardinal Wolsey seems to have been responsible for these arrangements. For a time Fitzroy's household was located at Wolsey's mansion of Durham Place. Ibid., p. 34.

26 LOADES, *Tudor Court*, p. 6. For a discussion of the early development of this genre of entertainment, see A. KELLY, 'Eleanor of Aquitaine and Her Courts of Love', *Speculum*, 12 (1937).

27 IVES, *The Life and Death of Anne Boleyn*, pp. 95–109.

28 This is my own speculation, based upon Ives's timetable of the relationship (in *The Life and Death of Anne Boleyn*, pp. 90–2). He dates the decision to marry to the summer of 1527, and points out that neither law nor custom were designed for long engagements.

29 'The noble triumphant Coronation of Queen Anne, Wife unto the most noble King Henry the VIIIth' (1533), printed in *Tudor Tracts*, pp. 9–28.

30 It has been suggested that the foetus that Anne miscarried was deformed in some way, which, to the contemporary eye, would have suggested unlawful conception. Retha M. WARNICKE, 'The Fall of Anne Boleyn', *History*, 70 (1985), pp. 1–15. IVES, in *The Life and Death of Anne Boleyn* (pp. 298–9), has rejected this interpretation, pointing out that it rests on the much later interpretation by Nicholas Sanders.

31 BL Cotton MS Otho. C. x, f. 289. *L&P*, X, 1136. LOADES, *Mary Tudor: A Life* (1989), pp. 101–2.

32 Retha M. WARNICKE, *The Marrying of Anne of Cleves* (2000), pp. 155–87.

33 LOADES, *Henry VIII and His Queens*, p. 124. The exact date is somewhat speculative.

34 TNA SP1/167, ff. 101–2. *L&P*, XV, 875.

35 Sir Harris NICHOLAS (ed.), *Proceedings and Ordinances of the Privy Council of England* (1877), VII, pp. 352–4.

36 LOADES, *Henry VIII and His Queens,* pp. 130–1.

37 Susan JAMES, *Kateryn Parr* (1999).

38 John FOXE, *Acts and Monuments* (1583), pp. 1242–3.

39 E.W. IVES, 'Faction at the Court of Henry VIII', *History,* 57 (1972). *The Life and Death of Anne Boleyn,* pp. 105–9.

§3 The King at War

1 SCARISBRICK, *Henry VIII,* p. 31.

2 Ibid. Henry VII had last asked for such a subsidy in 1489, to help with the Brittany campaign, and that had been very incompletely paid. S.B. Chrimes, *Henry VII* (1972), p. 199.

3 *L&P,* I, 1736, 2006. *Cal. Span.,* II, 91, 105, 106.

4 It was returned under the terms of the Treaty of London in 1518. For a full account of the campaign, see Charles CRUIKSHANK, *Henry VIII and the Invasion of France* (1990).

5 Richard GRAFTON, *A Chronicle at large and meere history of the affayres of England* (1568), edited by Henry Ellis (1809), pp. 268–72.

6 Peter GWYN, *The King's Cardinal* (1990), p. 15.

7 S.J. GUNN, *Charles Brandon, Duke of Suffolk* (1988), pp. 28–31. W.C. RICHARDSON, *Mary Tudor* (1970).

8 RYMER, *Foedera,* pp. 624–35. TNA SP1/17, f. 13.

9 For a full discussion of this encounter, see J.G. RUSSELL, *The Field of Cloth of Gold* (1969).

10 KNECHT, *Francis I,* pp. 146–60.

11 *L&P,* IV, 1379, 1380.

12 G.W. BERNARD, *War, Taxation and Rebellion in Early Tudor England* (1986). Knecht, *Francis I,* pp. 189–90.

13 On 6 May 1527 a mutinous army, operating in the Emperor's name, had sacked Rome and confined the pope to the Castel Sant'Angelo. Clement was subsequently released, but he was in no position to contravene Charles's wishes.

14 For a discussion of the rumours circulating about Charles's interest in Ireland, see S.G. ELLIS, *Tudor Ireland,* pp. 124–5.

15 Henry's negotiations with the Lutheran princes, like his marriage to Anne of Cleves, were means to avoid isolation in the event of Francis and Charles staying friends. SCARISBRICK, *Henry VIII,* pp. 368–75.

16 *L&P,* XVII, 63, 441, 447.

17 *L&P,* XVI, 1270, 1279; XVII, 818, 852–3, 862; XVIII, I, 44.

18 *L&P,* XVII, 1017, 1044. Scarisbrick, *Henry VIII,* pp. 440–1.

19 HALL, *Union,* p. 863. David Loades, *The Tudor Navy* (1992), pp. 131–2.

20 HALL, *Union,* pp. 865–6. *L&P,* XXI, I, 913. Loades, *John Dudley,* pp. 78–9.

21 He appointed one of his father's gunners, Humphrey Walker, as the king's gunfounder, and according to one Venetian report pushed up the price of tin with an ambitious plan to cast 100 bronze guns. *L&P,* I, 67, 287.

22 John B. HATTENDORF *et al., British Naval Documents 1204–1960* (1993), pp. 115–6.

23 Serpentines were wrought-iron, breach-loading guns, usually block mounted. They varied in size, but seldom fired a shot of more than 2–3 lbs. The *Regent* mounted 276 of them.

24 N.A.M. RODGER, *The Safeguard of the Sea* (1997), pp. 143–6.

25 Alfred SPONT, *Letters and Papers Relating to the War with France, 1512–13* (1897), pp. 121–4

26 HATTENDORF *et al., British Naval Documents,* pp. 83–5.

27 C.S.L. DAVIES, 'The Administration of the Royal Navy under Henry VIII', *English Historical Review,* 80 (1965).

28 Mark C. FISSEL, *English Warfare 1511–1642* (2004).

29 Jean Rotz, tempted from the service of Francis I.

30 COLVIN, *The History of the King's Works*, vol. IV (1982).

§4 The King's Great Matter

1 The precedent of Matilda in the 12th century, which is sometimes quoted, is not really relevant, because although she claimed the throne and held power for a short time, she was never generally accepted—nor crowned.

2 MURPHY (*Bastard Prince*, pp.41–69) discusses this option and explains why it was not adopted.

3 LOADES, *Mary Tudor*, pp.45–6. She was described as 'so thin, spare and small as to make it impossible to be married for the next three years'.

4 He was apparently persuaded by Robert Wakefield. BL Cotton MS Otho C.X, f.185. *The Divorce Tracts of Henry VIII*, ed. J. SURTZ and V. MURPHY (1988), p.xiii.

5 The king testified this before the legatine court in 1529. CAVENDISH, *Wolsey*, p.83.

6 Nicholas POCOCK, *Records of the Reformation: The Divorce 1527–1533* (2 vols, 1870), I, p.11.

7 Judith HOOK, *The Sack of Rome, 1527* (2005 edition).

8 SCARISBRICK, *Henry VIII*, p.227. HALL, *Chronicle*, p.758.

9 There are several full discussions of the theology and canon law of these proceedings: SCARISBRICK, *Henry VIII*, pp.163–97; SURTZ and MURPHY, *Divorce Tracts*, Introduction; Guy BEDOUELLE and Patrick LE GAL, *Le Divorce du Roi Henry VIII* (1987), pp.29–46.

10 BL Add. MS 40844, ff.31, 36.

11 E.W. IVES, *Anne Boleyn* (1986), p.154.

12 *State Papers of Henry VIII*, I, p.198. *L&P*, IV, 3231.

13 Graham NICHOLSON, 'The Act of Appeals and the English Reformation', in C. CROSS, D. LOADES and J. SCARISBRICK (eds), *Law and Government under the Tudors* (1988), pp.19–31.

14 This is speculation, but they were forced to spend ten days together housed in the Calais Exchequer, until the weather improved. By the middle of November there is some evidence that they were cohabiting. LOADES, *Henry VIII and His Queens*, pp.60–1.

15 The main statute was that of 1393 (16 Richard II, c.3). BL Harleian MS 431, f.42. E.F. JACOB, *The Fifteenth Century* (1961), pp.93–4.

16 *State Papers of Henry* VIII, I, no. 22. G.R. ELTON, *The Tudor Constitution* (1982), pp.327–30, 330–5.

17 *Letters and Papers*, VI, 1186, 1249, 1296. Mary's household was dismissed as a punishment for her recalcitrance, and she was placed, with a few servants, in the household that had just been created for Elizabeth. David LOADES, *Mary Tudor: The Tragical History of the First Queen of England* (2006), pp.34–5.

18 Statute 25 Henry VIII, c.22. *Statutes of the Realm*, III, pp.471–4.

19 IVES, *The Life and Death of Anne Boleyn*, pp.319–38.

20 LOADES, *Mary Tudor*, pp.103–3.

21 Henry and Anne had actually visited Jane's home at Wulf Hall during the previous year's progress, but there is no evidence that Jane was there. Her position at court was a relatively humble one in the queen's chamber.

22 *L&P*, VII, 1397.

23 Statute 28 Henry VIII, c.7. *Statutes of the Realm*, III, p.655.

24 HALL, *Chronicle,* p.825.

25 It is a popular myth that Edward was a sickly child. In fact he was robust and threw off the usual childish ailments easily, but he contracted pulmonary tuberculosis in the spring of 1553, and for that there was, at that time, no cure.

26 WARNICKE, *The Marrying of Anne of Cleves*, pp.127–54.

27 J. STRYPE, *Ecclesiastical Memorials* (1822), II, p.462.

28 WARNICKE, *The Marrying of Anne of Cleves*. J.G. Nichols (ed.), *The Diary of Henry Machyn* (Camden Society, 1848), pp.144–5.

29 35 Henry VIII, c.1 . *Statutes of the Realm*, III, p.955.

30 It was still being argued, as late as the early 17th century, that a statute was only valid if it was consistent with the law of God, but in practice that pass had been sold, not only by this succession act but also (more significantly) by the fact that Mary repealed her brother's and her father's statutes, instead of ignoring them as she was urged to do. ELTON, *The Tudor Constitution*, pp.233–45.

§5 The King's Laws

1 The common law was customary in origin, having been created jointly by the kings, thanes and freemen of the West Saxons. It had been the prevailing (but not the only) customary code of the Old English kingdom. The Mercians had their own laws, which were different in several respects, and there were other variants. At the Norman Conquest, these codes were rationalized, and added to from French sources. The result became the common law because, in the course of the 12th century, it was embraced by the Anglo-Norman and Angevin kings, and codified (in the *leges Henrici primi*), as part of their policy of increased central control. See W.S. HOLDSWORTH, *A History of English Law* (7th edition, by A.L Goodhart and H.G. Hanbury, 1956), vol. 1, pp.3–4.

2 Ibid., pp.357–65.

3 Diarmaid MACCULLOCH, 'Bondmen under the Tudors', in CROSS, LOADES and SCARISBRICK (eds), *Law and Government under the Tudors*, pp.91–110.

4 The Chancery had both a common law and an equity side, and it was the equity side that could be appealed to from the customary courts. David

LOADES, *Tudor Government* (1997) pp.66–7.

5 A situation addressed by the statute of 26 Henry VIII, c.6, which removed pleadings for felonies from the marcher lordships to the nearest adjacent English county. Peter ROBERTS, 'The Union with England and the Identity of "Anglican' Wales", *Transactions of the Royal Historical Society*, 5th series, 22 (1972), pp.49–70.

6 J.M.W. BEAN, *From Lord to Patron* (1989).

7 P. CLARK and P. SLACK (eds), *English Towns in Transition 1500–1700* (1976).

8 For a full and informative discussion of customary tenures and the problems relating to them, see Eric KERRIDGE, *The Agrarian Problem in the Sixteenth Century and After* (1969).

9 The owner of a freehold property held it in theory directly from the king, but in practice most freehold property was leased. These leases, and other issues of tenure, were pleadable in the king's courts and under the common law.

10 HOLDSWORTH, *A History of English Law*, I. pp.204–31. M. BLATCHER, *The Court of King's Bench 1450–1550* (1978).

11 Appeals were normally allowed only when an error of procedure was alleged, which led to some ingenious improvisations. Appeal from quarter sessions went to the assizes, but since the assize judges were the central courts on circuit, no appeal was possible from the assizes to King's Bench or Common Pleas. By an ancient practice, Common Pleas issues could be appealed to King's Bench, but until 1585 King's Bench issues could be appealed only to Parliament.

12 J.R. LANDER, *English Justices of the Peace 1461–1509* (1989). S.J. GUNN, *Early Tudor Government 1485–1558* (1995), pp.100–2.

13 Sir Thomas SMITH, *De republica anglorum*, ed. Mary Dewar (1982), p.104.

14 R.W. Heinze, *The Proclamations of the Tudor Kings* (1976). For the duties of the justices of the peace (admittedly at a slightly later date), see W. Lambarde, *Eirenarcha* (1602).

15 Smith, *De republica anglorum*, p.97. Loades, *Tudor Government*, pp. 111–13.

16 Ibid., pp.212–18.

17 This power went back to the 15th century, and during Henry's reign was regulated by the Bail Act of 1487 (3 Henry VII, c.4).

18 When an indictment had been returned, a writ of *capias* would be issued to the sheriff of the relevant county, ordering the arrest of the offender. If the sheriff could not (or did not wish to) find the offender, he returned the writ *non est inventus*. A fresh writ of *capias* would then have to be issued to the sheriff of the county where he was supposed to be lurking. This could go on for some time. If the person could not be apprehended, sooner or later he would be outlawed.

19 For discussions of the powers of equity jurisdiction, see J.A. Guy, *The Cardinal's Court* (1977) and W.J. Jones, *The Elizabethan Court of Chancery* (1967).

20 Elton, *Tudor Constitution,* pp. 163–6.

21 Smith, *De republica anglorum*, pp. 115–8.

22 A.F. Pollard, 'Council, Star Chamber and Privy Council under the Tudors', *English Historical Review*, 37 (1922). Blatcher, *Court of King's Bench*.

23 Beat Kumin, *The Shaping of a Community* (1996).

24 Visitations were carried out regularly by the archdeacons, spasmodically by the bishops, and very occasionally by the archbishops. For some examples, see W.H. Frere and W.M. Kennedy (eds), *Visitation Articles and Injunctions of the Period of the Reformation* (1910).

25 R.H. Helmholtz, *Canon Law and the Church of England* (1987).

26 E.W. Ives, *The Common Lawyers of Pre-Reformation England* (1983).

27 Susan Brigden, *London and the Reformation* (1989), pp.98–103, where numerous other references can be found.

28 2 Henry V, st.1, c.7. This act authorized bishops to call upon the secular magistrates for assistance.

29 David Loades, 'Anticlericalim in the Church of England before 1558', in Nigel Aston and Mathew Cragoe (eds), *Anticlericalism in Britain c.1500–1914* (2000), pp.1–17.

30 Frere and Kennedy (eds), *Visitation Articles and Injunctions*, II, pp. 1–11, 34–43.

31 Eamon Duffy, *The Voices of Morebath* (2001).

32 Smith, *De republica anglorum*, pp. 78–9.

33 J.H. Baker, 'Criminal Courts and Procedure at Common Law' in J.S. Cockburn (ed.), *Crime in England 1550–1800* (1977).

34 J.H.Baker (ed.), *The Reports of Sir John Spelman* (Selden Society, 2 vols. 1977).

35 See particularly the Treason Acts of 1534 and 1541 (26 Henry VIII, c.1 3 and 33 Henry VIII, c.23) and the discussion of them in Elton, *Tudor Constitution,* pp.59–87.

36 J.R.Tanner, *Tudor Constitutional Documents* (1951), p.423.

37 Statute 7 Richard II, c.5.

38 Statute 22 Henry VIII, c.12. *Statutes of the Realm*, III, p.328. Tanner, *Tudor Constitutional Documents*, pp.469–79.

39 Ibid., p.483.

40 Kerridge, *The Agrarian Problem*. Joan Thirsk, *The Agrarian History of England and Wales, 1500–1640* (1967).

41 Tanner, *Tudor Constitutional Documents*, p.95.

42 Ibid.

43 Statute 25 Henry VIII, c.14.

44 Statute 31 Henry VIII, c.14. *Statutes of the Realm*, III, p.739.

45 Peter MARSHALL, *Reformation England 1480–1642* (2003), pp. 48–57.

46 BRIGDEN, *London and the Reformation*, pp. 299–324.

47 David CRESSY, *Literacy and the Social Order* (1980), pp. 42–62.

48 Ibid.

§6 The King's Government

1 J.F. BALDWIN, *The King's Council in the Middle Ages* (1913).

2 C.L. KINGSFORD (ed.), *The Great Chronicle of London* (1905), p. 186.

3 Officers such as the treasurer of Calais or the lord deputy of Ireland were often councillors, but they attended only occasionally. Their membership was more in the way of recognition, and their advice would be communicated by letter.

4 There are many discussions of the origin of the Wars of the Roses. See R.A. GRIFFITHS, *Henry VI* (1981); J. GILLINGHAM, *The Wars of the Roses* (1981); and A.J. POLLARD, *The Wars of the Roses* (1988).

5 LOADES, *Tudor Government*, p. 20. G.R. ELTON, 'Henry VII's Council', in *Studies in Tudor and Stuart Politics and Government,* I (1974), pp. 294–9.

6 J.A. GUY, *The Cardinal's Court* (1977).

7 G.W. BERNARD, *War, Taxation and Rebellion in Early Tudor England.* Peter GWYN, *The King's Cardinal*, pp. 397–407.

8 ELTON, *The Tudor Constitution*, pp. 199–217.

9 G.R. ELTON, *Thomas Cromwell* (1990).

10 G.R. ELTON, in *Policy and Police* (1972), provides a full account of this role.

11 Susan BRIGDEN, 'Popular Disturbance and the Fall of Thomas Cromwell and the Reformers, 1539–40', *Historical Journal*, 34 (1981), pp. 255–78. Ibid., 'Thomas Cromwell and the 'Brethren', in CROSS, LOADES and SCARISBRICK (eds), *Law and Government under the Tudors*, pp. 51–66.

12 G.R. ELTON, *The Tudor Revolution in Government* (1953), pp. 316–69. J.A. GUY, 'The Privy Council', in David STARKEY (ed.), *Reassessing the Henrician Age* (1987).

13 G.R. ELTON, 'Tudor Government: Points of Contact: The Council', in *Studies,* III (1983).

14 S.E. LEHMBERG, *The Reformation Parliament 1529–36* (1988).

15 M.A.R. GRAVES, *The Early Tudor Parliaments 1485–1558* (1990).

16 P.J. HOLMES, 'The Great Council in the Reign of Henry VII', *English Historical Review,* 101 (1986).

17 A.R. MYERS, 'Parliament 1422–1509', in R.G. DAVIES and J.H. DENTON (eds), *The English Parliament in the Middle Ages* (1981). GRAVES, *Early Tudor Parliaments.*

18 After the submission of the clergy in 1534, all canons had to be approved by the king, and the main function of the convocations became the voting of clerical subsidies. Although some doubts were expressed during the reign, the convocations had never been part of the Parliament, although they met at the same time.

19 Statutes 24 Henry VIII c. 12 and 26 Henry VIII, c. 1. G.W. BERNARD, *The King's Reformation* (2005), pp. 199–212.

20 Statutes of 27 Henry VIII, c. 28 and 31 Henry VIII, c. 1 3. The houses deemed to be corrupt, and dissolved by the first statute, were those with incomes of less than £200 a year.

21 SMITH, *De republica anglorum*, p. 78.

22 This right had been established by Charles IX as early as 1439, on account of the continuing war with England. In the eyes of Sir John Fortescue this made France a *dominium regale* (absolute monarchy), in contrast to England. C. PLUMMER (ed.), *The Governance of England* (1885), p. 109.

23 LOADES, *Tudor Government,* p.62.

24 This figure is an average. F.C. DIETZ, *English Government Finance 1485–1558* (1964), p.162.

25 J.D. ALSOP, 'Innovation in Tudor Taxation', *English Historical Review,* 99 (1984). *Tudor Government,* pp.62–3.

26 ELTON, *Tudor Revolution in Government,* p.225.

27 ELTON, *Tudor Revolution in Government, passim.*

28 LOADES, *Tudor Government,* pp. 52–8.

29 LOADES, *The Reign of Mary Tudor,* pp.139–43. The reason why Wards and Liveries was exempted may have been the influence of the Marquis of Winchester, the long-time master and now lord treasurer.

30 W. MACCAFFREY, *The Shaping of the Elizabethan Regime* (1969).

31 ELTON, *The Tudor Constitution,* pp.118–20. W.J. Jones, *The Elizabethan Court of Chancery* (1967).

32 Writs were necessary for the authentication of process, and had been designed originally to prevent officers (and others) from acting on their own initiative. John Foxe, the Protestant martyrologist, accused some sheriffs in Mary's reign of burning heretics before the appropriate writ had been received — which technically turned due process into murder.

33 'Wapentake' was a word of Norse origin, used in the old Danelaw. Other alternatives were 'rape' (Sussex) and 'lathe' (Kent). All were administrative subdivisions of the shire.

34 LOADES, *Power in Tudor England* (1997), pp.10–23.

35 Peter CLARK, *English Towns in Transition 1500–1700* (1976).

36 Jasper RIDLEY, *Nicholas Ridley* (1957).

37. Stephen G. ELLIS, *Tudor Frontiers and Noble Power* (1995), pp.3–80.

38 ELTON, *The Tudor Constitution,* pp.200–3.

39 S.J. GUNN, *Early Tudor Government,* pp.67–70.

40. LOADES, *Power in Tudor England,* pp.1–10.

41. By far the best discussion of Henry VIII's various policies in respect of the aristocracy is contained in Helen MILLER, *Henry VIII and the English Nobility* (1986), which discusses Buckingham's case at length. See also Carole RAWCLIFFE, *The Staffords, Earls of Stafford and Dukes of Buckingham* (1978).

42. STONE, *The Crisis of the Aristocracy 1558–1641* (1965), pp.7–15.

43 *Report of the Deputy Keeper of the Public Records,* III (1842), pp.267–8. *Henry VIII and the English Nobility,* pp. 72–3.

44 MILLER, *Henry VIII and the English Nobility.* G.W BERNARD (ed.), *The Tudor Nobility* (1992).

§7 The King's Enemies

1 It is somewhat surprising that so obvious a rival as the Earl of Warwick was not disposed of earlier. There was some suggestion that he was a simpleton, or regarded as such, but Hazel Pierce is unconvinced. PIERCE, *Margaret Pole,* pp.23–4.

2 W.E. HAMPTON, 'The White Rose under the First Tudors: Part I', *The Ricardian,* 7 (1987), pp.414–20.

3 Richard de la Pole, although not strictly a member of the royal family, was Henry VII's half cousin, and a man in whom he placed high confidence. PIERCE, *Margaret Pole,* pp.14–15.

4 SCARISBRICK, *Henry VIII,* p.32.

5 S.J. GUNN, *Charles Brandon, Duke of Suffolk* (1986). W.C. RICHARDSON, *The White Queen* (1970). The only man with any legitimate claim to the throne in 1525 was the young James V of Scotland.

6 BL Cotton MS Titus B.I, ff.99–101. MILLER, *Henry VIII and the English Nobility,* p.72.

7 MacCaffrey, *The Shaping of the Elizabethan Regime*, pp. 199–220.

8 Rawcliffe, *The Staffords*, p. 1.

9 Scarisbrick, *Henry VIII*, pp. 120–1.

10 Miller, *Henry VIII and the English Nobility*, pp. 45–51.

11 W.H. Dunham, 'Wolsey's Rule of the King's Whole Council', *American Historical Review*, 49 (1944), p. 655. Rawcliffe, *The Staffords*, pp. 99–100.

12 Report of Ludovico Spinelli, *Cal. Ven.*, III, no. 213.

13 G.W. Bernard, *War, Taxation and Rebellion in Early Tudor England*, pp. 53–75.

14 Ibid., p. 114.

15 It was this fear that prompted Anne in the outburst to Henry, 'I see that some fine morning you will succumb to her reasoning, and that you will cast me off.' Loades, *Mary Tudor*, p. 57.

16 Clement threatened Henry with excommunication in July 1533 if he did not return to Catherine. This sentence should have come into force in September, but it was not promulgated. Scarisbrick, *Henry VIII*, pp. 318–20.

17 Elton, *Policy and Police*, p. 387.

18 Ibid., p. 407.

19 G.W. Bernard, *The King's Reformation* (2005), pp. 101–3.

20 Ibid., pp. 118–20.

21 J. Guy, *The Public Career of Thomas More* (1980).

22 G.R. Elton, 'Sir Thomas More and the Opposition to Henry VIII', *Bulletin of the Institute of Historical Research*, 41 (1968), pp. 19–34.

23 The Treasons Act of 1534 made it high treason to 'maliciously' deny the king any of his titles. However, this act did not receive the royal assent until December 1534, by which time More was already in the Tower.

24 Thomas F. Mayer, *Reginald Pole, Prince and Prophet* (2000), p. 5.

25 Ibid., pp. 34–7.

26 Ibid., pp. 13–61.

27 Scarisbrick, *Henry VIII*, pp. 346–7.

28 *L&P*, XII, ii, 174.

29 Pierce, *Margaret Pole*, p. 169.

30 Ibid., pp. 166–7. Loades, *William Paulet* (forthcoming, 2007).

31 *L&P*, XIII, ii, 802, 961.

32 There are numerous studies of the Pilgrimage of Grace, the most recent being R.W. Hoyle, *The Pilgrimage of Grace and the Politics of the 1530s* (2001).

33 M.E. James, 'Obedience and Dissent in Henrician England', *Past and Present*, 68 (1970), pp. 3–78.

34 Hoyle, *The Pilgrimage of Grace*, pp. 135–57.

35 David Loades (ed.), *The Papers of George Wyatt* (Camden Society, 1967), pp. 168–9.

36 Mattingly, *Catherine of Aragon*, p. 287.

37 'The Pontefract Articles' in Hoyle, *The Pilgrimage of Grace*, Appendix 5, pp. 460–3.

38 Ibid.

39 G.W. Bernard, *The Power of the Tudor Nobility* (1985).

40 Hoyle, *The Pilgrimage of Grace*, pp. 459–60.

41 Ibid., pp. 439–64.

42 Ibid., pp. 384–5.

§8 The King's Other Island

1 G.O. Sayles, *The Administration of Ireland 1172–1377* (1963).

2 S.G. Ellis, *Tudor Ireland* (1985), pp. 19–32.

3 Gunn, *Early Tudor Government*, pp. 62–70.

4 S.G. Ellis, 'Tudor Policy and the Kildare Ascendancy in the Lordship of Ireland 1496–1534', *Irish Historical Studies*, 20 (1976–7).

5 His son and heir was married in England, to Elizabeth Zouche, while two of his daughters were married to Irish chieftains.

6 Brendan BRADSHAW, *The Irish Constitutional Revolution of the Sixteenth Century* (1979), p.9.

7 H.G. RICHARDSON and G.O. SAYLES, *The Irish Parliament in the Middle Ages* (1952), p.274.

8 Appointed in 1513. William Rokeby, the Archbishop of Dublin, who had held the office before Compton, continued as his deputy, and regained the office in 1516.

9 ELLIS, *Tudor Ireland*, p.102.

10 S.G. ELLIS, *Reform and Revival* (1984), pp.157–8.

11 Ibid., pp.13, 16, 27. TNA SP60/3/162. *L&P*, III, 670, 899.

12 ELLIS, 'Tudor Policy and the Kildare Ascendancy', p.239.

13 *State Papers, Henry VIII* (1830–52) II, 60.

14 ELLIS, *Tudor Ireland*, p.115.

15 KNECHT, *Francis I*, p.147.

16 *L&P*, IV, 3698. Ellis, *Tudor Ireland*, pp.118–9.

17 See MURPHY (*Bastard Prince*, pp. 107–48) for a full account of FitzRoy's role (or lack of it) in this capacity.

18 D.B. QUINN, 'Henry VIII and Ireland', *Irish Historical Studies*, XII (1960–1), pp.338–9.

19 ELLIS, *Tudor Ireland*, pp.124–5. ELLIS, 'The Kildare Rebellion and the Early Henrician Reformation', *Historical Journal*, XIX (1976).

20 S.G. ELLIS, *Tudor Frontiers and Noble Power* (1995), p.176.

21 Both Francis I and Charles V were arming early in 1535 in preparation for a fresh round in their confrontation. Whenever such moves happened, it took the pressure off Henry. Knecht, *Francis I*, pp.274–6.

22 The 9th Earl had died in London in September 1534.

23 BRADSHAW, *The Irish Constitutional Revolution*, pp.154–9, and 'The Opposition to the Ecclesiastical Legislation in the Irish Reformation Parliament', *Irish Historical Studies*, 16 (1969).

24 ELLIS, *Tudor Ireland*, pp.135–6.

25 BRADSHAW, *Irish Constitutional Revolution*, pp.193–6

26 *State Papers*, III, p.326. Ellis, *Tudor Ireland*, pp.139–40

27 BRADSHAW, *Irish Constitutional Revolution*, pp.196–200.

28 For a discussion of the complexities of the Gaelic tenurial system, see K. NICHOLLS, *Gaelic and Gaelicized Ireland* (1972), pp.37–9, 57–67.

29 E.B. FRYDE, D.E. GREEWAY, S. PORTER and I. ROY (eds), *Handbook of British Chronology* (1986), pp.323–77.

30 B. BRADSHAW, *The Dissolution of the Religious Orders in Ireland* (1974).

31 ELLIS, *Tudor Ireland*, pp.200–4.

32 R.D. EDWARDS, 'The Irish Bishops and the Anglican Schism', *Irish Ecclesiastical Record*, 45 (1935).

33 R.D. EDWARDS, *Ireland in the Age of the Tudors* (1977).

34 State Papers, II, p.122.

35 BRADSHAW, *The Dissolution of the Religious Orders in Ireland*.

36 Ibid., pp.36–7. ELLIS, *Tudor Ireland*, pp.200–3.

37 NICHOLLS, *Gaelic and Gaelicized Ireland*, pp.107–9.

38 C. CONWAY, 'Decline and Attempted Reform of the Irish Cistercians, 1445–1531', *Collectanea Ordinis Cisterciensium Reformatorum*, XIX (1957), pp.146–62, 371–84.

39 ELLIS, *Tudor Ireland*, p.190.

40 BRADSHAW, *Dissolution of the Religious Orders*, pp.32–3, 47–77.

41 Ibid., pp.206–7.

42 Ibid., Appendix I. ELLIS, *Tudor Ireland*, pp.233–4.

§9 The King's Religion

1 *Calendar of the Patent Rolls 1494–1509*, p.72.

2 Lord Edward HERBERT, *The Life and Raigne of King Henry the eighth* (1672), p.2.

3 HALL, *Union*, p.519.

4 MATTINGLY, *Catherine of Aragon*, pp. 104–5. It was later said that the people of England loved the queen because she fed them.

5 In a Good Friday sermon of 1513, Colet attacked Henry's war with France, and the dean's enemies, who were numerous, expected this to lead to his arrest. Instead, Henry sought him out, professing that he had come to discharge his conscience, and ended the interview with the words 'Let every man have his doctor. This is mine.' ERASMUS, *Opus Epistolarum*, IV, p. 525.

6 Henry VII to Pope Innocent VIII, 5 July 1487. *Cal. Ven.*, I, p. 164. This related specifically to the sanctuary at Westminster.

7 A.G. DICKENS, *The English Reformation* (1964), pp. 90–1. Statute 4 Henry VIII, c.2.

8 Since the case was about a mortuary fee, it is not clear why such a writ was issued. A. OGLE, *The Tragedy of the Lollard's Tower* (1949).

9 DICKENS, *English Reformation*, pp. 92–4. Henry Standish, the king's spokesman, was summoned to appear before convocation, and the convocation was then threatened with *praemunire*.

10 The draft survives as BL MS Cotton Vitellius B. xx, ff. 98 *et seq.* SCARISBRICK, *Henry VIII*, pp. 110–15.

11 Ibid., p. 111.

12 G.W. BERNARD, *The King's Reformation* (2006), pp. 1–2.

13 The evidence for the manner in which this conclusion was reached has been carefully assembled by BERNARD, pp. 14–19.

14 Graham NICHOLSON, 'The Act of Appeals and the English Reformation', in *Law and Government under the Tudors*, pp. 19–30. MACCULLOCH, *Thomas Cranmer*.

15 For a full discussion of the assembly of Henry's case, see SCARISBRICK, *Henry VIII*, pp. 163–80, and for a more recent examination, BERNARD, *The*

King's Reformation, pp. 26–43.

16 Although Henry was excommunicated on the 30 August the bull was not promulgated until January 1536. *L&P*, IX, 207; X, 82.

17 Charles STURGE, *Cuthbert Tunstall* (1938), pp. 131–5.

18 FRERE and KENNEDY, *Visitation Articles and Injunctions*, II, pp. 35–6.

19 *Tudor Royal Proclamations*, I, pp. 301–2.

20 FRERE and KENNEDY, *Visitation Articles and Injunctions*, II, p. 39.

21 DICKENS, *English Reformation*, pp. 184–6.

22 Becket was removed from the calendar by proclamation on 16 November 1538. *Tudor Royal Proclamations*, I, pp. 27–76.

23 G.R. ELTON, *Thomas Cromwell* (1992), representing a modification of his view of 1953.

24 'A Chronicle and Defence of the English Reformation', in LOADES (ed.), *The Papers of George Wyatt*, pp. 159–60.

25 M.C. KNOWLES, *The Religious Orders in England*, III, *The Tudor Age* (1959).

26 The words used in the preamble to the statute 27 Henry VIII, c.28. *Statutes of the Realm*, III, pp. 575–8.

27 DICKENS, *English Reformation*, p. 143.

28 There are many discussions of this phenomenon, but see particularly Joyce YOUINGS, *The Dissolution of the Monasteries* (1972).

29 *L&P*, XIII, i, 173, 195, 231. TNA SP 1/129, f. 12.

30 *L&P*, XIII, ii, 347, 409, 709, 710.

31 BERNARD, *The King's Reformation*, pp. 453–4.

32 *L&P*, XIII, I, 926; ii, 1186.

33 DICKENS, *English Reformation*, pp. 149–50. The monastic chapters of Coventry, Rochester, Winchester, Ely, Durham, Carlisle and Norwich were also re-founded as houses of secular canons, and became known as the cathedrals of the 'new foundation'.

34 FOXE, *Acts and Monuments*, p.1123.

35 Ibid., p.1124.

36 Statute 31 Henry VIII, c.14. *Statutes of the Realm*, III, pp.739–43.

37 BERNARD, *The King's Reformation*, pp.501–4. MacCULLOCH, *Thomas Cranmer*.

38 BERNARD, *The King's Reformation*, pp.529–33.

39 D.G. NEWCOMBE, *John Hooper* (2007). House of Lords, Original Acts, 32 Henry VIII, c.60. SCARISBRICK, *Henry VIII*, pp.381–2.

40 DICKENS, *English Reformation*, pp.189–90.

41 Jennifer LOACH, *Edward VI* (1999).

42 C. LLOYD, *Formularies of the Faith* (1856). P. MARSHALL, 'Fear, Purgatory and Polemic in Reformation England', in W.G. NAPHY and P. ROBERTS (eds), *Fear in Early Modern Society* (1997), pp.150–65.

§10 The King's Last Years

1 This was well demonstrated in a testy letter he wrote to Francis I in 1543, justifying his declaration of war. *L&P*, XIX, ii, 19(2). TNA SP1/191, f.25.

2 The subject of Henry's glosses and annotations is a huge one in itself. For a way in to the discussion, see J.P. CARLEY, *Henry VIII and His Books* (2006).

3 *L&P*, X, 908. IVES, *Rise and Fall of Anne Boleyn*.

4 Those who were executed for affronting the king's honour tended to be dispatched by Act of Attainder rather than brought to trial, for the obvious reason that their offences were felt rather than seen. See, for example, House of Lords, Original Acts 32 Henry VIII, c.60.

5 L.B. SMITH, *Henry VIII: The Mask of Royalty* (1971), pp.230–1.

6 A.S. CURRIE, 'Notes on the Obstetric Histories of Catherine of Aragon and Anne Boleyn', *Edinburgh Medical Journal*, I (1888).

7 *Cal. Span.*, VIII, 291. SMITH, *Mask of Royalty*, p.233.

8 For example, the French ambassador commented (only a few days before being received by the king): 'Whatever his health, it can only be bad, and will not last long.' *Correspondence politique de Odet de Selve* (1888), vol. 90, p.85.

9 Examples of the armour can be viewed in the Royal Armouries.

10 LOACH, *Edward VI*. W.K. JORDAN, *Edward VI* (1968).

11 SMITH, *Mask of Royalty*, pp.262–74.

12 Glyn REDWORTH, *In Defence of the Church Catholic: A Life of Stephen Gardiner* (1990).

13 The king's words in this connection, as related by Foxe, are quoted with comments by J.A. MULLER, *Stephen Gardiner and the Tudor Reaction* (1970), pp.141–2.

14 LOADES, *Mary Tudor*, pp.144–5. See also Gardiner to Somerset, 21 May 1547, in J.A. MULLER, *The Letters of Stephen Gardiner* (1933), p.276.

15 Helen MILLER, 'Henry VIII's Unwritten Will', in E.W. IVES, R.J. KNECHT and J. SCARISBRICK (eds), *Wealth and Power in Tudor England* (1978), pp.88–91.

16 SMITH, *Mask of Royalty*, p.266.

17 *Acts of the Privy Council*, II, pp.15–20.

18 SMITH, *Mask of Royalty*, p.266. JORDAN, *The Young King*, pp.63–5.

19 Statute 35 Henry VIII, c.1.

20 JORDAN, *The Young King*, pp.54–7.

21 E.W. IVES, 'Henry VIII's Will', *Historical Journal*, 35 (1992), pp.779–804.

22 Gilbert BURNET, *The History of the Reformation of the Church of England* (1679), I, pp.267–70, from an original in the Petyt MSS.

23 TNA SP4, list 19, section 85. *L&P*, XXI, ii, 770 (85).

24 SCARISBRICK, *Henry VIII*, p.488.

25 L.B. SMITH, 'The Last Will and Testament of Henry VIII', *Journal of British Studies*, II (1962). M. LEVINE, 'The Last Will and Testament of Henry VIII', *Historian*, 26 (1964), pp.471–85.

26 LOADES, *John Dudley*, pp.86–7.

27 *Acts of the Privy Council*, II, pp.3–5.

28 *L&P*, XXI, ii, 713.

29 SCARISBRICK, *Henry VIII*, p.496, quoting FOXE, *Acts and Monuments*.

30 Ibid., p.497.

31 *Calendar of State Papers, Domestic 1547–81*, p.296.

32 ST JOHN HOPE, *Windsor Castle* (1913), pp.484 *et seq.*

33 Much of Mary's will consisted of provision for the various religious houses founded in her reign, all of which were dissolved within months of her death. LOADES, *Mary Tudor*, pp.370–83.

34 SCARISBRICK, *Henry VIII*, p.497, n.4. The story appears in PARSONS, *Certamen Ecclesiae Anglicanae*, ed. SIMONS (1965).

35 FOXE, *Acts and Monuments* (1583), pp.1950–64.

36 'The Count of Feria's Dispatch to Philip II of 14 November 1558', ed. M.-J. RODRIGUEZ SALGADO and Simon ADAMS, *Camden Miscellany*, 28 (1984), pp.302–37.

37 LOADES, *Tudor Navy*, pp.74–102.

38 MILLER, *Henry VIII and the English Nobility*. STONE, *The Crisis of the Aristocracy, 1558–1641* (1965).

Further Reading

J.M.W. BEAN, *From Lord to Patron: Lordship in Late Medieval England* (1989)

G.W. BERNARD, *War, Taxation and Rebellion in Early Tudor England* (1986)

—(ed.) *The Tudor Nobility* (1992)

—*The King's Reformation* (2005)

B. BRADSHAW, *The Dissolution of the Religious Orders in Ireland* (1974)

—*The Irish Constitutional Revolution of the Sixteenth Century* (1979)

S. BRIGDEN, *London and the Reformation* (1989)

J.P. CARLEY, *The Books of Henry VIII and His Wives* (2004)

H.M. COLVIN (gen. ed.), *The History of the King's Works* (1963–76)

F.C. DIETZ, *English Government Finance, 1485–1558* (1964)

E. DUFFY, *The Stripping of the Altars* (1992)

S.G. ELLIS, *Tudor Ireland 1470–1603* (1985)

—*Tudor Frontiers and Noble Power* (1995)

G.R. ELTON, *The Tudor Revolution in Government* (1953)

—*Policy and Police* (1972)

—*The Tudor Constitution* (1982)

—*Thomas Cromwell* (1990)

M.C. FRISSEL, *English Warfare 1511–1642* (2004)

S.J. GUNN, *Charles Brandon, Duke of Suffolk* (1988)

—*Early Tudor Government 1485–1558* (1995)

J.A. GUY, *The Cardinal's Court* (1977)

P. GWYN, *The King's Cardinal* (1991)

R.W. HEINZE, *The Proclamations of the Tudor Kings* (1976)

R.H. HELMHOLTZ, *Canon Law and the Church of England* (1987)

R.W. HOYLE, *The Pilgrimage of Grace and the Politics of the 1530s* (2001)

E.W. IVES, *The Life and Death of Anne Boleyn* (2004)

S. JAMES, *Kateryn Parr* (1999)

E. KERRIDGE, *The Agrarian Problem in the Sixteenth Century and After* (1969)

M.C. KNOWLES, *The Religious Orders in England*, vol. 3, *The Tudor Age* (1959)

S.E. LEHMBERG, *The Reformation Parliament, 1529–1536* (1970)

D. LOADES, *The Tudor Court* (1986)

—*Henry VIII and His Queens* (1994)

—*Princes of Wales: Royal Heirs in Waiting* (2008)

D. MACCULLOCH, *Thomas Cranmer* (1996)

R. MARIUS, *Thomas More* (1984)

P. MARSHALL, *Reformation England 1480–1642* (2003)

G. MATTINGLY, *Catherine of Aragon* (1963)

T.F. MAYER, *Reginald Pole, Prince and Prophet* (2000)

H. MILLER, *Henry VIII and the English Nobility* (1986)

J.A. MULLER, *Stephen Gardiner and the Tudor Reaction* (1926, 1970)

B. MURPHY, *Bastard Prince* (2001)

H. PIERCE, *Margaret Pole, Countess of Salisbury 1473–1541* (2003)

G. REDWORTH, *In Defence of the Church Catholic: A Life of Stephen Gardiner* (1990)

J.J. SCARISBRICK, *Henry VIII* (1968; new edition, 2000)

R.S. SCHOFIELD, *Taxation under the Early Tudor 1485–1547* (2004)

L.B. SMITH, *A Tudor Tragedy* (1961)

—*Henry VIII: The Mask of Royalty* (1971)

D. STARKEY, *The Reign of Henry VIII* (1985)

—(ed.) *The English Court* (1987)

J. SURTZ and V. MURPHY (eds), *The Divorce Tracts of Henry VIII* (1988)

R.M. WARNICKE, *The Rise and Fall of Anne Boleyn* (1989)

—*The Marrying of Anne of Cleves* (2000)

J. YOUINGS, *The Dissolution of the Monasteries* (1972)

Index

Numbers in *italic* denote plate numbers

ACT OF ... *see under* name of relevant
    act
Advancement of True Religion, Act
    for the (1543) 221, 223
Alexander VI, Pope 15
Alen, John 193
Allin, John 187
Amicable Grant (1525) 71–2, 136, 162
Anglo-French wars
    (1512–14) 30–2, 61–3, 79–81; (1523–
    5) 70–1, 72; (1543–6) 75, 77–80,
    146; cost of campaigns 80
Anne of Cleves *see* Cleves, Anne of
Appeals, Act of 142
Aquitaine campaign (1512) 30, 62
Arches, Court of 121
Arran, Earl of 76
Arthur (Henry's brother) *3*, 21, 153
Aske, Robert 173, 174, 177, 230
Askew, Anne *58*, 224
Assertio septem sacramentorum ('Assertion
    of the Seven Sacraments') 205
assize judges 116, 118
attainder, acts of 125
Audley, Sir Thomas 150
Augmentations, Court of 44, 148, 214,
    216
Augustinians 198, 215

BAINBRIDGE, Christopher
    (Archbishop of York) 27
Barnes, Robert 220
Beaton, Cardinal 77
Becket, Thomas 211
benefit of clergy 33, 204
benevolences 146
Bernard, George 227
Bible 208–9, 220–1
Bishops Book (1537) 209, 224
Black Death 10
Blount, Elizabeth 48–9
Blount, John 48
Blount, Walter *see* Mountjoy, Lord

Boleyn, Anne *6*, 39, 59, 75, 162–3, 230
    coronation 52, 99–100; courtship of
    by Henry and secret marriage 50–3,
    91, 96–7, 98–9, 162, 230; execution
    53, 103–4
Boleyn, Margaret 184
Boleyn, Mary 49–50, 230
Boleyn, Thomas (Earl of Wiltshire)
    49, 53, 154
boroughs 116
Boulogne, siege of (1544) 77–9, 80
Bourbon, Duke of 69–70
Boxley Priory (Kent) 214–15
Brandon, Charles *see* Suffolk,
    Duke of
Browne, Sir Anthony 234, 238
Buckingham, Duke of (Edward
    Stafford) 59, 136, 154, 158–62
Bulmer, Sir William 160
Burgo, Nicholas del 97
Butler, Sir Piers 185–6, 187
Butler, Thomas (Earl of Ormond) 184

CABOT, John 17
Camber Castle 86
Camp, Treaty of (1546) 80
Campeggio, Cardinal 94–5
canon law 121, 123–4, 130
Canterbury, Archbishop of *see*
    Warham, William
Cárceres, Francesca de 32
Caroz, Don Luis 32, 33
Catherine of Aragon *3*, 21–4, 59, 63,
    206, 207
    birth of Mary 48; death 53, 75;
    and death of children 26; household
    40; marriage to and relationship
    with Henry 21, 23–4, 25, 32–3, 48;
    marriage to Arthur 21; supporters
    162; *see also* 'Great Matter'
Cavendish, George 93–4
Cecil, Sir William 149
chamber 36, 43
chancery (lord chancellor) 150
Chapuys, Eustace 54–5, 82–3, 97, 102,
    163–4, 165, 195
Charles V, Emperor 68, 69, 70–1, 72, 75
    and 'Great Matter' 97, 102; and Ire-
    land 188; relationship with Henry
    70–1, 72–3, 75, 92, 97; signs treaty

with Henry (1543) 77; signs treaty of Toledo with Francis (1539) 73, 107; signs Truce of Crespy with Francis (1544) 79

charters 115–16

chastity 218

Church 245
  affect on ordinary people 13–14, 122; assessment of its wealth of 10, 212; Henry's campaign against pilgrimages and shrines 210–11; and heresy legislation 130; in Ireland 196; and legislation 120–2, 142–3, 144–5; reforms initiated by Henry as supreme head 122–4, 207–10; *see also* royal supremacy

Church courts 13, 120, 121–2, 123

churchwardens 120–1

Cistercians 199

Clement VII, Pope 72, 92, 207

clergy 121–2, 123, 131–2, 171, 196, 204–5, 208

Clerk, William 238

Cleves, Anne of 12, 56, 108–9, 231

Clifford, Henry (Earl of Cumberland) 155

Colet, John 203

'commissions of array' 85

commission(s) 116–17, 151, 152
  oyer et terminer 117, 120; of peace 117, 118, 151

common law 13, 113, 114, 118, 119, 124, 129

Common Pleas, Court of 116, 124

Commons, House of 140–1, 147–8, 155

Compton, Sir William 32, 38, 39, 183

council, king's *see* king's council

counting house 35

countryside 11

county courts 141, 151

court, king's 35–60, 81
  chamber 36, 43; companions to the king 38; cost of upkeeping 43–5; early festivities 37–8; factions at 58–9; household 35, 43, 46–7; movement of to king's residences 42–3; and politics 47–8; privy chamber 36, 38–9, 46; and prostitutes 47; security 45–7; separate

establishments for queens and children 40; shortage of women 47; staff 36; structural changes implemented 40–1

Courtenay, Henry (Marquis of Exeter) 169–70

courtly love 50

courts 119
  Church 13, 120, 121–2, 123; county 141, 151; customary 116; financial 139, 148, 247; manorial 13, 114, 116, 120; royal 13, 116

Cranmer, Thomas 52, 57, 60, 97, 207, 218, 242
  burning of 244; and 'Great Matter' 8, 98; relationship with Henry 222–3

Crespy, Truce of (1544) 79

Cromwell, Thomas 11, 40, 54, 55, 58, 59, 73–4, 229
  and Anne Boleyn 103; and Cleves marriage 108; and dissolution of monasteries 147, 211; downfall 39, 139, 219; enforcing of Henry's controversial policies 138; in the House of Commons 147–8; and Ireland 187; method of personal control 39, 138–9; and Pilgrimage of Grace 172; and reform of secretary's office 149–50; reorganization of financial administration 148–9; secret of success 138; as spymaster 73–4, 138, 149

Crowley, Robert 183

Culpepper, Thomas 56

custom of the manor 114

customary courts 116

DACRE, Lord 112

Damplip, Adam 219

Darcy, Lord 28, 172, 174, 176, 177, 183, 188, 230

de la Pole, Edmund (Earl of Suffolk) 17, 156, 157

de la Pole, Elizabeth 156

de la Pole, John 137

de la Pole, Richard 17, 156, 157, 186

de Selve, Odet 242

Denny, Sir Anthony 40, 44, 235, 237, 242, 243

Derby, Earl of 174
Dereham, Francis 56
Desmond, Earl of 186
Dissolution of the monasteries *see under* monasteries
Dominicans 198, 215
Dorset, Marquis of 30
'Drummer of Nickelhausen' 16
Dudley, Edmund 19–21, 204
Dudley, John *see* Lisle, Lord

EDICTS 113
Edward, Earl of Warwick 156
Edward IV, King 12, 125, 156
Edward, Prince (later Edward VI) *14,* 55–6, 76, 107, 110
elections 141
Elizabeth, Princess (later Elizabeth I) *6, 14,* 53, 111, 245–6, 247
Elizabeth of York 14, 26, 34, 107, 157
Elton, Geoffrey 115, 148
Empson, Richard 19–21
enforcement officers 118–19
Englefield, Sir Francis 244
equity jurisdiction 119, 150, 247
Erasmus 18, 202, 210
Essex, Earl of (William Parr) 58, 154, 155
'evangelicals' 59
exchequer 148, 149, 150
'Exeter conspiracy' 170

FERDINAND of Aragon 21, 22, 23, 25, 27, 30, 48, 62, 66, 68
fictional pleading 124
Field of the Cloth of Gold 69
financial administration, reorganization of under Cromwell 148–9
financial courts 139, 148, 247
First Fruits and Tenths 148
Fisher, John (Bishop of Rochester) 5, 73, 93–5, 101, 102, 162, 164–5
FitzGerald, Thomas, of Leixlip 186
FitzGerald earls of Kildare *see* Kildare
Fitzroy, Henry (Duke of Richmond) 49, 52, 55, 88–9, 107, 136, 153, 187, 190
Flodden, Battle of (1513) 63–5
fortification 86
Fox, Richard (Bishop of Winchester) 19

Foxe, Edward 97
Foxe, John 217–18, 224–7, 245
France
    relations with papacy 28–9, 30; treaty of peace with England (1514) 66, 67; wars with England *see* Anglo–French wars
franchises 114–15, 118, 138, 141, 153
    abolishment of 143–4
Francis I, King of France 38, 68, 69, 157
    failed invasion of England (1545) 79–80; and Field of the Cloth of Gold 69; and 'Great Matter' 98; relationship with Henry 69; signs Treaty of Camp with Henry (1546) 80; signs Treaty of Toledo with Charles 73, 107; signs Truce of Crespy with Charles (1544) 79; war with England 70–1
Franciscans 198, 215
friaries, dissolution of 122–3, 215–16
Fuensalida, Count of 18

GAELIC Church 197–8
Gardiner, Stephen (Bishop of Winchester) 58, 208, 218, 219, 224, 229, 234, 238, 243
Gates, John 238
General Surveyors 148
'gentleman of the privy chamber' 38
'gentlemen pensioners, the' 46
Geraldines 186
government 12–13, 133–55
Grafton, Richard 21, 49, 63–5, 66–7, 89–91, 135–6
Great Bible 221
'great council' 140
Great Galley (ship) 82
'Great Matter' 88–111, 142, 162
    attitude of Catherine to proposed annulment 91–2, 96; convincing by Henry that marriage was contrary to divine law 91, 206–7; defence of marriage by Bishop Fisher 5, 93–5, 162, 164; and Henry's 'scruple of conscience' 5, 89–91, 101–2, 206–7; international implications 92; legatine commission to hear case 92–3; and Parliament 101;

political fallout 101–2; pronounce-
ment of marriage as null and void *8*,
98–9; relations with pope 92, 96,
163, 207; secret marriage between
Anne and Henry and pregnancy
98–9; succession issue 88–9, 95;
and test of allegiance 162–3
Great Seal, Third *2*
Greenwich, Treaty of 80
Grey, Lord Leonard 191
groom of the stool 38, 43
Guistianni, Sebastian 159
guns 82–3, 86
deployment on ships 82

Hailes, blood of 215
Hall, Edward 30
Hall, Mary 57
Hampton Court 42
Hastings, Anne 32, 33, 39, 48
Hastings, George (Earl of Huntingdon)
155, 159
Henry V, King 24–5, 83
Henry VII, King 14, 16–17, 18, 20,
22–3, 24, 25–6, 34, 81, 134, 181, 202
Henry VIII, King *1, 9, 10, 15, 16*
  PERSONAL LIFE AND MARRIAGES
  attitude towards illness and death
  232–3; character and qualities 19,
  81, 248–9; courtship with and marriage to Anne Boleyn 50–3, 91,
  96–7, 98–9, 162, 230; death 242;
  deterioration of health 229, 231–3,
  21–2; education 202; funeral and
  fate of body 243–4; and honour
  229–31; and hunting 43; jousting
  fall 232; learned and humanist
  mind–set 202–3; love of big guns
  81–2; marriage to Anne of Cleves
  12, 56, 108–9; marriage to (and
  relationship with) Catherine of
  Aragon 5, *8*, 21, 23–4, 25, 32–3, 48;
  marriage to Catherine Howard 56–8;
  109–10, 231; marriage to Catherine
  Parr 58, 110; marriage to Jane
  Seymour *14*, 55, 105; mistresses
  48–9, 51; pastimes 38; physique
  17,34; religious beliefs 203, 206,
  231; 'scruple of conscience' 5, 89–91,
  102, 206–7; sex life 48, 230–1;

superstitious streak 203, 206;
upbringing 18; and upbringing of
son 233, 234–5; will 236–40, 243
  REIGN
  and army 85–6; campaign against
  pilgrimages and shrines 210–11;
  chivalric values and wanting to prove
  himself on battlefield 24, 25, 61, 63,
  87, 203–4; court of *see* court, king's;
  converting nobility from lineage
  mode to service mode 247; dealing
  with his council 138; and dissolution
  of monasteries 44, 75, 122–3, 127–8,
  147, 173, 200–1, 212–15; distribution
  of honours and rewards (1547) 235–6;
  enemies of 156–79; erratic behaviour
  60; excommunication of 52, 178,
  208; fear of attack from continent
  73–4; finances and private expenditure 43–5, 146; foreign policy aims
  81; and French failed invasion (1545)
  79; 'Great Matter' *see* 'Great Matter';
  interest in hydrography and fortification 86–7; interest in weaponry and
  ships 81–3; Irish policy 183, 184–5,
  193–5, 201; joins Holy League 27,
  28; last years 229–49; and law 112–
  13, 119; legacy of and achievements
  81, 245, 246–8; and navy reform
  83–5, 246; relations with senior
  peers 134–5; relationship with
  Emperor Charles 70–1, 72–3, 75, 92,
  97; religious policy 202–28;
  representation in drama 247–8;
  residences 42–3; and royal supremacy 102, 105, 111, 123, 129, 131, 138,
  147, 164, 165, 197, 207–8, 210–11,
  231, 234; Scottish campaign 75–6;
  tournaments 87; view of war 61;
  and wars against France 24–32,
  61–2, 65, 70–1, 72, 77–80
Henry VIII (Shakespeare) 248
Herbert of Cherbury, Lord 202
heresy 129–30, 205
Heresy Acts 129
Hertford, Earl of (Edward Seymour) *2*,
55, 154, 229, 234, 235, 241
Hilton, Sir Thomas 174
Holbein the Younger, Hans 7, *9, 15*,
217, 249

Holy League 27, 28
Hooper, John 220
Horenbout, Lucas *1*
household 35, 43, 46–7
Howard, Catherine 39, 56–8, 59, 109–10, 221, 231
Howard, George 53
Howard, Henry *see* Surrey, Earl of
Howard, Sir Edward 31, 33–4, 83
Howard, Thomas *see* Surrey, Earl of
Howard family 59, 154, 158, 221, 224, 235, 247
humanism *see* New learning
hundreds 13, 119, 151
Hunne, Richard 121, 205
Huntingdon, Earl of *see* Hastings, George
husbandmen 11–12
Hussey, Lord 172, 174, 177
hydrography 86

INDICTMENT 117, 118
indulgences 205
Ingworth, Richard 215
Ireland 179, 180–201
    Church 196–8; commission appointed to examine affairs of 191; Cromwell's policy in 187; decline of monasticism 199–201; division of into three zones 180; Henry's policy towards 183, 184–5, 193–5, 201; and Kildare Revolt (1534) 73, 187–91; and mendicant orders 198, 201; overlap between Irish and English law 182; Parliament in 182–3, 191; policy of surrender and regrant 193–5, 201; and royal supremacy 197; Surrey's lieutenancy 184–5
Isabella of Castile 22, 71

JAMES IV, King of Scotland 63, 64, 76, 157
James V, King of Scotland 75, 165
judicial system 13, 112–19, 150 *see also* courts
Julius II, Pope 27, 28, 30, 66, 95, 207
juries 117
jury of indictment 117
justices of the peace (JPs) 117, 118, 119, 125–6, 140, 151

KILDARE, 8th Earl of 181, 183
Kildare, 9th Earl of 183–4, 184–5, 185–6, 187
Kildare, 10th Earl of (Thomas, Lord Offaly) 187–90
Kildare Revolt (1534) 73, 187–91
King's Bench 116, 124
King's Book 224
king's coffers 43–4
king's council 133–4, 138–41, 153
Kite, John 183
knights of the Garter 204

LAMBERT, John, trial of 216–17
Lascelles, John 57
Latimer, Hugh 201, 220
law 13–14, 112–32
    canon 121, 123–4, 130; common 13, 113, 114, 118, 119, 124, 129
League of Cambrai 27, 28
legislation 124–5, 140
    against heresy 129–30; on poor and vagabonds 125–7, 128
Leo X, Pope 66, 205
Letters and Papers … of Henry VIII, extracts from 23–4, 41–2, 54–5, 71–2, 73–4, 103–4, 136–8, 176–7, 189–90, 191–2, 193–4, 212–13, 239–40
liberties 114
Lisle, Lord (John Dudley) 84, 155, 224, 234, 235
literacy 131–2
Livet, William 82
local government 13, 151–2
Lollards 15, 16, 129, 131, 202
London 11, 16–17, 131
London, Bishop of 204–5
London, Treaty of (1518) 68
Longland, John 206
lord chamberlain 36, 41
lord chancellor 150
lord privy seal 149, 150
lord protector 241
Lords, House of 140, 141, 155
Louis XII, King of France 25, 27, 28, 30, 66, 67, 157
Low Countries 69
Luther, Martin 205

MACCOUGHLAN, Cormac 197–8
Madrid, Treaty of (1526) 71
Maitland of Lethington 237
Malines agreement (1513) 62
Manners, Thomas (Earl of Rutland) 155
manorial courts 13, 114, 116, 120
marches of Wales *see* Wales, marches of
Margaret, Countess of Salisbury 169
Mary (daughter of James V) 76
Mary, Duchess of Suffolk (Henry's
    sister) 52, 65, 66–7, 157, 162
Mary, Princess (later Mary I) *14*, 48,
    54, 59, 71, 88, 242, 243, 244–5
    and Act of Succession (1544) 110;
    capitulates to father's demands 54–5,
    59, 105; and 'Great Matter' 102
Mary Rose 82
Matsys, Cornelis *15*
Maximilian, Emperor 63, 65, 68
Mellifont, Abbot Troy of 199
mendicant orders 198, 201, 215
Merchant Adventurers 16, 17
militias 85
monasteries 15–16
    dissolution of 44, 75, 122–3, 127–8,
    147, 173, 200–1, 212–15
monastic land, selling of 147, 214, 216
Montague, Lord (Henry Pole) 169
More, Sir Thomas 7, 101, 102, 150,
    165–7
More, Treaty of the (1525) 71
Mountjoy, Lord (Walter Blount)
    18–19, 48

NAVY 83–5, 246–7
Neville, Sir Edward 169–70
New Learning 15, 202, 223
Nine Years' War 180
Nonsuch, palace at 42
Norfolk, Duke of *13*, 39, 56, 158, 175,
    219, 234
Norris, Sir Henry 53
Northumberland, Earl of 174

OATLANDS hunting lodge 43
Offaly, Thomas Lord *see* Kildare, 10th
    Earl of
opus dei 15, 203
oyer et terminer 117, 120
Order of the Garter 12

PAGET, Sir William 234, 235, 236, 238
papacy
    relations with England 196;
    relations with France 28, 30;
    relations with Henry over 'Great
    Matter' 92, 96, 163, 207; *see also*
    individual popes
parish constable 119
Parliament 102, 111, 124, 140, 245
    change in functions and elevation
    of 141–5, 148; composition and
    structure 140–1; and 'Great Matter'
    101; in Ireland 182–3, 191; and
    legislation 125, 141–5; royal power
    subjected to consent of 145–6;
    sovereignty of 111; *see also* Com-
    mons, House of; Lords, House of
'parochiani' 121
Parr, Catherine 58, 59, 110, 242–3
plot against 224–7
Parr, William *see* Essex, Earl of
Parsons, Robert 244
Paul III, Pope 105, 109 165
Paulet, William (Lord St John) 41–2,
    149, 155, 169
peers 154–5
Percys 152, 154, 247
petitions 46
Philip, Duke of Burgundy 22
Pierce, Hazel 169
Pilgrimage of Grace 73, 155, 170–9,
    189, 213
pilgrimages, Henry's campaign against
    210–11
plague 10, 15
Pole, Sir Geoffrey 169
Pole, Henry *see* Montague, Lord
Pole, Margaret (Countess of Salisbury)
    154
Pole, Reginald 74, 108, 167–70, 224
Pollard, A.F. 100
poor, the 128–9
    legislation on 125–7
population 10–11, 128
Poynings, Sir Edward 182
Pragmatic Sanction of Bourges (1438)
    28
'Princes in the Tower' 157
privy chamber 36, 38–9, 46
privy council 139–40, 152

privy purse 43–5
proclamations 29–30
prostitutes 47

QUARTER sessions 117

RADCLIFFE, Robert (Earl of Sussex) 155
Ratcliffe, Elizabeth 32
Regent (ship) 82
regional councils 120, 153
religion 15–16, 202–28 *see also* Church; monasteries; royal supremacy
Requests, Court of 119, 136
retainers 29–30
revenues 146
Richard III, King 14, 157
Ridley, Nicholas 152
Rochester, Bishop of *see* Fisher, John
Rochford, Jane 57
Rochford, Lord 103
rowbarges 83
royal commission 13
royal courts 13, 116
royal injunctions 122, 209–10, 221
Royal Navy 83, 246–7
royal supremacy 102, 105, 111, 123, 129, 131, 138, 147, 164, 165, 197, 207–8, 210–11, 231, 234
Rutland, Earl of *see* Manners, Thomas

ST LEGER, Anne 184
St Leger, Sir Anthony 191, 193, 195
saints 211
Scarisbrick, J.J. 244
Schmalkaldic League 75, 108
Scotland 63, 79, 85
Henry's campaign against 77–7
secretary's office 149
serpentines 82
'service nobility' 12
Seymour, Edward *see* Hertford, Earl of
Seymour, Jane 14, 55, 59, 105–7, 230, 243
Seymour, Sir John 105
Seymour, Thomas 235
sheriff 117–18, 151
ships 82–4, 86, 246
Shrewsbury, Earl of 174
shrines, demolishing of 211

Simnel, Lambert 180–1
Sittow, Michel 3
Six Articles, Act of (1539) 130, 201, 218, 219–20
Skeffington, William 187, 188, 189
Smith, Lacey Baldwin 273
Smith, Sir Thomas 145
social scale 12
Solway Moss, Battle of (1542) 76
'spears, the' 45
Spurs, Battle of the (1513) 63
Stafford, Edward *see* Buckingham, Duke of
Star Chamber 119, 134, 136
steward 35, 40
Stone, Lawrence 154
subsidy 146, 171
Succession, Act of (1534) 102–3; (1536) 106; (1544) 110–11, 240
Suffolk, Duchess of *see* Mary, Duchess of Suffolk
Suffolk, Duke of (Charles Brandon) 38, 67, 154, 158, 171
Supremacy, Act of (1534) 102, 142–3
Surrey, Earl of (Henry Howard) 154, 158, 233
Surrey, Earl of (Thomas Howard) 184–5
Sussex, Earl of *see* Radcliffe, Robert

TAILBOYS, Gilbert 49
taxation 146, 247
and Amicable Grant 71–2, 136, 162; and subsidy 146, 171; 'tenth and fifteenth' 146
Ten Articles (1537) 211
'tenth and fifteenth' tax 146
Thirlby, Thomas (Bishop of Westminster) 238
Toledo, Treaty of (1539) 73, 107
Tournai, siege of (1513) 63, 66
tournaments 87
towns, governing of 152
trade 16
transubstantiation 218, 221, 227
treason 124–5, 163, 164
treasury of the chamber 148
'trespass on the case' 124
trial jury 117
Trykhay, Christopher 123

Tunstall, Cuthbert 208
Tyndale, William 208, 221

UNEMPLOYMENT, rural 128

VAGABONDS, legislation on 125–7,
   128
Valor ecclesiasticus 10
Venetians 27
village life 11–12

WALES, marches of 13, 114–16, 143,
   153, 159
wapentakes 151
Warbeck, Perkin 181
Wards and Liveries 149
Warham, William (Archbishop of
   Canterbury) 19, 52, 71–2, 97
Wars of the Roses 12, 14, 34, 134
Warwick, Earl of 14
weaponry 81–2, 86
Westminster, Bishop of *see* Thirlby,
   Thomas
Wills, Act of 178
Winchester, Lord Treasurer 149
Wolsey, Thomas 4, 7, 33, 39, 40, 59,
   69, 119, 121, 154, 162, 229
   as adviser to Henry 33, 66, 69; and
   Amicable Grant 71–2, 162; and
   Duke of Buckingham 136; fall of
   136–8; and government 136; and
   'Great Matter' 91, 92, 95; influence
   on Henry 134–5; and Ireland 187;
   and king's council 134–5; and
   military logistics 33–4; overreaching
   of 135–6, 146; and taxation 146
Wriothesley, Sir Thomas 58, 150, 229,
   234, 235
writs 150
Wyatt, George 172
Wycliffe, John 15

YEOMAN of the guard 115
yeomanry 12
York, Duke of 133

ZWINGLI, Ulrich 216

Picture Credits
(by plate number)

Author's Acknowledgements

I am grateful to The National Archives
for the opportunity to write this
book and particularly to the following
individuals who had a hand in its
emergence: Mark Hawkins-Dady,
for his initiative and encouragement;
Gwen Campbell for diligently
researching the illustrations; Ian
Crofton for copy editing; and Ken
Wilson who brought everything
together in a pleasing design.